Media Scandals

MediaScandals

Morality and Desire in the
Popular Culture Marketplace

EDITED BY
James Lull and Stephen Hinerman

Polity Press

Copyright © this volume Polity Press 1997

First published in 1997 by Polity Press
in association with Blackwell Publishers Ltd.

Editorial office:
Polity Press
65 Bridge Street
Cambridge CB2 1UR, UK

Marketing and production:
Blackwell Publishers Ltd
108 Cowley Road
Oxford OX4 1JF, UK

ISBN 0-7456-1885-5
ISBN 0-7456-1886-3 (pbk)

A CIP catalogue record for this book is available from the British Library.

Typeset in 10.5 on 12 pt Palatino
by Graphicraft Typesetters Ltd., Hong Kong
Printed and bound in Great Britain by MPG Books Ltd, Bodmin, Cornwall

This book is printed on acid-free paper.

Contents

Editors   vii

List of Contributors   viii

Acknowledgments   x

1 **The Search for Scandal**   1
  James Lull and Stephen Hinerman

2 **Scandal and Social Theory**   34
  John B. Thompson

3 **"And Besides, the Wench is Dead"**: Media
  Scandals and the Globalization of Communication   65
  John Tomlinson

4 **Anxiety, Desire, and Conflict in the American
  Racial Imagination**   85
  Herman Gray

5 **What a Story!** Understanding the Audience for
  Scandal   99
  S. Elizabeth Bird

6 **Character, Celebrity, and Sexual Innuendo in the Mass-Mediated Presidency** 122
Bruce E. Gronbeck

7 **(Don't) Leave Me Alone**: Tabloid Narrative and the Michael Jackson Child-Abuse Scandal 143
Stephen Hinerman

8 **Producing Trash, Class, and the Money Shot**: A Behind-the-Scenes Account of Daytime TV Talk Shows 164
Laura Grindstaff

9 **Apollo Undone**: The Sports Scandal 203
David Rowe

10 **Church, Media, and Scandal** 222
Paul A. Soukup

11 **Pushin' it to the Limit**: Scandals and Pop Music 240
Javier Santiago-Lucerna

Index 255

Editors

James Lull is Professor of Communication Studies at San Jose State University. He is author of *Media, Communication, Culture: A Global Approach*, *China Turned On: Television, Reform, and Resistance*, and *Inside Family Viewing*. He is editor of *Popular Music and Communication* and *World Families Watch Television*. He holds an honorary doctorate in Social Science from the University of Helsinki.

Stephen Hinerman currently teaches in Communication Studies at San Jose State University. He has written extensively on cultural studies and rhetoric in academic and popular publications. He writes regularly on popular music for several newspapers, and was music critic for Denver's *Westword* and the *Colorado Daily*.

Contributors

S. Elizabeth Bird is Professor of Anthropology at the University of South Florida. She is author of *For Enquiring Minds: A Cultural Study of Supermarket Tabloids* and editor of *Dressing in Feathers: The Construction of the Indian in American Popular Culture*.

Herman Gray is Professor and Graduate Director of Sociology at the University of California–Santa Cruz. He is author of *Watching Race: Television and the Sign of Blackness* and *Producing Jazz: The Experience of an Independent Record Company*.

Laura Grindstaff is Assistant Professor in the Annenberg School for Communication, University of Pennsylvania. Her doctoral degree is in Sociology from the University of California, Santa Barbara. She has published in several journals, and holds a master's degree in journalism, with a speciality in documentary video.

Bruce E. Gronbeck is A. Craig Baird Distinguished Professor of Public Address in the Department of Communication Studies at the University of Iowa. He is past president of the National Communication Association and author or editor of many books on rhetoric, communication, and media criticism.

David Rowe is Senior Lecturer in Leisure and Tourism Studies at the University of Newcastle, Australia. He is author of *Popular*

Cultures: Rock Music, Sport and the Politics of Pleasure, and co-editor
of *Power Play* and *Sport and Leisure.*

Javier Santiago-Lucerna is Director of Treatment for Hogar CREA,
Inc., a drug rehabilitation program, in the Carolina District, Puerto
Rico. He is finishing a doctoral degree in psychology at the University of Puerto Rico, and has published many articles on rock and
salsa music.

Paul A. Soukup, S.J. is Associate Professor of Communication at
Santa Clara University, California. He also serves on the Communication Committee of the United States Catholic Conference. He is
author of *Communication and Theology* and *Christian Communication,*
and co-editor of *Media, Consciousness and Culture, Faith and Contexts: The Essays of Walter J. Ong,* and *Mass Media and the Moral
Imagination.*

John B. Thompson is Reader in Sociology at the University of
Cambridge and Fellow of Jesus College, Cambridge. He is author
of *The Media and Modernity: A Social Theory of the Media, Ideology and
Modern Culture: Critical Social Theory in the Era of Mass Communication,* and *Studies in the Theory of Ideology.*

John Tomlinson is Head of the Centre for Research in International Communication and Culture at the Nottingham Trent University. He is author of *Global Modernity* and *Cultural Imperialism.*

Acknowledgments

We would especially like to thank Bo Reimer, who was a colleague of ours in the Department of Communication Studies at San Jose State University in 1995–6, for his thoughtful comments on this book, and for his personal and professional friendship. John B. Thompson made many contributions to the book. We also want to acknowledge the help given by Aggie Silva, Dawn Mills, Tim Hegstrom, Lotta Kratz, and Helen Quinn. Julia Harsant managed the project for Polity Press, Ann Miller for Columbia University Press. Pamela Thomas supervised production of the book with great skill and good humor. Fiona Sewell contributed a particularly thorough and insightful editorial reading. Portrait photography was by Aggie Silva.

1 The Search for Scandal

James Lull and Stephen Hinerman

"This is an investigation in search of a scandal. This is not about finding out the truth."

Hillary Clinton answering questions before a United States Senate sub-committee regarding her financial interest in the Whitewater land deal

Scandals are pervasive today. They have become the dominant feature of tabloid journalism, have vaulted tabloid values to the forefront of mainstream news practice, and define topic after topic on that staple of American daytime television, the talk show. The prevalence of scandals can be seen as a distinctive sign of the "Murdochization" of modern media, where shocking stories are packaged to appeal to the prurient interests, star-gazing curiosities, and moral requirements of a global audience. Truth is always at issue. In the quote above, Hillary Clinton conveniently positions scandal *against* truth, but is it not also the case that scandals often pull back the curtains of privacy to *reveal* (ugly) truths and expose those responsible? Is that not what the search for scandal is all about?

No doubt the effects of the media scandal are socially significant, and the connotations are usually negative. Some forms of the media scandal have even been identified as unmistakable signs of moral decay. William Bennett, former United States secretary of education and a leading conservative political figure, has labeled scandalous TV talk shows as "perpetrators of cultural rot" and "the force of decomposition" in society. But at the same time, one of America's best-known TV talk-show hosts, Jerry Springer, insists that the scandalous genre is central to democracy and the upholding of a high moral standard: "This is America ... we will never keep off the air a point of view, opinion, or lifestyle just because it is unpopular. And when moral questions are involved, we've got to come down on the right side. Exposure is the way to stop Nazism!" Indeed, everywhere we look, sordid stories of how personal desire triumphs over conventional morality are told for profit. And, yes, people everywhere are watching, reading, listening, and talking.

Before one decides whether media scandals are perpetrators of cultural rot or the last defense against Nazism, a close examination of their production and reception should be undertaken. The purpose of the present volume is to help initiate this process, assessing not only the history and defining characteristics of scandal as the symbolic representation of acts deemed morally reprehensible, but also the social and cultural consequences their extensive media coverage produces. In the pages that follow, an international group of authors representing a variety of academic disciplines and theoretical viewpoints discuss how media scandals enter and influence popular culture. The authors explore the ways media construct representations of scandal and what impact these constructions have on an increasingly globalized audience. We believe that the modernday scandal provides a clear and compelling entry point for criticism of contemporary media in society. Whatever is striking about the mass media generally is made considerably more dramatic when scandals appear as media content and become the subject matter for analysis.

Media scandals and the postmodern morality play

Such analyses are pertinent today, particularly for those parts of the world where the circulation of symbolic forms and the construction of cultural identities has accelerated at a frantic, some would say "postmodern," pace. We live in an increasingly dangerous, "risk"-oriented society (Beck 1992) which brings with it a profound moral dualism. Within the complexities, uncertainties, and threats of postmodernity, the scandal functions simultaneously as a moral anchor in a sea of conventionality, and as a vigorous challenge to mainstream social values conditioned by the substantial forces of ideological and cultural hegemony.

Scandal serves as a term to delineate a breach in moral conduct and authority. *A media scandal occurs when private acts that disgrace or offend the idealized, dominant morality of a social community are made public and narrativized by the media, producing a range of effects from ideological and cultural retrenchment to disruption and change.* The transgressions assume additional impact when markers of human difference such as race, gender, class, and sexual orientation are involved. Scandals fascinate at the same time as they infuriate. No one is immune – not celebrities, or ordinary people, or institutional employees. The secrets of desire are unlocked; the curtains of privacy are pulled back. The unspoken is articulated, observed, and pondered.

All this is done via the media narrative, the story which frames the scandal, populates it with characters, gives it a structure and longevity. Within the narrative the privileges of privacy are disrespected, given coherence, and converted into media products and profits. With the once private act now exposed, the scandal narrative becomes a resource circulating in the mediated public sphere (Thompson 1995 and this volume). Competing emergent interpretations of what the narrative means are negotiated against a backdrop of a dominant moral code articulated and reinforced by major social institutions. Scandals, thus, provide symbolic terrain on which the terms and boundaries of public morality are negotiated within the provisional framework of postmodernity. While the facts comprising any particular scandal may be contested, and while the creation, interpretation, and use of scandals may be widely divergent, what audiences want is a moral code they can use to understand and evaluate human conduct. Scandals provide just such opportunities (see Bird, this volume).

When the public believes that the dominant morality of the day has been violated by someone – especially if that someone is famous or holds power – we have an opportunity for a media scandal: Were Charles and Diana adulterous? Are the top executives at a major oil company blatantly racist? Did Hugh Grant unzip his pants for Divine Brown? Could O.J. Simpson really kill Nicole and Ron? Did Bill Clinton inhale? Media scandals thus direct attention to the problematic ethicality of human decisions made within the confines of a ruling value structure. True enough, the dominant morality of any society is never completely fixed. Furthermore, some people (famous persons in particular) are held to differing moral standards. And when news travels from place to place around the globe it will be read from differing moral perspectives. Given these important limitations on morality as a universal operative, what is at issue is whether or not individual people have acted in ways that violate social norms. Those norms *do* remain relatively unchanged over time, providing coherence and continuity to the dominant morality. Scandals, thus, are powerful partly because of their situated *lack* of moral ambiguity.

Scandal and the moral panic

Understanding of the media scandal can be enhanced by comparing it to a related concept which is quite familiar in the sociological literature, particularly in the United Kingdom. This is the "moral panic" (see especially Watney 1987; Cohen 1980; Young 1971; Pearson 1983). The moral panic is a reaction to an apparent social movement which generally and permanently threatens the stability of the dominant morality. The moral panic menaces the status quo precisely because of the numbers of people thought to be involved. So a "deviant" trend such as the increasing prominence of gay people in society (and the AIDS threat that it implies), a rise in juvenile crime, the sexual and cultural presence of immigrants of color, or an upswing in drug use among youth, to name some actual historical examples in the United Kingdom, can stimulate a moral panic.

As we shall see in a later section, the scandal differs in some ways substantively and discursively from the moral panic in that *scandals must be traceable to real persons who are held responsible for their actions*. It is precisely this personalization process that turns a news story from a rumor into a scandal. But the media scandal and the moral panic are not mutually exclusive. The behavior of individuals who create scandals can even stimulate a moral panic when their actions are interpreted as symptomatic of a larger social problem. Furthermore, in many scandals the manner of the moral violation overshadows the actual persons involved. When ordinary people are exposed on TV talk shows, for instance, audiences probably do not care much about them as individuals. Instead, the *actions* of talk-show guests are what is relevant. If their actions are thought to be sufficiently deviant and widespread throughout the population, a moral panic is possible. As one example, the recent glut of talk shows focusing on specific cases of childhood sexual abuse and repressed memory in America has created considerable social concern.

The discourses of the moral panic and the scandal require that a societal moral baseline is challenged. Their very discussion in the media assures that conventional morality is once again asserted as normal. Drawing on normative sociocultural codes, the moral panic can "act as a form of ideological cohesion which draws on a complex language of nostalgia" and "act on behalf of the dominant social order" by "orchestrating consent" (McRobbie and Thornton 1995: 562). In the United States, the media scandal is, in one instance, part of an ultra-conservative overall trend in popular culture where Rush Limbaugh preaches reactionary politics to dittoheads, Dr Laura Schlesinger scolds her radio talk-show callers for not conforming to "family values," the tabloid press blames Hollywood stars for not being faithful in marriage, and TV talk-show audiences scream disapproval at guests who fail to conform to normal lifestyles.

Moreover, the contrast between conventional social behavior and the forms of "deviance" that make social action scandalous is part of an ideological system that defines media practice and popular culture generally. All media depend on the pervasiveness and functionality of dominant morality to define, for instance, what is funny in situation comedies, what qualifies as a front-page newspaper story, what topics should be raised on a radio or TV talk show, or what solution the actress should find in order to solve a social problem on a daytime soap opera. The media scandal is but the most extreme example of how, in practice, individuals are held to an imagined, idealized standard of social conduct. In this way, mass media become reflexive agents implicitly representing those whose interests are served by the constant reassertion of dominant modes of thought, driving mainstream values and lifestyles into the assumptive worlds of audience members.

But do moral panics and media scandals inspire only such conservative reactions? Do cultural conditions today signify an end to the hegemony of any dominant morality? Has the exercise of moral judgment become decentered through the redistribution of global authority (LaClau 1990)? Angela McRobbie and Sarah Thornton have addressed questions such as these recently in their own work and together (McRobbie 1994; Thornton 1995; McRobbie and Thornton 1995). They argue overall that the idea of a moral panic needs to be reconsidered in the era of multimedia and contemporary culture. The traditional standoff between convention and deviance is upset in a world where new communication technologies routinely disrupt traditional forms of human interaction, and where deviance itself has become normative and desirable for certain segments of the public.

The rave-culture/acid-house phenomenon is one splendid example of the role of technology in culture, and of the dubious nature of morality as consensual, particularly in the United Kingdom, where:

> youth are inclined *not* to lament a safe and stable past, but to have over-whelming nostalgia for the days when youth culture was genuinely transgressive. The 1990s youth culture is steeped in the legacy of previous "moral panics"; fighting mods and rockers, drug-taking hippies, foul-mouthed punks, and gender-bending New Romantics are part of their celebrated folklore. (McRobbie and Thornton 1995: 572)

In America, the appearance, attitude, and antics of popular-culture stars such as Madonna, Beavis and Butthead, and Dennis Rodman have taken Generation-X challenges to conventional morality to an ever more shocking level. And because they deliver socially-disruptive content with such speed, facility, and appeal, communications media themselves have become synonymous with scandal, and with the moral panic, as the new "folk devils" (Boethius 1995).

Living scandalously on purpose, thus, is a viable way to organize one's worldview, and such decisions and lifestyles do not just please the resistant, subcultural souls who choose them. Scandals are entertaining, and as such they are marketable to a much wider audience. The market for popular music, for instance, depends on controversy (see Santiago-Lucerna, this volume). As McRobbie and Thornton argue, a threat of censorship, sexual scandal, or subversive act often serves the interests of the culture industries well:

> The promotional logic is twofold: first, the cultural good will receive a lot of free, if negative publicity because its associations with the moral panic have made it newsworthy; second, rather than alienating everyone, it will be attractive to a contingent of consumers who see themselves as alternative, avant-garde, rebellious, or simply young. (McRobbie and Thornton 1995: 572)

Similarly, where would the tabloid press be without the scandal? How could jurors from the O.J. Simpson case write best-selling books? Who would watch TV talk shows? How could Divine Brown turn a five-minute affair with Hugh Grant into half a million dollars? Clearly, the media try to move many stories to scandal status. Scandal can therefore be considered an *accomplishment* with real ideological, cultural, and material winners and losers.[1]

Birth of the media scandal

We find gossip, the whispering campaign, and mudslinging in much ancient literature, and societies have always devised ways to punish and try to contain those who would violate social norms (see Soukup, this volume). The naming of certain such violations as "scandal," however, elevates social retaliation to a more formal and powerful level. This is a relatively recent development. While "scandal" can be found as a descriptive lexeme in courts of law as early as the 1750s, its circulation as a legal term does not occur for another century. According to the *Oxford English Dictionary* (1989), at that time scandal came to mean, for legal purposes, "Any injurious report published concerning another which may be the foundation of legal action." The scandal, thus, was a precursor to the development of libel and slander law. For scandal to mature comprehensively as a social concept, however, it needed a development in communications that was at the heart of early modernity – the birth of the publishing industry and the subsequent introduction of the popular press. With the rise of literacy, the development of the high-speed printing press, and the marketplace drive of capitalism all working together, news became a viable commodity in Europe and the United States. To attract, inform, and – not least of all – entertain readers, newspaper editorial practices were redefined to meet the growing demand. The tabloid press, complete with sensational stories of "sin and corruption," made possible the very first media scandals (Tebbel 1974), and the laws which would be necessary to settle the claims of damaged reputation that scandals provoked. Scandal thus was institutionalized into social life in the Western world by the middle of the nineteenth century.

Because communication technologies allow information to be cast over larger and larger areas, scandals cannot be easily managed by those at risk from its influence. So: *Scandal is always shaped and given force by the technological means through which information is transmitted to the public as news.* The media scandal born of the penny press is still with us today, but its form changes continuously as media technologies expand. Consider, for example, the nature of the TV quiz-show scandals of the 1950s or the payola scandals of the American commercial radio industry a decade later. The recent cyberspace scandals even call into question the very meaning of scandal. (What is a private act? Is virtual sex adulterous? Who is the audience? How do audiences chat about scandals?) Communications technology ranging from print on paper to megabytes in cyberspace thus shape the media scandal narrative, give it wide exposure, and influence the scandal's effects by making stories readily available for simultaneous exercises in moral judgment and entertainment, rendered by audience members worldwide using a myriad of mass and micro technologies. Following the church and the state, the media have become the third major player in the history of modern social influence, including the construction of moral discourses resulting from the intentional production of scandals.

Scandal and mediated visibility

John B. Thompson has focused considerable attention in recent writing on how communications media have changed the nature of social interaction generally – the "mediazation" process – and political and social accountability in particular (Thompson 1995). Drawing on the early work of Erving Goffman (1959) and interpretations given it by Joshua Meyrowitz (1985), Thompson problematizes the "shifting boundaries between the public and the private" (1995: 145) in media terms, noting that it has become far more difficult today for power holders in society to keep "back region" (private) separate from "front region" (public) behaviors. Maintaining distance between these regions has always been linked to the effective exercise of (political/economic/cultural) power. Those with power often prefer to operate in the back region, so to turn their dealings into public knowledge is to threaten their power base. It is the media that provide just such visibility and accountability.[2]

Scandals lurk when morally-transgressive private acts become public, and it is the powerful who are particularly vulnerable because their actions are watched so closely by the media. It is increasingly difficult nowadays to manage visibility and to limit the damage information can bring about: "Scandal is an occupational hazard of politics in the age of mediated visibility" (Thompson 1995: 144). Implied in all this is the expectation of a moral code of behavior which media visibility and accountability threaten to deconstruct. This is dramatically the case for Britain's royal family, for instance, where the media have brought about not only greater visibility, but greater intimacy:

> in an increasingly mediated world, it is difficult for the temporal representatives of the monarchy to avoid appearing as ordinary individuals, as

men and women who are little different from other individuals apart
from the accident of their birth, and who are prone to the same temptations, driven by the same desires and subject to the same weaknesses as
ordinary mortals. (Thompson 1995: 201)

The increased visibility and intimacy made possible by the media
have also made the British monarchy more familiar than it has ever
been, and, as we know, familiarity breeds contempt. The royal family
is more like us than we would likely ever know without the media.
Media scandals have thus transformed political leaders of all stripes
from public servants to public characters whose primary impact
more and more is becoming their entertainment value, and that
value grows as the subject matter becomes scandalous. But the
dangers of the increased visibility that media technologies bring do
not only impact on famous or powerful people. Micro technologies
in particular can be used for surveillance at all social levels in the
more developed societies, and, as the Rodney King incident clearly
illustrates (see Gray, this volume), institutions – like the police
department, or the monarchy itself for that matter – are also vulnerable. As we shall soon see, while scandals *must* be of a personal
nature, it is not just persons who are perceived to act scandalously.
We also hold modern institutions responsible for breaches in moral
conduct.

What is a media scandal?

Managers of modern news media actively try to turn stories into
scandals. To call a story a scandal is to give it a bizarre kind of
journalistic appeal and integrity ("This must *really* be something!").
Not every controversial story qualifies. Certain criteria must be
met to achieve scandal status. To sort this all out, we are going to
use three news stories that broke more-or-less simultaneously in
the United States to help define one variety of media scandal – the
institutional scandal – and show how scandals work generally. In
late fall 1996, American news media reported the following stories:

- Texaco (a multinational oil company) was accused of blatant
  racism.
- The United States military was accused of systemic sexual harassment and rape.

- A California natural-juice company was blamed for the outbreak of a bacterial infection that killed a young girl and made hundreds of people seriously ill.

Were these stories scandals? What criteria do we use to determine whether a news story has become a scandal? Let us analyze what happened in each case to see how we might answer these questions.

The Texaco racism story

The Texaco oil company was already under fire for what many of its minority employees called racist practices in hiring and promotion; black employees in particular were not being treated fairly, according to the complainants. A lawsuit had been pending for years. In November, 1996, an audiotape was produced wherein some top company executives responsible for personnel decisions were heard to make unmistakable racial slurs. They even ridiculed the company's official pro-diversity campaign by referring to the minority employees as "black jelly beans." The tape was made available to the media, which circulated it widely.

The military sex story

Several female members of the United States military brought charges against the government for sexual harassment, attacks, and rape suffered in training and later service. The *Washington Post* broke the story that the military was investigating the possibility that the attacks had taken place in Maryland, Missouri, and elsewhere. High-level, senior officers were accused of "fostering the wrong atmosphere" so that such events could happen. A national television network newsmagazine also picked up the story, interviewing the victims and naming those charged as perpetrators of the alleged sexual crimes.

The natural-juice poisoning story

A California natural-juice company, Odwalla, sold bottles of unpasteurized apple juice that had been contaminated by *E. coli* bacteria. The bacteria was deemed responsible for the death of a 3-year-old girl, and for serious illnesses suffered by many other consumers throughout the western United States. A media blitz warned people not to buy the juice. The company recalled all its apple-juice products and accepted responsibility for the problem.

What about the status of these stories as scandals? For the term "scandal" to have significance, we must be able to separate a scandal from a non-scandal. Scandals, thus, must meet specific criteria. We propose a set of ten criteria for making just such determinations. The first of these is that (1) *social norms reflecting the dominant morality must be transgressed*. This criterion is fundamental. Without it, no story can be regarded as a scandal. Considering the three stories above, each qualifies. Texaco: racism is wrong. Military: rape is wrong. Natural-juice: death or illness of innocent consumers is wrong.

Now come crucial, compound considerations. The transgressions must be performed by (2) *specific persons* who carry out (3) *actions* that reflect an exercise of their desires or interests. So real persons must do (not just think about) something where their selfish interests override social norms and dominant moralities. Further, individual persons must be (4) *identified* as perpetrators of the act(s). They must be shown to have acted (5) *intentionally or recklessly* and must be (6) *held responsible* for their actions. The actions and events must have (7) *differential consequences for those involved*.

Let us return to our three examples and see what happens when we match these criteria with those actual events.

In the Texaco case, the story qualified for scandal status precisely when the executives were captured on audiotape making racist remarks. They were specific persons, acting in ways that reinforced their own race-based privilege. They had been identified by name and were shown conspiring together to limit opportunities for minority employees in the company. In fact, the guilty executives had even undermined the supposed good intentions of the company's sensitivity training, wherein different-colored jelly beans are used analogously to represent diversity, by referring to minority employees in a derogatory way as "black jelly beans." Scandals feed on repugnant revelations such as this. Upon these disclosures, the chief executive officer at Texaco and the public at large held the executives responsible for their actions. Texaco was guilty too, of course, for having these men in decision-making positions. The anonymous "breakdown in responsibility" had been personalized while it simultaneously implicated the institution which sponsored it. The "morality" of Texaco's inner circle was exposed to be in conflict with the imagined dominant morality of the broader society.

Figure 1.1 Personalization. The scandal develops when media identify actual persons responsible for moral violations.
(A.P. Wide World Photos)

Similarly, the story about sexual abuse in the military became a scandal when the moral breakdown was shown to be something more than just a largely unspoken, undocumented institutional problem. The media discovered that male drill sergeants in training units were forcing females to have sex with them, and that senior officers were covering up the problem. The persons involved were named and acknowledged to be acting intentionally (sex is never an accident). The perpetrators of the sexual assaults had benefitted from their acts while the victims suffered. The public, and later the military itself, held the men responsible for the sexual abuses, and for the cover-up.

Next, we turn to the story about the natural-juice poisoning. This story had great scandal potential when it first broke. The public was outraged to find that a profitable corporation could be responsible for distributing bottles of juice that contained deadly bacteria. Even more sinister was the expectation that the juices were supposed to be "natural, healthy, and good for you." The poisoning certainly had differential consequences for those involved. In this alarming search for scandal, however, several criteria were not met. Although specific persons could be located who were responsible for the bottling process, and executives could be found who were ultimately responsible for the company's policies and activities, investigators could not show that the personal interests or desires of Odwalla employees were exercised in an abusive way. Yes, there was an institutional interest – turning a profit – and there was potential to show the exercise of intentionality or recklessness. Had the media found that a product-safety manager was sleeping or gambling in Las Vegas when she should have been overseeing health standards, for example, a scandal would surely have been born, particularly if the story were to have been drawn out into a series of mediated accusations and denials. But nothing like that happened.

The public finally decided that the natural-juice poisoning was an accident, not a scandal. The processing plant was inspected and found to be clean. In the end, officials decided that the poisoning was a "natural" consequence of a "natural" (unpasteurized) product. The company apparently had innocently bought some apples that had fallen into manure. Furthermore, the type of company it is – a natural-juice company operated by homespun folks in a small California town – provided a context for interpretation quite different from that of a multinational oil company or the United States military. One consumer quoted in the press even defended Odwalla: "Sometimes bad things happen to good companies." Like those physically harmed by the bacterial infection, Odwalla was deemed by the public to be a victim. To further inoculate the company against scandal potential, Odwalla recalled all its apple juices, and compromised the integrity of its market niche by promising to pasteurize all juices in the future.

Three additional criteria must be met before news events can become scandals. The revelations must be (8) *widely circulated via communications media* where they are (9) *effectively narrativized into a story* which (10) *inspires widespread interest and discussion*. We cannot overstate the importance of the concept "story" when analyzing scandals. The need for stories is basic to all societies, even preliterate ones. A scandal is not just a logical reporting of damaging facts, no matter how shocking they may be. In a scandal, the story triumphs over the facts at some point and in doing so takes on a life of its own. The scandal story arouses the curiosity of a substantial

Figure 1.2 Visibility. Modern communications technology provides new avenues of access to scandalous activity.
(By permission of Mike Luckovich and Creators Syndicate)

audience who encourage the media to continue "telling the story." The scandal continues as long as the public remains interested in the story. Closure requires some kind of social consensus, which often demands a final "truth," "moral lesson," or "justice served." Terms of closure rest ultimately with the public. The numbing longevity of the O.J. Simpson debacle is one particularly clear example of how the "not guilty" verdict in the criminal trial was an official ending to the story that the public would not accept.

Returning to our three examples, we are left with the Texaco and military stories to evaluate along these lines. It was a combination of micro and macro media that made the Texaco scandal possible. The audio recording of private conversations was turned over to television news agencies, where it was played repeatedly for several days, accompanied by a word-for-word written translation of the racially-tinged words being spoken by the disgraced executives. Audiences could *hear* and *see* the insults for themselves. What is more, audiences were exposed not only to the unacceptable words, but to the ideas behind them. Texaco's executives discussed shredding documents and keeping false records of hiring and promotion that disguised the company's employment practices.

The factual information about the taped incident was easily developed into a story. Texaco's problem with the executives' comments was connected to the *past*. It was put into the context of their institutional history of racism, a sorry chronology that was then told to a public whose interest had now been piqued by the incident. These revelations attracted a large and indignant public reaction, including lots of interpersonal and mediated talk, as well as a company boycott. But as was pointed out above, a scandal, like all stories, begs for an ending too – maybe not a "happy ending," but at least a satisfactory one. So the story simultaneously called out for *future* action. The details of the future were in the hands of Texaco. Right on cue, the company CEO said he was "shocked and angered" (the right emotional reaction) as were "all decent people" (admitting a moral violation). He said the racial slurs were "utterly reprehensible and deplorable" and would not be tolerated (the proper moral corrective). Punitive action was then taken against the "guilty" executives, a major financial settlement was reached, and fair hiring and promotion procedures were to be installed and monitored. The company was doing its best to "put an end to the story." That objective was met, however, only when the measures taken by Texaco were deemed sufficient by civil rights organizations which had intervened, and by the wider public.

Like the scandal itself, news of Texaco's corrective actions was made known to the public by means of the mass media. The media also spread the word that one of the most serious allegations made about the executive's racist remarks had apparently been reported incorrectly. What at first sounded like a man making the most callous reference to African Americans (the infamous "n" word, "niggers") turned out to be "Nicholas," according to sound experts who digitized and enhanced the audiotape. So it must be stressed that the media not only have the ability to ignite and fuel scandals; they can also relativize, downgrade, and extinguish them. Indeed, "scandal management" is the ultimate challenge of corporate public relations, but corporations must depend on the willingness of the media to report their responses, and hope that the public will accept the explanations.

The military sex scandal is similar to that of Texaco in that serious indiscretions on the part of some employees put a large institution under close scrutiny by the media. Beginning with one woman in Maryland who risked much by disclosing what had happened to her, more than 50 others brought charges of sexual abuse against the military. The military story became a bona fide sex scandal when officers were named, questioned by military authorities, and interrogated by the press. The unflattering personal background of several of the accused men was reported, giving the necessary historical perspective. The developing story took an ironic, newsworthy twist when victims and commentators pointed out that the attacks had taken place in a publicly-supported institution charged to protect people. As had been the case with Texaco (and many other scandals), military authorities had exacerbated the problem by trying to cover it up. The cover-up, of course, then became a central part of the story. The female victims *and* the dominant morality had been abused in multiple ways. But in a manner also resembling the Texaco story, the military sex scandal was attenuated months later when several of the women recanted their accusations, and blamed the army for coercing them into making untrue allegations in the investigation of rape charges.

As we have already seen, scandals are, in the first instance, events wherein moral boundaries are transgressed. Yet how do we know that the boundaries have been crossed unless the events are made available to an audience, who then decide the seriousness of the transgression? A scandal does not materialize until events are shaped into narrative form and those narratives are made accessible to a consuming public, who interpret and use the symbolic resources scandals provide for their own purposes. Media scandals (like media content generally) are predigested events which enter a network of personal relationships, where the scandal is implicitly evaluated and granted its moral intensity through personal reflection and social interaction. The scandal, thus, is produced not only by the media, but by audiences. Circulating as a social resource via media and interpersonal channels, scandals take their place as striking features of popular culture (Fiske 1989; Lull 1995).

Treatment of a potentially-scandalous event must take the form of a story complete with believable characters, motives, and plot lines. The shocking narrative is presented in a way appropriate to the content and genre of the story, but also by taking full advantage of the intrinsic characteristics of the communications medium. Because visual media can best capture the essence of a transgression by reducing it to a clear and understandable image, TV, newspapers, magazines, and on-line graphics are the best conveyors of the narrative (who could forget Nicole Simpson's bruised and bloody face on international TV, for instance, or the Duchess of

York stepping out of her lover's swimming pool onto the front pages of the tabloid press?). Of course, most media scandals are multimedia events: the tabloid press, trash TV video, on-line services, mainstream TV news, even radio all construct versions of the story fitting to their technologies and audiences. The TV narrative of the media scandal, for example, blends empirical events with visual techniques (e.g. close-up shots, fast-cut editing, slow motion) and an audio narration. The presentation must appear to be "news," so it should resemble other news stories, particularly other scandals. It must evoke a "master narrative" of scandal, even if what this construction finally produces does not authentically reflect the event itself.

A free-falling, expectation-raising quality to the story becomes a central characteristic of the scandal. Various media outlets compete with one another to create the next chapter to the story; the more repugnant, the better. Because media scandals tend to unravel slowly, they are profitable in the same way as other aspects of popular culture make money; they are milked for all they are worth until the opinion polls and ratings show that the audience has tired of the story.

The ecology of scandal

Media scandals, like all symbolic displays, exist in a complex relation to a wide range of sociocultural influences, including other symbolic forms, even other scandals. Given this, we want to bring the following four considerations into play about media scandals:

1 Some people and institutions are more vulnerable to scandal than others. There are differences, therefore, in *scandal susceptibility*.
2 Scandals are never interpreted uniformly by audiences, so they are *polysemic*.
3 Scandals frequently inform each other in a process of *scandal intertextuality*.
4 Scandals' relationship to one another are sometimes perceived by news agencies and by audiences in terms of a *scandal hierarchy*.

Specific scandalous acts performed by individuals often are perceived within a structure of expectations related to that person, as in the case of a celebrity involved in a scandal, or framed in terms of the institutions with which the person is associated. There is a

disreputable history of scandal, for instance, related to the environment of politics – "Politicians and government are inherently
corrupt." Watergate and Richard Nixon have become synonymous
with scandal. Any scandalous misdeeds attributed to a politician
today necessarily will be read against this generalized reputation
of party politics. Big business also has a history of abuse related
to greed with which to contend. Because Western, capitalist societies have endured numerous scandals in politics and business,
we are hardly surprised when new allegations are made. Such
institutions, therefore, have a high degree of scandal susceptibility.
In the final analysis, though, this same history imbues us with a
pervasive cynicism that can make it quite difficult for scandals
about politics or business to reach epic proportions. The Whitewater
financial scandal plagued the Clinton administration for years,
for instance, but it certainly did not deny him an overwhelming
victory in 1996, and most Americans did not even claim to be
much bothered by the story (see Gronbeck, this volume).

Fairness is an issue in cases such as these too. Scandals such
as Texaco's and the US military sexual assaults discussed previously become especially horrific, and attractive to media audiences,
when the moral violations in question occur under conditions of
structural inequality. Differences in power are endemic to institutions. In the Texaco case, the rich, white executives were abusing
the career potential of lesser-paid, black employees. In the military
case, strong men took advantage of their position to abuse physically weaker, younger women of lower rank. Returning to politics,
Bill Clinton's alleged extramarital sexual adventures were perceived
to bring harm not only to those female acquaintances who accused
him of the misdeeds, but also to his wife and daughter.

The way the media represent the scandal suggests the inflection,
clarity, and intensity of the transgressive events, and encourages
audience members to make preferred moral judgments. But these
judgments are not so predictable. The scandal narrative is always
read differentially by various audiences. Furthermore, audience readings take the form of both the abstract/universal and the concrete/
particular (Johnson 1986). So, for example, the scandal can be seen
by any one person simultaneously as a sign of a nation or culture's
moral decay (as in a moral panic), but also in terms of the actual
circumstances pertaining to the subjects of the story. These understandings are then further shaped by the way they enter the lived
cultures and social relationships of their interpreters–users. In
any case, scandals become the stuff of modern-day conversation

that is told and retold in the employee lounge, around the TV set in the sitting room, and in chat rooms on the Internet.

The polysemy, intertextuality, and hierarchical nature of scandal (see Tomlinson, this volume) are well illustrated by the O.J. Simpson scandal, which will likely go down in history as the "scandal of scandals." The Simpson case shows how conditions can even be interpreted in a way favorable to a person who is negatively implicated in a scandal. For the mainly black jury serving in that trial, and for the vast majority of black Americans, the "scandal" deemed more harmful than the former football star's alleged murders was the perceived racism and police abuse sensed by black residents of Los Angeles and elsewhere. The police department was more susceptible to scandal in the minds of the jurors than Simpson was. For many, Mark Fuhrmann (the white policeman who had been audiotaped using racial slurs against black Americans, and who was also accused by Simpson's lawyers of planting evidence) was more guilty than Simpson, not least because his racist remarks and perjury became a symbol of police racism and corruption (see Gray, this volume, for a discussion of how scandals related to blackness may take form). The Simpson scandal is not contained within the margins of its own storyline either. A spokesperson for the National Urban League, a civil rights organization in the United States composed mainly of black Americans, said that when he heard the audiotapes from the Texaco scandal, the emotional impact was similar to hearing Mark Fuhrmann's racial slurs during the Simpson trial the previous year.

Scandals sometimes compete with each other. Besides market saturation, the biggest ratings enemy of the scandal-ridden daytime TV talk show in America in the 1990s was the year-long Simpson trial. Even the tedious explanation of DNA and forensics tests in the trial overcame competing topics like "Pregnant women confront the unemployed father of their children," "Dating virgins to avoid contracting AIDS," "Promiscuous women with a weight problem," and "Highlights of conflicts between guests on previous shows" scheduled on other channels.

A typology of scandals

What we have discussed in the case of Texaco and the US military is what we call the *institutional scandal*. This is the first type

Table 1 Typology of media scandals

Scandal type	Platform	Key characteristics
Institutional	• Bureaucratic matrix • Institutional history, reputation	• Personalization • Institution held publicly responsible
Star	• Name recognition • Celebrity image system	• Intense media scrutiny • Moral contextualization • Fiction/reality blurred • Public sanctions
Psychodrama	• Basic cognitive-emotional structures • Cultural pressure points • Strong stories • Character "types"	• Moral violations by "ordinary people" • Turns persons into "stars" • Cultural contextualization • Societal psychic release

of scandal in our typology (table 1). The institutional scandal, as we have seen, develops when actions that disgrace or offend the dominant morality take place in settings such as government offices or corporate suites. While we live in a world that is increasingly characterized by abstract systems and vast, distant bureaucracies that carry out their work, the seemingly anonymous institutions of late modernity remain *social* ones. The real persons who make up the institutions of politics, education, business, military, and religion are motivated not only by professional objectives, but by private desires that sometimes conflict with prevailing moral standards. Their indiscretions become scandalous because these persons represent not only themselves, but the institutions in which they are professionally situated.

The institutions are held publicly to a moral standard that individual persons associated with them fail to meet. So, for example, Prince Charles's infidelities scandalized the monarchy; Bill Clinton's love affairs and financial dealings said something about politics and the presidency; the Texaco executives embarrassed their company; child-abusing Catholic priests put the church in trouble; and so on. Modern institutions are, in some respects, even more vulnerable than individual persons to the social backlash that media visibility produces because institutions often pretend to set moral examples (through institutional advertising and public relations) which can quickly turn into empty promises. Scandals thus relativize the image and integrity of institutions by putting a human face (and body) on the transgression. Stories of institutional scandals also remind us that whatever trust we place in abstract systems is ultimately subject to radical violation and social revision.

Just as familiar as the institutional scandal, and often more interesting to the public, are the two other types of scandal in the basic typology presented here. The *star scandal*, our second category, is a prime focus of this book. As its name suggests, a star scandal erupts when the mass media reveal an instance of how the desires of famous people overrule social expectations, norms, and practices. The private behavior of a public persona enters the public arena under circumstances that are outside the star's control. That behavior then becomes evaluated according to the dominant moral code. Stars are in a paradoxical position. They may be given more moral leeway in expectations about their social behavior, but at the same time they endure closer scrutiny than other people.

Narratives of the star scandal are fleshed out dramatically with real-world characters, motivations, and plots, which appear chapter by chapter in news programs, on talk shows, and in the tabloid and mainstream press. The media narratives become widely-circulated conversational touchstones at home, at work, at school, and on the street. In the process, the star scandal not only raises questions about the integrity of individual celebrities, but reinforces the idea that even famous people finally must be held responsible to society's moral expectations.

A star's moral violations, however, are always contextualized in terms of his or her "image system" (Lull 1995). By this we mean that any particular transgression is constructed and read against an image in circulation. Of course, image systems differ widely. Take, for instance, Madonna, Michael Jackson, and Hugh Grant as three exemplars of the star scandal. Madonna has constructed her success partly by creating a scandalous style. Michael Jackson has done so too; however, his image system has always been far more ambiguous and conservative than Madonna's (see Hinerman, this volume). Hugh Grant, of course, was perceived to be a choir boy, probably a tenor, until he invited Divine Brown to try out the leather seats of his BMW one lonely Los Angeles evening. So while all three of these stars have been implicated in moral violations involving sex, the nature of the scandals constructed about them differs greatly owing to considerable variation in their public image. That public image, of course, commutes between the star as a person, and the star as a performer. The image system is an amalgam of impressions that blurs any boundary between reality and fiction, as in the case of soap-opera stars or movie stars who may be judged as much by their dramatic roles as by their "real" personalities and situations. The private act(s) in which stars engage thus are interpreted according to the dominant morality, but they are simultaneously relativized in terms of the moral character and boundaries of the star's complex image system. The star scandal forges an intersection composed of three semiotic trajectories: society's dominant morality, the particular image system of the star in question, and the actual events as reported in the news. The dynamic interplay of these factors gives each star scandal its particular platforms for interpretation.

Just as stars earn fame and fortune from the power of media and popular culture, they also suffer at the hands of the same devices. Consider, for instance, how the scandals of Richard Nixon, Magic Johnson, O.J. Simpson, Jim Bakker, and John Profumo altered the consciousness of their publics. What will Charles and Diana's legacy be for citizens of the United Kingdom? Will Maradona be remembered mainly as a great football player in Argentina? Carlos Salinas as the president who modernized Mexico? Rock Hudson as an accomplished actor?

Our third main category of scandals is the *psychodrama*. These scandals are not about celebrities, but the stories they entail frequently make stars out of ordinary people. While the star scandal makes the indiscretions of well-known persons public, the psychodrama scandal turns ordinary persons who do extraordinary things into public figures. Two ingredients are crucial. First, the psychodrama scandal story must be compelling in a particular way, and, second, the characters ("stars") should reflect stereotypes fitting to the story. The chemistry between the narrative and the characters is what creates the charm of the story, generating the psychodrama scandal's popular appeal.

Specifically, how does a good psychodrama scandal take form? Many of the most significant media scandals are born when a narrative representing acts undertaken by ordinary people is transgressive in ways that tap into fundamental and powerful cognitive-emotional structures, though these structures always take culturally-specific forms. These scandals resonate with our core emotions by touching basic human predicaments, fears, passions, and weaknesses. One major focus of media attention is the human body – a sensual body situated within the normative expectations and practices of a dominant morality, but subject nonetheless to life's parade of temptations. Psychodrama scandals, thus, often deal with our sexual preoccupations, fantasies, and insecurities. We deal with such quandaries and internal struggles vicariously through the scandal. By making moral issues so visible and entertaining, while at the same time so distant and impersonal, the psychodrama scandal gives its interpretants a viable and safe channel through which to release psychic tension.

The psychodrama scandal also usually features characters who epitomize particular "types." The players in the scandal should be attractive or interesting in a very familiar or extreme way. They could be babes, bitches, dopes, machos, nerds, or sluts. They could be geeks, freaks, bullies, fools, devils, or angels. Heroes and villains should be clearly identifiable. The psychodrama scandal succeeds in part when audiences recognize the characters in the play. The more a scandal's characters resemble ideal or stereotypical people doing extraordinary things in everyday settings, the better the chance for a media scandal to emerge.

For example, consider the "love triangle," a psychodrama story structure dating back to the beginning of human history. Unique variations on the emotional and sexual aspects of the love triangle have definite scandal potential. One paradigmatic instance of this was the Joey Buttafuoco–Mary Jo Buttafuoco–Amy Fisher triad of the early 1990s that captured much attention in America. The basic story has a sultry, teenage sex kitten (Amy) who meets a married, middle-aged, blue-collar hustler type (Joey); they then have an affair. When Amy is unable to win Joey's long-term affections, she buys a gun and tries to solve the problem by killing Joey's wife, Mary Jo. She fails. Amy is sent to jail for attempted murder, while Joey is left to explain his professed moral innocence to an increasingly hostile (especially female) public. The story fits the classic mold and the characters are perfectly cast. Even better, we have a double transgression with a twist: adultery, then violence from an unlikely source (girl to wife). Amy is the pouty-lipped seductress. Joey is the dirty old man. Mary Jo is the loyal, forgiving victim. The unusual murder attempt is what first made the story intriguing to the media; then the stereotypicality of the characters took hold as the story progressed in time, creating an attractive and durable scandal.

Such stories bring moral predicaments to light, make good drama out of the way the predicament unfolds, and populate the narrative with believable, real-world characters. In the Buttafuoco–Fisher story, a fundamental social concern and moral dilemma is narrativized.

Just the right mixture of moral predictability (young girl tempts married man) and unpredictability (girl tries to kill her lover's wife) were brought together in story form. And, because the stars were *not* actors and actresses – but fit the character mold perfectly – the "reality is better than fiction" effect contributed to the scandal's "hit" potential with audiences. When stories like this catch on as scandal narratives, the characters begin to appear everywhere on the media. For instance, two of the major television networks in the United States aired a miniseries on the Buttafuoco–Fisher scandal. Especially when the characters fit role stereotypes as neatly as they did in this story, they can quite easily become fixed in the popular consciousness as scandal stars. Even the jilted wife became a stereotype of passivity; the relatively little media attention given her compared to Joey and Amy only reinforced her pathetic background role as victim in the scandalous drama of sex and romance.

Psychodrama scandals must be able to shock on the strength of the story. They do so first by making moral predicaments explicit, then by revealing how moral expectations are transgressed. The stars of other recent psychodrama scandals where morality and desire collide are Lorena Bobbitt, the Venezuelan-American woman who cut off the penis of her abusive husband (John Wayne Bobbitt) and threw it out a car window, and Susan Smith, who locked her children in a car which she pushed into a lake, telling authorities the youngsters were "kidnapped by a black man." Television talk shows often rely on short-lived psychodramas for their appeal too. As Laura Grindstaff explains in her chapter in this volume, TV talk-show guests are encouraged to unpack, even brag about, their private behaviors for the amusement of audiences.

Some of the most famous media scandals combine features of the psychodrama scandal with the star scandal. The Tonya Harding –Nancy Kerrigan story discussed in this volume by David Rowe is a good example. Tonya, a short, muscular, working-class girl, conspired to have Nancy, a tall, elegant, upper-middle-class girl, physically assaulted while the two competed for places on the US Olympic figure skating team. While the two skaters were somewhat famous prior to the event, the psychodrama quality made the story fascinating and greatly enhanced their visibility and fame. Or how about Selena, the beautiful Tejana singer who was shot to death in a motel room by the much older, physically unattractive president of her fan club? Even the enormous appeal of the O.J. Simpson star scandal had a complex psychodramatic dimension:

interracial marriage, an untold history of domestic abuse, Ron Goldman killed while carrying out a good deed, an acquittal most people feel is based on race, the triumph of golf over O.J.'s promise to dedicate his life to finding the "real killers," the custody battle for the children, and so on.

Shame, guilt, and community

> You are a person who knows how to defend her principles and values. And you look a lot prettier in person than you do on television.
>
> *Abdala Bucaram, former president of Ecuador, upon meeting*
> *Lorena Bobbitt*

The disgrace that scandals bring presumes the presence of a community to which individual persons are held accountable. Whether these are communities of neighborhood, culture, gender, class, race, or nation, *the disgrace of scandal lies in the collective willingness of others to impose shame and even bring damage upon the scandalizer*. The scandalizer is disgraced because he or she is believed to have violated norms which are then read by members of the culture as known-in-common markers of the offense. Every cultural community has norms and moral standards which are taught by society's institutions as social rules (see Lull 1995). Violation of the norms leads to sanctions, which promote outrage that threatens to expel the scandalizer from the community. One need only think in our own time about the O.J. Simpson scandal, where, even long after his courtroom acquittal on criminal charges of murder, so much negative attention was given him that he was *de facto* expelled from the larger community despite his "innocence" (or lack of proven guilt). Such expulsion included golf courses denying him admittance, members of the public jamming telephone lines so he could not sell his self-promoting videos, and women's rights groups making him the poster boy for domestic violence. Many of his Los Angeles neighbors implored him to sell his home and leave town: "And go where?," O.J. asked; "They want me to go back to Africa, that's what some of these people want!" Indeed, after the unanimous civil court finding of liability, rumors immediately surfaced that he was moving from California to escape such intense public scrutiny.

We must understand that the shame that scandals inflict reflects a unique kind of social accountability, different from guilt, and influenced greatly by the mass media. Differentiating between guilt and shame has been a common interest of psychologists and sociologists for decades. Essentially both guilt and shame are about social transgressions or violations, but guilt has more to do with individual misdeeds while shame is about the integrity of the person. One can be guilty of a crime, for instance, but feel no shame as a person. Guilt derives from "feelings of wrongdoing" while shame demeans the "integrity of the self" (Giddens 1991: 65) and the person's self-esteem (Giddens 1992: 108). Guilt can be repaired and managed. A person can apologize, pay a fine, serve time in jail, change behavior, or combine these in various ways. That feelings of guilt can be fixed by therapy is a cornerstone of Freudian psychoanalysis. Guilt is a contextualized lapse in conduct; shame reflects much more deeply and permanently on a flawed person. Guilt is what you have done; shame is who you are.

Clearly, shame is far more condemning than guilt. Although shame is about self-integrity and respect, it is a quintessential *social and cultural* construct. It has to do with how others view the self as a long-term project. Shame results when a person's hidden traits are exposed for social sanction, thereby compromising the inner narrative of self-identity (Giddens 1991: 67). The shamed person may feel disrespected, unwanted, unloved, undesirable, unintelligent. Because shame is socially constructed as a permanent condition, the shamed person is without hope and is, therefore, undesirable to the community.

We believe the media scandal disturbs conventional distinctions made between guilt and shame. The media scandal disembeds human actions and recontextualizes them into far-reaching, symbolic realities. The media make moral transgressions profoundly visible to an interpretive community, and in doing so make the perpetrators of such actions shameful. Those scandals call attention to particular moral transgressions, string them out for maximum entertainment value, humiliate the "guilty" party as an essential programmatic ingredient in the process, then send the whole package deep into the social fabric where severe moral judgments are enthusiastically rendered by a large audience. Such judgments may comfort "readers" of scandals who search their "internal referential systems" for stability and love in modernity's climate of uncertainty and moral permissiveness, particularly when sexual conduct is at issue (Giddens 1992: 175–6).

But the effect of the media scandal need not solely extend guilt into shame. In the case of O.J. Simpson, the media scandal even helped make a person who was found "not guilty" shameful. This happened precisely because the scandal narrative was more powerful socially than the legal judgment (a fact which then made the judgment itself scandalous), keeping in mind that it is what the audience does with the narrative that determines its outcome. In the end, the jury at large for O.J. Simpson may have been far more influential than the twelve sequestered souls who sat in the courtroom. The process can work the other way too. Lorena Bobbitt could have been guilty in a court of law, but given the conditions of patriarchy generally, and her marriage in particular, the world audience was more likely to impose shame on her abusive husband than on her. It was a classic case of "victim rises up." The scandal thus can also make a "guilty" person less shameful.

Just the mention of people and institutions implicated by scandals can stimulate an emotional response, a reaction conditioned by the fact that we know a moral standard we have been taught to respect has been violated, even though we may be not completely innocent of such violations ourselves. Indeed, the impact of scandals may well be exacerbated by the discontinuity between the high moral standard of the idealized dominant culture (the "good life" or "superculture") that is reinforced by the media, and the far less honorable realm of our own everyday lives. We must distinguish, therefore, between the moral contours of the dominant culture, and the lived realities of culture in practice. So racism is wrong, but practiced; sexual inequality is wrong, but practiced. Part of the appeal of the media scandal may be that it touches our own individual human weaknesses, providing us an opportunity to deal with such thoughts vicariously, and to render a safe moral judgment. We can displace the shame of our own transgressions by observing and talking about the well-publicized misdeeds of others.

Shame as a consequence of scandal bears not only on the minds of individuals. There is collective shame too. With his presidential hopes fading at the same time as fresh allegations about the incumbent's sexual and financial dealings were front-page news, a frustrated Ross Perot berated the American public: "Why isn't there any shame about this in our country?" The Republicans (Colin Powell in particular), too, said it was time to "restore a sense of shame in society." But recalling our discussion of moral panics early in this chapter, we know that the dominant morality is becoming less and less certain.

Even with the uncertainties and limitations, media scandals function uniquely and powerfully as subject matter for the exercise of an interpretive community's conscience by telling sensational stories of right versus wrong. The scandal is the consummate content display of the media cultural forum (Newcomb and Hirsch 1987), where the dominant morality is negotiated through public media. So while communication technologies make media scandals possible, this fact should not be judged too harshly. The common condemning view of scandal does not explain their significance well. The media have the ability to demystify as well as mystify, to descandalize as well as scandalize, to calm as well as agitate.

Media scandals and the fourth estate

In their discussion of moral panics, Angela McRobbie and Sarah Thornton argue that the communications media assume the societal role of "moral guardian, ever alert to new possibilities for concern and indignation" (McRobbie and Thornton 1995: 570). One motive for such activity, no doubt, is financial gain. Competing voices in the crowded media marketplace today scream for attention more loudly than ever before. The media scandal is one proven means to stimulate public outrage and corporate profits. It is certainly true that the media scandal sometimes represents the worst of yellow journalism.

But that is not the end of the story. The media scandal is also a popular forum for public awareness and debate of moral questions – issues that often have strong implications for public policy. From Watergate to O.J. Simpson and beyond, the news media try to uncover hidden truths and expose those responsible. In one sense, then, constructing certain media scandals is a major contribution to the mediated public sphere in modern society. One can argue, therefore, that such often-derided activity is in fact a modern-day exercise of "fourth estate" responsibilities, wherein the press keeps close tabs on those in society who wield tremendous political, economic, and cultural power. A more comprehensive view credits scandal as one form of vigorous investigative journalism. Any analysis of contemporary media ethics, therefore, cannot fairly dismiss the media scandal as nothing more than sensationalism.

Sometimes the journalistic vigilance characteristic of the media scandal even threatens the profit-driven interests of the news industries. The Texaco racism case, for instance, was interesting partly because the multinational oil giant is a national advertiser of considerable proportion. The media thus were biting one of the hands that feed them by investigating the company so closely and by disclosing such clear and shocking evidence. So while scandals may attract audiences and ratings points, the critiques they feature can also drive a wedge between the culture industries and the advertisers they depend on.

The discursive implications of media scandals are paramount. Scandals are more than just the sum of disgraceful details told in any interesting way. They encourage public discussions of sensitive, controversial issues. But the role of communications media is not only to call attention to such issues. The media also have the capacity to expose those responsible for moral violations, hold them accountable, and turn active scandals into history by providing a publicly-acceptable end to the story. The media thus not only stimulate moral outrage, but can also reduce public fears and concerns by relativizing scandals and by descandalizing topics.

Communications media technologies have proliferated with unprecedented rapidity during recent years. Along the way, established news sources such as the American commercial networks and the BBC have seen their market shares dwindle under the crush of competition from a myriad of cable and satellite channels, most of which offer news coverage. The look of that news, of course, does not necessarily follow traditional patterns. The advent of alternative, personality-driven news in television programs and tabloid newspapers has made the media scandal a foundational content area. The Internet also comes into play these days, opening more opportunities for media scandals and changing the way they are produced. Internet news groups now make it possible for people to gossip about Hollywood stars, for instance, in ways that have made some kinds of scandal production much faster and more socially interactive than ever before.

Through it all, however, the core polemic remains constant: human populations construct codes of moral conduct which are violated by individuals who privilege their personal desires over the rules of society. As we have seen, certain stories of such violations routinely attract the rapt attention of media audiences, sometimes even at a global level. The negotiation of moral standards is a never-ending social process, facilitated in no small measure today by the provocative images and discourses of the media scandal. To ignore or underestimate the role of the media scandal in modern societies is to miss an increasingly conspicuous and vital phenomenon. Indeed, in the fast-paced, media-dependent world we live in, can we even argue against the proposition that the media scandal is a crucial outpost for moral thinking and decision making? Can we afford not to take the media scandal seriously?

Scandals just ahead . . .

In the next chapter John B. Thompson reviews scandal as a sociological concept and develops several themes from his earlier work. He is particularly interested in the crucial question of how communications media have dramatically increased the visibility and accountability of public figures in late modernity, and the role that scandal plays in that. Then John Tomlinson explores the nature of media scandals in an international, intercultural frame. He relates media scandals to debates about a global public sphere and cosmopolitan cultural values. Tomlinson interrogates the problem of why some issues attract global scrutiny while others do not, and how a hierarchy of scandal might relate to conceptualizations of universal human interests. Herman Gray argues overall that the term "scandal" itself must be problematized. From whose point of view is a scandal a scandal? Gray explains how the black social and corporal body is central to media representations of scandal and moral panic in the late twentieth century. He concludes that such representations may be in and of themselves scandalous. S. Elizabeth Bird continues her theoretical and empirical work on the popular appeal of scandalous news by analyzing how readers and viewers actually use scandals. She argues that scandals enter the culture orally, via daily conversations, and become above all else a kind of modern-day oral folklore serving to socialize audience members culturally, while at the same time serving as an outlet for fantasy and wish fulfillment.

Bruce E. Gronbeck explores how the media scandal has seriously remade American presidential politics in recent years. The author describes how erasing the line between public and private and between politics and entertainment has conflated "character" with "celebrity." He then shows how changes in the political process have impacted on the national sense of public morality. Stephen Hinerman then analyzes how the tabloid TV and press have represented the alleged sexual transgressions of pop music superstar

Michael Jackson. Because the tabloids ultimately could not fix the "truth" of either Jackson's sexual persona or his apparently untoward adventures, they were left with endless speculation. Hinerman shows how such ambiguity is turned into a narrative about morality, helping to create a scandal in the process. In the next chapter Laura Grindstaff explains how the much-maligned, but frequently-viewed, American TV talk show constructs scandalous discourses as one of its main themes. Her analysis derives from long-term ethnographic research conducted on the set at two well-known daytime shows. This chapter reveals how the everyday norms, routines, and practices of talk-show production are put to work in order to make scandalous content appealing to a large audience. David Rowe then takes up the ways sports scandals highlight and problematize structures of social and cultural power. He presents the anatomy and "natural history" of the sports scandal, its appeal to the audience, the metonymic functions of the athletic body, the ethics of Olympism, and the kinds of conclusions that can be drawn from the scandals of Magic Johnson, O.J. Simpson, Mike Tyson, and Tonya Harding.

We then turn to the site where the term "scandal" was originally used – the church. Paul Soukup shows how an ideological and cultural tension between the church and the media has developed in the concrete instance of the religious scandal. By analyzing televangelism, allegations of pedophilia against priests and ministers, and financial misdealings by church members, Soukup describes how the scandal differentiates the church and media as social, cultural, and rhetorical forces. Finally, Javier Santiago-Lucerna traces the origins of scandal in contemporary popular music and explains the impacts and limitations of scandals as a cultural phenomenon and market force. He analyzes the genesis of the Sex Pistols, and the extraordinary scene created by Madonna's visit to Puerto Rico, in order to show how the complex roles of the media scandal take shape in the spectacle of performance, and in the creation of marketable imagery in popular music.

Notes

1 Scandals do not always pay. For example, O.J. Simpson memorabilia do not fetch much money. Nicole Brown Simpson's condominium sold for considerably less than market value two years after the murders. The president of Argentina, Carlos Menem, suffered politically from his friendship with

football star Maradona after the athlete was busted for cocaine possession and distribution. James Hewitt had a difficult time selling his story
of a five-year love affair with Princess Diana. Personalities and property
associated with scandals frequently become ostracized by the societies in
which they occur (see the later section in this chapter on "Shame, guilt, and
community").

2 We should point out that the increased visibility does not just threaten to
discredit famous people or powerful institutions. They gain much favorable
public recognition from media exposure too. Furthermore, these people and
institutions have learned many effective techniques for managing the exposure they receive from the media (Reimer 1995).

References

Beck, U. (1992). *Risk Society*. London: Sage.

Boethius, U. (1995). Youth, the media, and moral panics. In J. Fornas and
G. Bolin (eds), *Youth Culture in Late Modernity*. London: Sage.

Cohen, S. (1980). *Folk Devils and Moral Panics: The Creation of the Mods and
Rockers*. Oxford: Blackwell.

Fiske, J. (1989). *Understanding Popular Culture*. Boston: Unwin-Hyman.

Giddens, A. (1991). *Modernity and Self-Identity*. Cambridge, UK: Polity Press;
Stanford, CA: Stanford University Press.

Giddens, A. (1992). *The Transformation of Intimacy*. Cambridge, UK: Polity Press;
Stanford, CA: Stanford University Press.

Goffman, E. (1959). *The Presentation of the Self in Everyday Life*. New York:
Doubleday.

Johnson, R. (1986). The story so far: And further transformations. In D. Punter
(ed.), *Introduction to Contemporary Cultural Studies*. London: Longman.

LaClau, E. (1990). *New Reflections on the Revolution of Our Time*. London:
Verso.

Lull, J. (1995). *Media, Communication, Culture: A Global Approach*. Cambridge,
UK: Polity Press; New York: Columbia University Press.

McRobbie, A. (1994). *Postmodernism and Popular Culture*. London: Routledge.

McRobbie, A. and Thornton, S.L. (1995). Rethinking "moral panic" for multi-
mediated social worlds. *British Journal of Sociology* 46: 4(559–74).

Meyrowitz, J. (1985). *No Sense of Place: The Impact of Electronic Media on Social
Behavior*. New York: Oxford University Press.

Newcomb, H. and Hirsch, P. (1987). Television as a cultural form. In H.
Newcomb (ed.), *Television: The Critical View*. New York: Oxford University
Press.

Oxford English Dictionary (1989). Prepared by J.A. Simpson and E.S.C. Weiner,
2nd edn, vol. 14. Oxford, UK: Clarendon Press.

Pearson, G. (1983). *Hooligans: A History of Respectable Fear*. London: Macmillan.

Reimer, B. (1995). The media in public and private spheres. In J. Fornas and
G. Bolin (eds), *Youth Culture in Late Modernity*. London: Sage.

Tebbel, J. (1974). *The Media in America*. New York: Thomas Y. Crowell.

Thompson, J.B. (1995). *The Media and Modernity: A Social Theory of the Media*.
Cambridge, UK: Polity Press; Stanford, CA: Stanford University Press.

Thornton, S.L. (1995). *Club Culture: Music, Media, and Subcultural Capital*. Cambridge, UK: Polity Press.

Watney, S. (1987). *Policing Desire: Pornography, AIDS and the Media*. London: Methuen.

Young, J. (1971). *The Drugtakers: The Social Meaning of Drug Use*. London: Paladin.

2 Scandal and Social Theory

John B. Thompson

Domestic treachery, systematic and long-continued deception, the whole squalid apparatus of letters written with the intent of misleading, houses taken under false names, disguises and aliases, secret visits, and sudden flights make up a story of dull and ignoble infidelity . . . The popular standard of morality may not be too exalted, but even the least prudish draw the line for public men above the level of a scandalous exposure like this, and cynically observe that, when the man of loose life is found out, he must take the consequences.[1]

Such was the judgment of *The Times*, commenting more than a century ago on the well-publicized affair of Mr Charles Parnell and Mrs Katherine O'Shea, an affair which eventually culminated in a successful divorce action brought by Captain William O'Shea on grounds of adultery. The affair might have generated relatively little interest in the press had it not been for the fact that Mr Parnell was a pivotal political figure at the time. Heralded as "the uncrowned King of Ireland", Parnell was the Member of Parliament (MP) for Cork and the charismatic leader of the Irish parliamentary party at Westminster; he was also a fervent advocate of Irish Home Rule, a cause to which Gladstone's Liberal Party had lent its support but which the Tories, among others, opposed. It was in this sensitive political context, where Parnell was a key power broker in the complex negotiations concerning the future of British–Irish relations, that the affair with Katherine O'Shea suddenly burst into public view.

Charles Parnell and Katherine O'Shea had met in the summer of 1880, at a dinner party to celebrate Captain O'Shea's election as MP for County Clare. It seems likely that the affair began soon afterward. Captain O'Shea spent much time abroad, while Mrs O'Shea resided with their three children at their home in Eltham, Kent, where Parnell was a regular visitor. Rumors circulated about a possible affair, but speculation was curtailed by repeated denials until 1886, when the *Pall Mall Gazette* reported rather discreetly, under the headline "Mr Parnell's suburban retreat," that the MP for Cork had been involved in a collision with a market gardener's cart shortly after midnight on a Friday evening. "During the sitting of Parliament," the *Gazette* continued, "the hon. member for Cork usually takes up his residence at Eltham, a suburban village in the south-east of London."[2] Discretion notwithstanding, the implications of this report were perfectly clear. Relations between Captain O'Shea and his wife deteriorated, further revelations ensued, and on December 24, 1889, the captain filed for divorce, naming Charles Parnell as co-respondent.

When the trial opened on November 16, 1890, it was the focus of intense interest and was widely reported in the press. Mrs O'Shea denied the charges of adultery and alleged, in turn, that her husband had been guilty of neglect, cruelty, and misconduct, and that he himself had committed adultery. Neither Mrs O'Shea nor Parnell turned up to defend the action; Captain O'Shea's counsel, on the other hand, produced a string of letters and called witnesses – including former servants whose vivid testimonies were reported in the press – which seemed to establish a pattern of infidelity and deceit that had continued for several years. The jury found in favor of the plaintiff and granted the divorce.[3] In the days and weeks following the trial, the press was filled with speculation about Parnell's political future. Parnell rejected calls for his resignation, but his position as leader of the Irish parliamentary party became increasingly untenable. In December 1890 the party split into two factions, one supporting Parnell and the other opposed to him. In the following months Parnell campaigned in several by-elections in Ireland; in each case the Parnellite candidate lost and Parnell's position was weakened further. In June, 1891, Parnell married Katherine O'Shea, but their marriage was not to last for long. Addressing a crowd in the rain during a by-election in September 1891, Parnell caught a severe chill and died of rheumatic fever several days later, at the age of 45.

This sorry tale of a lofty career undone by scandalous disclosures has, in the late twentieth century, a wearisomely familiar ring. John

Profumo, Jeremy Thorpe, Cecil Parkinson, Richard Nixon, Edward Kennedy, Gary Hart: these are but a few of the more recent names in a long list of public figures, stretching back into the nineteenth century and well before, whose lives and careers have been indelibly marked by the scandals that unfolded around them. Of course, not all scandals have consequences which are as devastating for the individuals concerned, and as serious for the causes they pursue, as the affair between Charles Parnell and Katherine O'Shea had been for them and for the cause of Irish Home Rule. But some scandals do have consequences which are as great as (perhaps even greater than) these, and there are few scandals that do not represent at the very least a serious threat to the reputations of the individuals who are embroiled in them.

Despite the long history of scandal and the profusion of scandalous disclosures of various kinds in the public domain today, there is a dearth of serious scholarly literature on the subject. There are several anthologies which offer informative but rather light-hearted tours of a terrain strewn with the damaged reputations of politicians and other public figures;[4] and there are many books and articles, written both by journalists and by participants who have varying degrees of insider knowledge, which retell the stories of particular scandals from differing points of view. But there are very few scholarly studies which seek to examine, in a more analytical fashion, the nature of scandals and the social conditions which shape their emergence, development, and consequences.[5] No doubt scandal is viewed by many academic commentators as a subject too frivolous and a phenomenon too ephemeral to warrant serious and sustained attention.

In this chapter I shall adopt a different view. I shall contend that scandal is a more significant phenomenon than many commentators are inclined to assume, and I shall argue that the growing significance of scandal is symptomatic of certain broad changes in the development of modern societies – symptomatic, in particular, of the changing nature of communication media, which have transformed the nature of visibility and altered the relations between public and private life. Not all scandals are mediated scandals; like gossip and rumor, which are similar in some respects,[6] scandal is a fairly common feature of social life and does not necessarily presuppose disclosure through the media. But the great scandals which have featured – and no doubt will continue to feature – so prominently in the public domain are generally linked to the activities of media organizations. I shall attempt to shed some light on the nature of this connection and to draw out some of its implications.

However, we cannot explore the relation between scandal and the media unless we first get clear about the nature of scandal itself. What exactly is a scandal? What are the origins of the word "scandal" and what does it mean today? These are the questions I shall address in the first section of this chapter before turning, in the second section, to the relation between scandal and the media. In the third and final section, I shall try to assess some of the broader social and political consequences of scandal. Before I begin, I should add one qualification. If one looks through the history of scandal, it quickly becomes clear that this is an extremely complex and varied phenomenon. Scandals occur in many different social settings and their characteristics vary from one historical and cultural context to another. In the space of this chapter I shall not attempt to examine all forms of scandal, or to explore the cultural variations in any detail. I shall concentrate on a particular type of scandal – namely, those that break out in the political sphere – and I shall draw my examples primarily from the Anglo–American world. But my general arguments can be extended (at least in certain respects) beyond this domain, and the theoretical approach outlined here could perhaps provide the basis for a broader and more comparative study.

The concept of scandal

The word "scandal" first appeared in European languages in the sixteenth century, but the concept has a long and complex history which can be traced back to Greek, Latin, and early Judeo–Christian thought (see Soukup, this volume). In terms of its etymological origins, "scandal" probably derives from the Indo-Germanic root *skand-*, meaning to spring or leap. Early Greek derivatives, such as the word *skandalon*, were used in a figurative way to signify a trap, an obstacle or a "cause of moral stumbling."[7] The word was first used in a religious context in the Septuagint, the Greek version of the Old Testament. The idea of a trap or an obstacle was an integral feature of the theological vision of the Old Testament. It helped to explain how a people indissolubly linked to God could, nonetheless, begin to doubt Him and to lose their way: such doubt stemmed from an obstacle, a stumbling block placed along the path, which was intended to test people and to see how they would react.[8] This idea was expressed in the Septuagint by the word *skandalon*.

The notion of a trap or obstacle became part of Judaism and of early Christian thought, but it was gradually prised apart from the idea of a test of faith. Christian theology placed more emphasis on individual culpability; if individuals stumble and lose their way, if they commit sinful acts, this may stem from their own inner weakness and fallibility. Moreover, with the development of the Latin word *scandalum* and its diffusion into Romance languages, the religious connotation was gradually attenuated and supplemented by other senses. Hence the word *escandre* in Old French (eleventh century); this was derived from *scandalum* and meant both "scandal" and "calumny." Hence also the Old French word *esclandre*, from which the English word "slander" was derived.

The word "scandal" first appeared in English in the sixteenth century. Similar words appeared in other Romance languages at roughly the same time (in Spanish, *escándalo*; Portuguese, *escandalo*; Italian, *scandalo*). "Scandal" was probably derived from Latin, and probably from the French word *scandale*, which had been introduced to convey the strict sense of the ecclesiastical Latin term *scandalum*, as distinct from the senses that had been developed by *esclandre*. The early uses of "scandal" in the sixteenth and seventeenth centuries were, broadly speaking, of two main types.[9] First, "scandal" was used in a religious sense to refer (1a) to the conduct of a religious person which brought discredit to religion, or (1b) to something that hindered religious faith or belief. The latter usage retains the sense, derived from the original Greek, of scandal as a moral lapse or stumbling block.

The second type of usage was more secular in character and had to do with any or all of the following: (2a) actions or utterances which damaged an individual's reputation; (2b) actions, events, or circumstances that were grossly discreditable; or (2c) conduct which offended moral sentiments or the sense of decency. The use of "scandal" to refer to actions or utterances which damage reputation attests to the fact that, in terms of their etymological origins, "scandal" and "slander" were very close. Both words were used to refer to damaging or defamatory imputations, but they differed in an important respect: the use of "scandal" did not generally imply, whereas the use of "slander" did, that the imputations made were false.

As "scandal" was increasingly used in the senses of 2b and 2c, it acquired an additional and important implication. In its religious uses, "scandal" involved a relation between an individual or individuals (believers or waverers) and a religious doctrine or system of belief. But when "scandal" was used to describe grossly discreditable actions, events, or circumstances, or to describe conduct which offended moral sentiments or the sense of decency, a different kind of relation was implied – a relation between, on the one hand, an individual or humanly created event or circumstance and, on the other hand, a social collectivity whose moral sentiments were offended.[10] Scandal thus involved a transgression of moral codes which could be, but did not have to be, religious in character, and with reference to which the action or event was denounced.

It is the latter presuppositions which underlie the most common uses of the word "scandal" today. They refer primarily to actions or events involving certain kinds of transgression which become known to others and are sufficiently serious – though not too serious[11] – to elicit a public response. More precisely, I shall propose that, in its current usage, "scandal" refers primarily to actions, events, or circumstances which have the following characteristics:

1 Their occurrence or existence involves the transgression of certain values, norms, or moral codes.
2 They are known or strongly believed to occur or exist by individuals other than those directly involved (I shall refer to these individuals as "non-participants").
3 Some non-participants disapprove of the actions or events and may be offended by the transgression.
4 Some non-participants express their disapproval by publicly denouncing the actions or events.
5 The disclosure and condemnation of the actions or events may damage the reputation of the individuals responsible for them (although it does not always or necessarily do so, as we shall see).

Let us briefly examine each of these characteristics in turn.

(1) The most obvious aspect of scandal is that it involves actions or events which transgress or contravene certain values, norms, or moral codes. Some form and some degree of transgression are a necessary condition of scandal: there would be no scandal without them. Of course, there is a great deal of diversity and variability in the nature of the values, norms, and moral codes which are relevant here: what counts as scandalous activity in one context – e.g. extramarital affairs among members of the political elite – may

do no more than raise an eyebrow elsewhere. Values and norms have differing degrees of what we could call "scandal sensitivity," depending on the social-historical context and the general moral and cultural climate of the time, and depending on the extent to which these values and norms matter to particular individuals or groups. The disclosure of Parnell's relationship with Katherine O'Shea was particularly damaging for the man and his cause precisely because it occurred in the context of late Victorian Britain, when adultery was condemned by an influential moral purity lobby within Gladstone's Liberal Party, with which Parnell was temporarily allied in the pursuit of Home Rule, and by the Catholic church, which remained a powerful force in Ireland.

While there is a great deal of diversity and variability in the nature of the values and norms which are relevant to scandal, nevertheless there are certain types of norm which are more scandal-sensitive than others. Norms and moral codes governing the conduct of sexual relations are particularly prone to scandal: to transgress these norms is, depending on the context and the specific circumstances of the individuals concerned, to run a serious risk of scandal. Norms governing financial transactions are also scandal-prone, especially when the transgressions involve serious fraud or corruption. A third type of scandal-sensitive norm is that of the rules, conventions, and procedures which govern the pursuit and exercise of political power. Scandals stemming from the transgression of this type are probably most likely to occur in liberal democratic regimes, since these regimes place particular emphasis on a formal system of laws and other procedures which are intended to apply equally and in principle to all individuals.[12] Sex, money, power: it is little wonder that scandal has exerted, and no doubt will continue to exert, a degree of fascination on the popular imagination.[13]

Just as certain norms are more scandal-sensitive than others, so too some individuals are more likely to be confronted by scandal on the occasion of transgressing a norm. All citizens may be formally equal before the law, but not all transgressors are equal in the court of scandal. This differential susceptibility to scandal is linked in part to the degree of visibility of the individuals concerned: some individuals, by virtue of their positions, achievements, or responsibilities, are much more visible than others, and therefore more vulnerable to scandal in the event of transgressing a norm. Moreover, individuals who, by virtue of their positions or affiliations, espouse or represent certain values or beliefs (such as those advocated by a religious organization or a political party) are especially vulnerable to scandal, since they run the risk that their private behavior may be shown to be inconsistent with the values or beliefs which they publicly espouse. Many scandals involve an element of hypocrisy – not just the transgression of norms, but the transgression of norms by individuals whose practice falls short of what they (or their organizations) preach for themselves and others. We could describe this circumstance as "Parkinson's predicament," in reference to the British Conservative MP and former party chairman who found himself in the uncomfortable position of leading a party committed to the defense of traditional moral values at the very moment when his long-standing affair with his former secretary became public.[14]

I have suggested that the transgression of a value or norm can give rise to a scandal only if the value or norm has some degree of moral force or "bindingness" for some of the individuals who become aware of its transgression. But this is neither to say that these values or norms are likely to elicit general or widespread consensus in a particular social-historical context, nor to say that they are matters about which most people feel very strongly and with reference to which they organize their own lives. On the contrary, values and norms are often contested features of social life, adhered to by some individuals and groups and rejected (or simply ignored) by others. Hence scandals are often rather messy affairs, involving the alleged transgression of values and norms which are themselves subject to contestation. Moreover, values and norms are always embedded in relations of power; they structure social life in ways that permit certain kinds of activity and exclude or forbid others (or force them underground). In many cases, scandals are not just about actions which transgress certain values or norms: they are also about the cultivation or assertion of the values or norms themselves. Thus the making of a scandal is often associated with a broader process of "moralization" through which certain values or norms are espoused and reaffirmed – with varying degrees of effectiveness and good faith – by those who denounce the action as scandalous.

Scandals are often messy affairs not only because values and norms are commonly contested, but also because, in the unfolding sequence of actions, utterances, and events that constitutes a particular scandal, a multiplicity of values and norms may be implicated. A specific transgression may lie at the origin of a particular scandal and may form the initial focus of attention, but the unfolding sequence of actions and events may shift the focus elsewhere, in such a way that the initial transgression is overshadowed by other concerns. Many scandals involve what I shall describe as "second-order transgressions" where attention is shifted from the original offense to a series of subsequent actions which are aimed at concealing it. The attempt to cover up a transgression – a process that may involve deception, obstruction, false denials, and straightforward lies – may become more important than the original transgression itself, giving rise to an intensifying cycle of claim and counter-claim that dwarfs the initial offense and fuels a scandal which escalates with every twist. That Watergate had such disastrous consequences for Nixon and his administration was due not so much to the discovery of the original break-in at the Democratic National Committee headquarters, but rather to the fact that, in the course of subsequent inquiries, it became increasingly clear that the White House was involved in a cover-up and that the president himself had sought to obstruct the FBI's investigation of the affair. Similarly, it seems clear that second-order transgressions played a crucial role in the fall of John Profumo,[15] a point which was captured rather well in an anonymous rhyme:

> Oh what have you done, cried Christine,
> You've wrecked the whole party machine!
> To lie in the nude may be terribly rude,
> But to lie in the House is obscene.

It would not be implausible to suggest that some political leaders and others have come to appreciate the significance of second-order transgressions and have sought – as Bill Clinton did when faced with allegations concerning an affair with Gennifer Flowers – to pre-empt or deflate an incipient scandal by explicitly or implicitly admitting the original offense, thereby depriving their opponents of the advantages that can be gained by further attempts to demonstrate the falsity of public denials.

(2) A second characteristic of scandal is that the actions or events concerned must be known or strongly believed to exist by non-participants. If knowledge of an action or event is restricted to those who are directly involved in it – if, for example, knowledge of an illicit affair is shared only by the two lovers, or knowledge of a bribe is restricted to the giver and the recipient – then a scandal will not arise. To become a scandal, an action or event must

be known about by others, or strongly and plausibly believed by others to exist (in practice, most scandals involve a mélange of facts and more-or-less well founded suppositions). Unlike corruption and bribery, which can exist (and often do exist) when others do not know about them, scandal is always to some extent a "public" affair.

Since non-participant knowledge is a necessary condition of scandal, many scandals are characterized by a kind of drama of concealment and disclosure. Individuals involved in potentially scandalous activities may devote a great deal of effort to developing strategies of concealment – that is, methods of ensuring secrecy or of coping with unintended and unwanted revelations – since they know that the emergence of a scandal is dependent on the knowledge of others. On the other hand, when non-participants suspect the existence of potentially scandalous activities they may redouble their efforts to uncover the truth: the mere whiff of scandal is often sufficient to drive a scandal forward.

This enables us to see that scandal involves more than the actions and events which are, in any particular case, its principal focus, and more than the values and norms which these actions transgress. Scandal also involves (a) a degree of public knowledge of the actions or events, (b) a public of non-participants who know about them, and (c) a process of *making public* or *making visible* through which the actions or events become known by others. Activities that remain invisible to non-participants cannot, *ipso facto*, be scandalous. They can, at most, be potentially scandalous, and the transition from a potential to an actual scandal requires, among other things, a process of making public. This is one reason why communication media play a crucial role in many scandals, as we shall see.

(3) Scandal not only presupposes some degree of public knowledge: it also presupposes some degree of public disapproval. In order for a scandal to emerge, some non-participants must feel, on hearing or learning about it, that the transgression is (or was) a morally discreditable action. Non-participant knowledge of the action coincides or overlaps with disapproval of it; epistemic and evaluative judgments are fused together in the responses of some individuals who learn or hear about the transgression.

Undoubtedly there are some occasions when individuals not only disapprove of an action but are also offended or even shocked by it. The action may flout values or norms which are so fundamental to their sense of self and well-being that they are deeply upset – truly "scandalized" – by it. But reactions of this kind are the exception rather than the rule, and they are probably increasingly rare in many Western societies today, as the pluralization of value systems and the weakening of some traditional norms have gradually attenuated their moral force. Today many scandals involve the transgression of values and norms which have become fairly routine features of social life. They are adhered to loosely (if at all) by most people, and may be adhered to more in principle than in practice. They are token values to which many people may pay lip service but which, when it comes to making key decisions, play a relatively marginal role in their lives. When scandals involve the transgression of token values and norms of this kind, they have a certain formulaic character and a certain moral vacuousness. Genuine scandals they may be (and serious consequences they may have), but the values and norms whose transgression lies at the heart of these scandals may have little practically binding significance for most people. This is why some scandals – such as the British Conservative MP David Mellor's much-publicized affair with a Spanish actress[16] – can easily take on the appearance of a low-budget bedroom farce. Few people are shocked or offended by what they hear, but many are mildly amused by the sight of a minister on stage with his pants down.

(4) For a scandal to arise, it is not sufficient for some individuals to disapprove of the actions or events: it is also necessary for some to *express* their disapproval to others. A transgression that became known to others but elicited no response from them would not give rise to a scandal, since scandal is shaped as much by the responses of others as it is by the act of transgression itself. If no non-participants are sufficiently interested in or concerned about a transgression to express their concern to others, then a scandal will not arise. The phenomenon of scandal is constituted by both acts and speech-acts: by acts of transgression and by the speech-acts of others who respond to these acts with suitable forms of expression.

The responses of others thus have what we could call, following Austin, a performative role.[17] These responses do not merely describe a state of affairs – a scandal – that exists independently of them: on the contrary, in uttering these responses individuals are performing actions which are partly constitutive of the state of affairs. The responses of others are integral to the scandal, not retrospective commentaries on it. In short: no responses, no scandal.

What forms of expression by non-participants are suitable for accomplishing this performative role? Although these forms can be extremely varied, there is one feature they share: they are all forms of what I shall call "opprobrious discourse." This is a kind of moralizing discourse which reproaches and rebukes, which scolds and condemns, which expresses disapproval of actions or individuals. It is discourse which carries the implication that the actions are shameful or disgraceful, and hence that the actions bring shame, disgrace, or discredit to the individual or individuals who performed them.

Opprobrious discourse can express differing degrees of reproach, from mild scolding and faint, even teasing disapproval to unrestrained moral outrage. It can also be expressed in different ways and contexts. But for a scandal to emerge, at least some of the opprobrious discourse of non-participants must assume the status of public speech-acts: that is, it must be uttered (or otherwise produced) in a way that can be heard (or otherwise received) by a plurality of others. If the opprobrious discourse exists only as a private communication between friends or acquaintances, uttered *sotto voce* and in confidence, then it may constitute gossip or rumor or some other form of privately articulated belief, but it will not constitute a scandal. Of course, gossip and rumor can fuel scandal, and many scandals are in fact preceded by rumors which circulate among interested parties, such as journalists and politicians, or simply among individuals who are in the know. But a scandal can arise only if the tacit agreement which keeps gossip and rumor at the level of a private communication among friends or acquaintances is broken and the revelations, together with some suitable forms of opprobrious discourse on the actions or events in question, are articulated in public – that is, in a manner which is to some extent "open" and available for a plurality of others to see or hear or hear about.

Since scandal presupposes the public articulation of opprobrious discourse, it lends itself with particular ease to the use of communication media. Of course, opprobrious discourse can be articulated publicly without using the media (in a speech at a public meeting, for instance), and the use of communication media does not by itself ensure that the articulation of discourse will be public (a telephone conversation can remain private and confidential, provided that certain precautions are taken). Nevertheless, by using communication media such as printed materials (newspapers, magazines, pamphlets, etc.) or electronic media (such as radio and television), individuals can express opprobrium in ways which, by virtue of the medium itself, endow the expressions with the status of public speech-acts. I shall return to this point later.

(5) The final characteristic of scandal has to do with the reputations of the individuals involved. Since scandals involve the disclosure of hitherto covert activities which transgress some values or norms, and whose disclosure elicits opprobrious discourse of varying kinds, they may (and often do) seriously damage the reputations of the individuals whose actions lie at the center of the scandal. I say "may" advisedly: the damage or loss of reputation is neither a necessary feature nor an inevitable consequence of scandal (indeed, there are cases where individuals' reputations have been appreciably enhanced). But the damage or loss of reputation is a *risk* which is always present as a scandal erupts and unfolds. We could put it like this: scandal is a phenomenon where individuals' reputations are at stake. Of course, the threat to reputation is not the only issue at stake in many scandals. If the covert activities involve the contravention of legally binding norms or formally established procedures, the individuals may also face criminal prosecution and/or dismissal from their posts. In the most serious scandals (Watergate, the Iran–Contra affair, the corruption scandals in Italy, the Lockheed scandal in Japan, etc.), the revelations often result in an array of criminal prosecutions, sackings, and broken careers; for the individuals involved, the marring of reputation is by no means their only concern. Nevertheless they know very well that, just beyond the legal wrangling, just above the fray and fury of courtroom proceedings and special congressional inquiries, lurks the question of reputation, of one's "name" – that is, one's standing as a person of honesty, integrity, and good character.

From this viewpoint one can understand why scandals are often characterized by what we could describe as "struggles for 'name.' " Knowing that their reputations are at stake, the individuals at the center of a scandal may make a concerted effort to defend their reputations, or clear their names, by launching a counter-attack. They can do this in various ways. They can threaten legal action and, if necessary, seek to resolve the issues in a court of law. Whether this is a prudent strategy depends very much on the nature of the case and the strength of the evidence available to one's opponents. Alternatively individuals can simply reject the allegations and deny that the transgressions took place, or deny that they were involved. But this too can be a risky strategy, since it can shift the focus of attention to the possibility of second-order transgressions, which, if demonstrated, can be even more damaging for an individual's reputation than the disclosure of the original offense. A different strategy is to go for the moral high ground, to appeal to higher values in the name of which the original actions were carried out, in the hope of persuading others that the ends justified the means. This was the strategy used by Oliver North, who, while admitting his involvement in the Iran–Contra affair, sought (not without some success) to redeem his reputation by showing that his illicit activities were justified – morally if not legally – by the resolute pursuit of a higher good (the defeat of the communist threat and the maintenance of US national security).

Other strategies are commonly used in the struggle for name. Sometimes individuals take the route of open confession, publicly acknowledging their guilt in the hope that honesty in the face of adversity will elicit sympathy from others – the route taken, with varying degrees of success, by Clinton in the Gennifer Flowers affair, by Paddy Ashdown when news broke of an affair with his former secretary,[18] and by Prince Charles and Princess Diana when faced with allegations about their extramarital affairs. In other cases, individuals may admit that the original actions took place but contest or play down their significance, arguing that the furor created by the scandalmongers is disproportionate to the seriousness of the offense.

More generally, the importance of reputation enables us to understand why scandal (and the threat of scandal) has such significance in politics and in other spheres of social life. Reputation is a kind of resource, a sort of "symbolic capital,"[19] that individuals can accumulate, cultivate, and protect. It is a valuable resource, because it enables individuals to exercise a certain kind of power – what we could call "symbolic power"[20] – and to elicit the support of others. While the use of symbolic power is important in many spheres of social life, it is particularly important in the political field, since anyone who wishes to acquire political power and to exercise it in a durable and effective fashion must use symbolic power to some extent in order to cultivate and sustain the belief in legitimacy. In liberal democratic regimes, this use of symbolic power is shaped by a distinctive double logic.[21] On the one hand, political representatives are members of a professionalized political sub-field – that is, a sphere of action and interaction occupied by professional or semi-professional politicians and their associated personnel – and, in their day-to-day activities, their conduct and strategies are governed above all by the logic of this sub-field, by the demands of party loyalty, the maintenance of alliances, and so on. On the other hand, as elected officials, political representatives are also linked to a broader political field of citizens or non-professionals to whom they are accountable in some sense, and on whose support they crucially depend from time to time. Both within the political sub-field and in relation to the broader field of non-professionals, political representatives must constantly use symbolic power to persuade and confront, to influence actions and beliefs, to cultivate relations of trust, and to shape, as best they can, the course of actions and events.

Scandal (and the threat of scandal) has such significance in the political field because it can destroy (or threaten to destroy) a vital resource upon which the power of political representatives depends – namely, their reputation and good name, and the respect accorded to them by other politicians and by the public at large. Since the conduct of politics depends on the effective use of symbolic power (among other things), politicians are especially vulnerable to anything which threatens to undermine their reputation. To damage or destroy their reputation is to damage or destroy their credibility and thereby weaken or undermine their capacity to persuade and influence others, to secure and maintain a bond of trust, and to turn their words into deeds.

It would therefore be short-sighted to think of scandal as an altogether unimportant phenomenon or as a frivolous distraction from the real substance of political life. No doubt there are many reasons why scandals feature so prominently in social and political life, and many reasons why people are often absorbed, even enthralled, by them. But the salience of scandal is also a reflection of the fact that it can and often does impinge on real sources of power, and that it can and often does have substantial material consequences for the individuals and organizations affected by it.

Scandal and the media

The salience of scandal is also linked to the fact that the most prominent scandals are interwoven in various ways with mediated forms of communication. This is not to say that all scandals are "mediated" affairs: there are many scandals which have existed (and continue to exist) on a local level, erupting and unfolding in contexts of face-to-face interaction and involving little or no use of mediated forms of communication. But it is nevertheless clear that the media play a major role in many scandals, and indeed that the very nature of these scandals – their emergence, their developmental logic, their prominence, the ways in which they are experienced by both participants and non-participants, their consequences – are shaped by the media. Most "mediated scandals" are not simply scandals which are reported by the media and exist independently of them: they are, in varying ways and to some extent, constituted by mediated forms of communication.

Why does scandal lend itself to exposure in and through the media? How can we understand this intimate connection between scandal and mediated forms of communication? One factor, by no means insignificant, is that media organizations are themselves key players in the fields of social and political life. As commercial enterprises concerned with the commodification of symbolic forms, newspapers, magazines, and most other media organizations have a financial interest in maintaining or increasing the sale of their products, and scandals provide vivid, racy stories that can help splendidly to achieve this aim: in short, scandal sells. Moreover, some media organizations and personnel (as well as advocacy groups of various kinds which make heavy use of the media) explicitly position themselves in a political field, and the disclosure of scandals and commentary on them may concur both with their political aims and with their professional self-conceptions.

While these considerations are certainly important and merit more detailed investigation, they are not, in my view, the only factors that account for the affinity between scandal and the media. If we wish to understand this connection we must see that the rise of mediated scandals is to some extent a product of the transformations wrought by the development of communication media: these scandals are symptoms of a profound set of transformations which extend well beyond the sphere of scandal as such. We must also see that many of the properties of mediated scandals are shaped by the fact that they are constituted in and by the media.

If we look back at the historical development of mediated forms of communication, we can see that, with the rise of print in fifteenth-century Europe and with the subsequent emergence of electronic media in the nineteenth and twentieth centuries, new forms of visibility and publicness were created in the modern world.[22] Prior to the emergence of print, the visibility and publicness of individuals, actions, and events were linked to the sharing of a common locale.

An action or event was visible and observable by others, and was in this sense a "public" action or event, by virtue of being performed or staged before a plurality of individuals who were physically present at the time and place of its occurrence. A public action or event was a spectacle which could be seen or heard by a plurality of co-present others. But with the development of print and the subsequent emergence of electronic media, the visibility and publicness of actions and events were severed from the sharing of a common locale. Increasingly, actions and events could be seen and heard by others who were not present at the time and place of their occurrence. The media were endowed with the capacity to make actions and events visible to others in a way that was qualitatively different from anything that had existed previously: the process of making visible was severed from the constraints of physical co-presence and reconstituted in extended stretches of time and space.

The rise of mediated visibility altered the very conditions of public life and created new opportunities, but also new problems and new risks, for political leaders and other public figures. It created new opportunities because political leaders and public figures could now convey their views to others, and appear before others, in ways and on a scale that had never existed before. Information, images, and opinions could be circulated far beyond the sphere of co-present others, and social relations (between ruler and ruled, celebrity and fan, etc.) could be created or reshaped on the basis of social bonds formed primarily or even exclusively through mediated forms of communication. But the rise of mediated visibility also created new problems and new risks, because the mediated arena of modern public life is much more open and accessible than public life was in the past. With the development of print and other media, political leaders and public figures were increasingly drawn into an arena of mediated visibility where they could be seen or heard or read about by others with whom they did not interact directly, but on whose support they depended in various ways. Increasingly, political leaders and public figures were obliged to preoccupy themselves with the management of their self-presentation before distant others, but they could not completely control this. In most contexts the arena of mediated visibility was (and is) simply too complex, with too many sources of information and too many channels of information diffusion, for particular individuals or organizations to be able to control every detail. Moreover, given the nature of the media, the messages produced by political leaders and public figures may be received and understood in ways that cannot be directly monitored and determined in advance. Hence the rise of mediated visibility has become the source of a new and distinctive kind of fragility. However much political leaders and public figures may seek to manage their self-presentation, they cannot completely control it; the media can make visible actions and aspects of self which compromise or undercut the image that leaders or other public figures seek to project of themselves.

From this perspective we can appreciate the historical significance of the rise of mediated scandals. Unlike scandals that occur in localized settings, where the mechanisms of concealment and disclosure are linked only to strategies of face-to-face interaction, mediated scandals are intrinsically connected to the new forms of visibility and publicness created by the media. Mediated scandals arise when activities hitherto concealed are disclosed or made visible through the media: the media become the principal mechanisms through which the activities are made visible to others. Disclosure through the media endows the activities with a public status in a new and distinctive sense: they are now visible, observable, and knowable by others who are widely dispersed in time and space, and whose knowledge of the activities and of the individuals concerned may be (and often is) derived exclusively from the media.

From this perspective we can also understand why individuals who are actual or aspiring political leaders or prominent public figures are particularly vulnerable to mediated scandals. For these are individuals who, in an age of mediated visibility, are known to many people primarily through the media; they are individuals who, in varying degrees, may be preoccupied with their self-presentation in the media, and who are likely to be the focus of intense media scrutiny. Mediated scandals are a constant risk for individuals whose lives are played out in the public domain, precisely because these are the people who have come to depend on mediated visibility and who have to some extent built their careers upon it. Those who live by the media are most likely to die by the media.

So far I have been concerned to show that the rise of mediated scandals was to some extent symptomatic of the transformations brought about by the historical development of communication media, which created new forms of visibility and publicness in the modern world and new ways of making things visible to others. But there are other aspects of communication media which render them conducive to the occurrence of scandal and which shape the character and development of scandals once they are underway. One of the most important aspects of communication media in this regard is that they *fix* information or symbolic content in a relatively durable medium. In the temporal flow of social interaction in day-to-day life, the contents of symbolic exchange may have a fleeting existence: words uttered may rapidly fade away, and the preservation of symbolic contents may depend on the fallible and contestable faculty of memory. However, by using certain technical media of communication – paper, photographic film, electromagnetic tape, digital storage systems, etc. – the contents of symbolic exchange can be fixed or preserved in a relatively durable fashion. Different media have different degrees of durability, and they vary in the extent to which they allow symbolic contents to be altered or revised. A message written in pencil is easier to alter than one inscribed in ink, and words exchanged in face-to-face interaction are easier to renounce than utterances recorded on tape or images preserved on film.

This feature of communication media has come to play a crucial role in many scandals, precisely because they often involve contested claims concerning actions which allegedly occurred. Fixed symbolic materials such as letters, photographs, or tape-recorded conversations can provide vital evidence concerning the existence or otherwise of the alleged actions. Moreover, if these materials are subsequently relayed to a broader range of non-participants through the mass media, they can fuel the kind of public awareness and reproach which underpin the phenomenon of scandal. If one examines the scandals which have featured most prominently in public life in recent decades, one is struck by the role played by fixed symbolic materials of various kinds – a role that is probably growing in importance as methods of surveillance become increasingly sophisticated. The most obvious example is, of course, Watergate: it is certain that the scandal would not have unfolded as it did, and it is at least questionable whether it would have had such dramatic consequences (culminating in the resignation of a president in the face of his imminent impeachment), had it not been for the existence of a "smoking-gun" tape which recorded a crucial and incriminating conversation between Nixon and one of his aides shortly after the original break-in. But fixed symbolic materials of this kind have played an important role in other scandals too: Profumo's hastily scribbled note to Christine Keeler which began with the much-discussed epithet "Darling"; Jeremy Thorpe's letter to Norman Scott which contained the infamous line "Bunnies can (+ will) go to France";[23] and, of course, the tape-recorded telephone conversations allegedly picked up by amateur scanners and purportedly conveying the details of intimate conversations between Prince Charles and Camilla Parker-Bowles (the so-called "Camillagate" tape) and between Princess Diana and James Gilbey (the "Squidgygate" tape). In these and other cases, fixed symbolic materials provide forms of evidence which may not be entirely conclusive, but which are much more difficult to deny or explain away than unwitnessed and unrecorded conversations. And when these forms of evidence are propelled into the public domain by being printed in newspapers or otherwise made available, it may be difficult for the individuals implicated in them to limit the damage.

Once mediated scandals begin to emerge, their character and subsequent development – and, indeed, whether they develop at all – are shaped by the distinctive pattern of revelations, allegations, and denunciations which unfolds in the media. These are scandals which are literally played out in the media, and in which the activities of media personnel and organizations, with their distinctive practices and rhythms of work, play a determining role. The media operate as a framing device, focusing attention on an individual or an alleged activity and refusing to let go. Denials are commonly met by intensified efforts at disclosure, in the knowledge that the impact of further revelations can be greatly enhanced by the demonstration of second-order transgressions. The individuals at the center of the scandal, together with their advisors, solicitors, and supporters, may become locked in a strategic battle with media organizations; each move may be met by a counter-move, threats of disclosure may be met by threats of libel, and so on, in the hope either of flushing out a confession or of throwing the dogs off the scent.

In the midst of this strategic confrontation, it may be quite unclear to the protagonists just how the battle will unfold. The individuals at the center of the scandal may believe that, if they firmly and repeatedly deny their involvement in the alleged activities and if they can (should it be necessary) plug any leaks and prevent any incriminating evidence from emerging, then the public will eventually grow weary of a story that increasingly seems trumped up, and the scandal will gradually dissolve. On the other hand, journalists and other media personnel may be convinced that some kind of transgression or wrongdoing has occurred and may believe that, if they can keep up the pressure by disclosing new material, making new connections, and expressing opinions and judgments of various kinds, then the scandal will acquire a momentum which will become irreversible, eventually forcing the individuals to admit their culpability and accept the consequences.

As events which are shaped by and played out in the media, scandals take on the character of stories with continuously evolving plots, where each day, following the rhythms of newspaper publications or televised hearings, one may be confronted by new twists and turns, where old certainties may suddenly crumble and new hypotheses suddenly emerge, and where the plot may occasionally become so thick that even the dedicated followers begin to lose their way.[24] These are sometimes gripping stories with villains and heroes, with secret rendezvous and false clues, and in which the staple ingredients of sex, money, and power are mixed together in various heady combinations. They are stories often told with verve and vividness, where factual evidence is enlivened with illustrations, speculations, and – especially in the tabloid press – a generous dose of opprobrium. But often they are also stories in which serious issues are at stake, and where careers and reputations as well as policies and institutions may be significantly affected by the outcome.

Just as mediated scandals are largely played out in the media, so too, for most individuals, they are events which are known about and experienced only or primarily through the media. Of course, those individuals at the center of a scandal will have other sources of knowledge; they and their associates, as well as some non-participants, are likely to know certain things, or have good reason to believe certain things, on the basis of their personal experience and their familiarity with the individuals in question. But for the vast majority of people, knowledge of the actions and of the *dramatis personae* at the center of a scandal is based solely on media sources. (Of course, some of their knowledge may stem from conversations with friends and family members, but this knowledge too is ultimately based on media sources.) The scandal is not a "lived experience" – that is, an experience which they live through in the practical contexts of their daily lives and which impinges directly on them – but rather a "mediated experience" which is shaped by the distinctive mode of its acquisition.[25] For most people, these scandals are events which afflict distant others, individuals who are remote in space (perhaps also in time) and whom one would probably never encounter in the course of one's daily life. They are often also prominent public figures, and therefore, for most people, remote in terms of their relative status, power, and wealth. Through mediated scandals we experience the traumas of these distant others whose lives are laid bare before us. Therein lies part of the fascination that scandal holds for many: it is a stage on which the private lives of public figures are played out with a vivid, almost uncanny, openness. Mediated scandals are windows onto a world which is generally hidden from view, which lies behind the carefully managed self-presentation of political leaders and others who may be in the public eye. As these scandals unfold we experience a world – sometimes shocking, sometimes mildly amusing, often quite absorbing – which is at odds with the images projected of it. (Who would have thought, for example, that the President of the United States would conduct policy discussions in the White House in a manner indistinguishable from the scheming of a petty gangster?) The more elevated the individual (or the institution of which he or she is part), the greater the gulf is likely to be between the images projected and the realities disclosed, and the more interested we are likely to be in revelations which show that, despite pretensions to the contrary, these individuals are prone to the same temptations, driven by the same desires, and subject to the same weaknesses as ordinary mortals. The fascination that scandal holds for many stems not so much from the pleasure derived from witnessing the misfortunes of others (though there may be an element of this, especially when the others hold positions of power and authority), but rather from the tension that exists between the projected aura of public figures and the disclosed realities of their private lives.

The consequences of scandal

Scandals may be fascinating for some, intermittently absorbing for others, but do they really matter? Are they merely a form of entertainment drummed up by a media industry eager to exploit our prurient interest in the affairs of others? Or are they events which raise serious issues about the use and abuse of power, about the importance of reputation, and about the changing nature of public life? Undoubtedly these are among the most important questions to ask about the phenomenon of scandal, but they are also among the most difficult to answer in a clear and convincing fashion. The difficulty stems in part from the sheer diversity and complexity of the events we are inclined to bring together under the label "scandal." Each event is rooted in circumstances which make it unique, and each involves individuals whose lives are shaped by their own peculiar motivations, ambitions, opportunities, and faults. Sometimes a scandal has ruinous consequences for an individual, effectively terminating his or her career, whereas in other circumstances a person may survive unscathed. Moreover, it is quite possible that some types of scandal may have consequences which are different in character – both in terms of the kinds of consequence and in terms of the significance attached to them – from other types; a scandal involving large-scale corruption or fraud, for example, is likely to have consequences which are different in certain respects from a scandal based on an extramarital affair.

Given this diversity and complexity, any attempt to generalize about the consequences of scandal is likely to be a hazardous undertaking. I wish nevertheless to take a few small steps in this direction. Although there is not an established body of literature dealing with this issue, there are several different ways of approaching it. I shall try to identify some of these approaches and point to some of their shortcomings before raising, by way of a conclusion, a few considerations which might form the basis of an alternative approach.

One way of thinking about scandal is to see it as an ephemeral event, largely fabricated by the media, which has little or no bearing on the material factors and processes which shape social and political life – let us call this the "no-consequence theory." There is, undoubtedly, a good deal of *prima facie* evidence to support this theory. For all of the pages of newsprint devoted to scandals of various kinds, for all of the revelations concerning the private lives of public figures and all of the agonized debate about Watergate or the Iran–Contra affair (to mention only two), what difference has it made, at the end of the day, to the institutional organization and practical conduct of social and political life? The careers of some individuals may have been affected (some detrimentally, while others find themselves thrust unexpectedly and perhaps even advantageously into the public domain); but apart from these personal and largely unpredictable consequences, scandals have – or so it could be argued – no significant and determinate impact on social and political life.

Although the no-consequence theory has some plausibility, it does not offer, I think, a very compelling account of the social and political significance of scandal. Even if one were to accept the limited terms of reference of this theory, it would be difficult to maintain that scandals have had no significant and determinate impact: although Watergate was no doubt rather exceptional, it did have a discernible impact on the practical conduct of American presidential politics and on the legislative activity of Congress.[26] Moreover, if one takes a broader view of what might count as a "significant impact," then the no-consequence theory is rather misleading. For it obscures the fact that, in a world where symbolic capital is a scarce and valuable resource, reputation really does matter. Damage to one's reputation can (and often does) result in a damaged career and even a damaged life; and damage of this kind can (and sometimes does) have consequences which spread beyond the lives of the individuals concerned, weakening or even undermining the institutions or policies with which they are or have been linked.

There is a second way of thinking about scandal which acknowledges that scandals can have important consequences but maintains that these consequences are essentially conservative, in the sense that scandals involve a reaffirmation and consolidation of the status quo. Scandals are rituals of collective absolution: moments when a society confronts the shortcomings and transgressions of its members and, by working through the sometimes painful process of disclosure, denunciation, and retribution, ultimately reinforces the norms, conventions, and institutions which constitute the social order. This "functionalist theory of scandal," as I shall call it, is indebted to Durkheim's account of religion; just as religious practices serve to reaffirm the collective sentiments and ideas which give unity to social groups, so too scandals serve to reinforce the norms and conventions which were transgressed by the activities in question. In our modern, mediated world, scandal is a secularized form of sin.

Once again, this theory is not altogether implausible. Many scandals seem to involve a temporary disruption of the social or political order, in which the individuals responsible for the disturbance are punished and the status quo is restored more or less unchanged; belief in the social order is reaffirmed by the public demonstration of its capacity to expose and condemn – and perhaps eventually to forgive and pardon – the transgressor. Sex scandals lend themselves readily to this kind of interpretation, but even Watergate could be viewed in this way.[27] Yet this approach, while illuminating in some respects, suffers from some of the same shortcomings which vitiate most functionalist accounts. It tends to assume that there is a social and political order which has certain identifiable needs (scandals fulfill a need for the periodical reaffirmation of social norms) and to emphasize social cohesion at the expense of dissensus, fragmentation, and chronic conflicts of interest.

So neither the no-consequence theory nor the functionalist theory provides, in my view, a compelling account of the social and political consequences of scandal. Are there any alternatives? Is it possible to develop a more plausible theoretical perspective? Here I can do no more than point to a few considerations which arise from the study of scandal and which might provide some of the elements of a more plausible account. In the first place, it seems clear that scandals can have serious consequences for the careers and reputations of the individuals involved. These consequences are not always deleterious, as we have seen; but deleterious consequences are always a risk for those individuals who have relatively high reputations and whose careers may depend to some extent on the protection of their name. If we understand reputation as a kind of resource that individuals can accumulate and protect, then we can see why scandals often involve much more than the transgression of values or norms: they are also struggles over power and the sources of power. And in certain respects, struggles over the sources of symbolic power can be more consequential for individuals (and the organizations of which they are part) than struggles over the sources of economic power: the loss of a substantial sum of money can often be recouped, but a tarnished reputation can last for ever. (Who remembers John Profumo for his achievements as a minister of war?) We can disregard this aspect of scandal, or treat it as an entirely personal matter, only at the cost of a seriously deficient conception of social and political life.

Scandals are consequential not just for the lives and reputations of the individuals immediately affected by them: they can also have long-term consequences for the character of the social relations and institutions associated with them. Most social relations and institutions in modern societies are based to some extent on forms of trust; that is, on presumptions concerning the reliability, competence, and good intentions of other agents or systems of action.[28] But when other agents are remote in time and space, forms of trust must be built up and maintained on bases other than the practical testing ground of face-to-face interaction. Institutions and more abstract systems of action – from political parties and governmental institutions to systems of banking and finance – also depend to some extent on the capacity to cultivate and maintain forms of trust under conditions which largely preclude a reliance on routinized encounters.

It is precisely under these conditions that scandals can have consequences which extend well beyond the particular circumstances in which they occur: scandals can have a corrosive impact on the forms of trust which underpin social relations and institutions. This is one of the reasons why major scandals, or a series of connected but relatively minor ones, are often followed today by some kind of formal or official inquiry, like a Senate investigation, a royal commission, or a committee of inquiry established by the government of the day. Inquiries of this kind may be attempts to discover what really happened, but they are also and perhaps even primarily repair mechanisms concerned with mending and strengthening the delicate fabrics of trust which have been torn by a series of damaging revelations.

To say that scandals can have a corrosive impact on forms of trust is not to say, of course, that they will always have this impact, nor is it to say that the impact, when it does occur, will necessarily weaken social institutions. (One can cease to trust an individual without necessarily losing trust in the institutions with which he or she is linked.) No doubt it would be equally imprudent to suggest, as some commentators are inclined to do, that the surge of scandals in recent decades has created a pervasive culture of mistrust, in which new laws and regulations have proliferated with counterproductive effects and in which ordinary citizens have become thoroughly disillusioned with public life.[29] One does not have to endow scandals with such world-historical significance in order to accept that, over time and in conjunction with other factors, they may contribute to a gradual corrosion of the forms of trust upon which modern social and political institutions are based.

What remains unclear (and exceedingly difficult to determine with any degree of precision) is whether the corrosive impact of scandals and related phenomena is likely to have a long-term impact on the stability, credibility, and efficiency of modern institutions. In the age of mediated visibility, many institutions, and the individuals who occupy prominent positions within them, have developed elaborate strategies for managing their public appearance and for limiting the damage caused by scandals and other forms of trouble. But it is the very unpredictability and uncontrollability of mediated scandals (among other things) which threaten to undermine the efforts of the managers of visibility and which could, perhaps, impinge on the practical operation of the institutions themselves. Governments racked by scandal, political leaders struggling to limit the damage caused by leaks and disclosures of various kinds: these are not the conditions under which decisive leadership can readily be shown but are, on the contrary, conditions which may lead to weakened government and to a kind of political paralysis. Rather more worryingly, they are also the conditions which could lend support to aspiring leaders whose claim to credibility stems less from their proven capacity to govern effectively than from their claim to stand above the scandals and murky dealings which have tainted their contemporaries.

In pointing to these possible consequences of scandal, I have gone well beyond a description of the discernible effects of particular scandals in particular circumstances. I have suggested that it is possible to offer a more general theoretical account of scandals and their consequences precisely because these very particular events are embedded in, and symptomatic of, a broader set of social relations and transformations which have shaped the modern world, creating fields of interaction and forms of visibility within which and through which actions can have consequences which extend far beyond their immediate locales. Scandals are by no means the only or even the most striking illustration of how, in our age of mediated visibility, activities conducted behind closed doors can suddenly be thrust into the public domain, with unpredictable and sometimes uncontrollable consequences. But the scandals that feature so prominently in the media are a good illustration of this distinctively modern predicament and therefore deserve, for this reason alone, a good deal more scholarly attention than they have received hitherto.

Notes

1 *The Times*, November 18, 1890, p. 9.
2 *Pall Mall Gazette*, May 24, 1886, p. 8.
3 For a fuller account of the circumstances surrounding this affair and its aftermath, see Trevor Fisher, *Scandal: The Sexual Politics of Late Victorian Britain* (Stroud: Alan Sutton Publishing, 1995), ch. 7.
4 For a selection of anthologies and general surveys of scandal, see Colin Wilson and Donald Seaman, *Scandal! An Encyclopaedia* (London: Weidenfeld and Nicolson, 1986); Sean Callery, *Scandals: Gripping Accounts of the Exposed and Deposed* (London: Apple Press, 1992); Bruce Palling (ed.), *The Book of Modern Scandal: From Byron to the Present Day* (London: Weidenfeld and Nicolson, 1995); Matthew Parris, *Great Parliamentary Scandals: Four Centuries of Calumny, Smear and Innuendo* (London: Robson Books, 1995). I draw on these various sources, and especially on Matthew Parris's informative book, in describing some of the examples used in this chapter.

5 Among the more serious and systematic studies of scandal are the following: Eric de Dampierre, "Thèmes pour l'étude du scandale," *Annales*, 9.3 (1954), pp. 328–36; Maxime Rodinson, "De l'histoire de l'antisemitisme à la sociologie du scandale", *Cahiers internationaux de sociologie*, 49 (1970), pp. 143–50; Manfred Schmitz, *Theorie und Praxis des politischen Skandals* (Frankfurt: Campus Verlag, 1981); Dirk Käsler et al., *Der politische Skandal: zur symbolischen und dramaturgischen Qualität von Politik* (Opladen: Westdeutscher Verlag, 1991); Anthony King, "Sex, money, and power," in Richard Hodder-Williams and James Ceaser (eds), *Politics in Britain and the United States: Comparative Perspectives* (Durham, NC: Duke University Press, 1986), pp. 173–222; Andrei S. Markovits and Mark Silverstein (eds), *The Politics of Scandal: Power and Process in Liberal Democracies* (New York: Holmes and Meier, 1988); Suzanne Garment, *Scandal: The Culture of Mistrust in American Politics* (New York: Doubleday, 1992).

6 Here I shall not discuss gossip and rumor and their relation to scandal in any detail, although these issues have attracted some interest from anthropologists, social psychologists, and others. See, for example, Max Gluckman, "Gossip and scandal," *Current Anthropology*, 4.3 (1963), pp. 307–16; Robert Paine, "What is gossip about? An alternative hypothesis," *Man*, 2 (1967), pp. 278–85; Sally Engle Merry, "Rethinking gossip and scandal," in Donald Block (ed.), *Toward a General Theory of Social Control*, vol. 1: *Fundamentals* (Orlando, FL: Academic Press, 1984), pp. 271–302; Ralph L. Rosnow and Gary Alan Fine, *Rumour and Gossip: The Social Psychology of Hearsay* (New York: Elsevier, 1976).

7 *Oxford English Dictionary*, second edition (Oxford: Clarendon Press, 1989), vol. XIV, p. 573.

8 See Rodinson, "De l'histoire de l'antisemitisme," p. 147.

9 See *Oxford English Dictionary*, vol. XIV, pp. 573–4.

10 See de Dampierre, "Thèmes pour l'étude du scandale," p. 330: "scandal, in its current sense, is no longer a relation between two people, between someone who scandalizes and someone who is scandalized, but rather an event which breaks out at the heart of a collectivity of people."

11 We would hesitate, for example, to use the word "scandal" to describe an event such as the Holocaust, where the scale of the calamity was far in excess of the kind of offense usually associated with scandal.

12 This point is made very forcefully by Markovits and Silverstein in their introduction to *The Politics of Scandal*: "the critical feature of any political scandal," they argue, "is the presence of any activity that seeks to increase political power at the expense of process and procedure" (p. 6). However, while Markovits and Silverstein are right to call attention to this feature, it seems to me that they adopt an overly restrictive conception of political scandal. They regard one dynamic – the pursuit of power at the expense of due process – as the defining characteristic of political scandal; hence any scandal that does not involve this dynamic is *ipso facto* non-political. But this leads to some rather paradoxical and unnecessarily self-limiting conclusions (e.g. political scandals involving illicit sexual affairs cannot, on their definition, be treated as political scandals – unless, for example, the conduct of the affair leads the politician to violate due process in the interests of protecting his or her career). It would, in my view, be prudent to adopt a more flexible approach to political scandal, one which does not

try to force a varied and often extremely complex phenomenon into the framework of a single model.

13 A more thorough analysis of scandal would have to examine the similarities and differences between scandals involving these different types of norm and convention. For a preliminary and insightful attempt to develop an analysis of this kind, see King, "Sex, money, and power."

14 A Member of Parliament since 1970, Cecil Parkinson became secretary of state for trade and industry and chairman of the Conservative Party in 1981, organizing Margaret Thatcher's landslide general election victory in 1983. Parkinson had everything going for him – he was charming, successful, popular, good-looking; his career seemed likely to go from strength to strength. But in the summer of 1983 a story began to emerge which would have disastrous consequences: Parkinson had had a long-standing affair with his former secretary, Sarah Keays, who had become pregnant and was expecting their child in the autumn. According to Sara Keays, Parkinson had promised to divorce his wife and to marry her instead, but subsequently changed his mind. On September 14, 1983, Parkinson suddenly resigned as party chairman. On October 5, the satirical magazine *Private Eye* broke the news that his secretary was pregnant; the same day, Parkinson issued a statement admitting his involvement in the affair. Parkinson remained a MP until 1992, but his career never regained the momentum it had had in the early 1980s. What made the affair particularly damaging for Parkinson's career, and acutely embarrassing for the government, was the fact that it occurred at a time when Thatcher and her associates were attempting to build a political program around the theme of a return to traditional values, a theme which emphasized the importance of the nuclear family. For Thatcher's erstwhile party chairman to be exposed as the man who made his secretary pregnant, and whose wife and family had to suffer the consequences, could hardly be seen in that context as anything other than scandalously hypocritical.

One could cite numerous other examples of Parkinson's predicament. Consider, for instance, the case of Tim Yeo, a Conservative MP and junior minister for the environment in John Major's government. In January, 1994, he was forced to resign as environment minister when it was disclosed in a tabloid newspaper that he had fathered a child in an extramarital affair. This revelation came at a time when Major's government was pursuing a "back-to-basics" policy and placing particular emphasis on "traditional family values." Yeo was one of several Conservative MPs who were caught out by the ill-conceived and scandal-prone back-to-basics policy.

15 On March 22, 1963, amid much speculation in the press and at Westminster, Profumo made a personal statement in the House of Commons in which he explicitly denied that there had been any impropriety in his acquaintanceship with Christine Keeler, a denial that he was subsequently obliged to retract in his letter of resignation.

16 David Mellor was elected as a MP in 1979, and was made secretary of state at the new Department of National Heritage created by John Major after the April, 1992, general election. In July, 1992, the *People* broke a story about his affair with a 31-year-old actress, Antonia de Sancha, whose London flat had been bugged by journalists. The tabloid press had a field day. Stories proliferated about Mellor's sexual proclivities, including the

suggestion (quite possibly fabricated) that the minister had a penchant for toe sucking. Since one of his responsibilities at the Department of National Heritage was to oversee a review of press freedom, he had placed himself in a rather compromising position. By September he was forced to resign – "Toe job to no job: Minister finally sunk by scandals" was the merciless headline in the *Sun.*

17 See J.L. Austin, *How To Do Things with Words,* second edition, ed. J.O. Urmson and Marina Sbisà (Oxford: Oxford University Press, 1976).

18 In 1987 the British MP Paddy Ashdown had a short-lived and secret affair with his secretary, Tricia Howard, before he became leader of the Liberal Democratic Party. Several years later, in January, 1992, reporters from the *News of the World* descended on Tricia Howard's home, having caught wind of a possible scandal. (It appears that a confidential document written by Paddy Ashdown and locked in the safe of his London solicitor had been stolen during a burglary.) Rather than trying to deny the affair or waiting until he was lampooned by the press, Ashdown convened a press conference and, with his wife standing by him, openly admitted to and apologized for his earlier indiscretions. Ashdown's personal popularity was not significantly dented by the affair and he continued as party leader.

19 The concept of symbolic capital is developed by Pierre Bourdieu; see, for example, *The Logic of Practice,* tr. Richard Nice (Cambridge: Polity Press, 1990), ch. 7.

20 I regard symbolic power as one of four basic forms of power; it is the capacity to use symbolic forms to intervene in and influence the course of actions and events. See John B. Thompson, *The Media and Modernity: A Social Theory of the Media* (Cambridge: Polity Press, 1995), pp. 12–18.

21 See Pierre Bourdieu, "Political representation: Elements for a theory of the political field," in his *Language and Symbolic Power,* ed. John B. Thompson, trs Gino Raymond and Matthew Adamson (Cambridge: Polity Press, 1991), pp. 171–202.

22 For more discussion of this theme, see Thompson, *The Media and Modernity,* ch. 4.

23 The scandal which eventually destroyed the career of Jeremy Thorpe – leader of the Liberal Party in Britain from 1967 to 1976 and highly regarded by many of his contemporaries – was certainly one of the most bizarre of recent decades. In 1961, shortly after being elected as a MP, Thorpe met a young man who worked in a friend's riding stables. The young man, who subsequently changed his name to Norman Scott, was later to allege that, soon after meeting Thorpe, he visited him at the House of Commons and was driven by him to his mother's house in Surrey. There, alleged Scott, Thorpe entered his bedroom, climbed into bed with him, hugged him and called him "poor bunny" before forcefully having sex with him. In the following months and years, Thorpe tried to help out Scott, who was an unstable and unreliable fellow; he found jobs for him and placed ads in magazines on his behalf. In 1962 Thorpe wrote to Scott and, knowing that Scott wanted to study dressage in France, he remarked at the end of the letter "Bunnies can (+ will) go to France." As Thorpe's career began to take off, Scott's life disintegrated and he made growing demands on Thorpe, who became increasingly concerned about Scott's behavior and about the possibility that damaging allegations could be made

in public. A bizarre series of events followed, including an alleged plot to murder Scott which – whether erroneously or intentionally remains unclear – resulted instead in the shooting of his dog on a deserted moor in Devon. When the scandal began to break in the spring of 1976, Thorpe denied that he had ever had a homosexual relation with Scott and denied any involvement in the shooting of Scott's dog, claiming that he was the victim of a smear campaign. But the pressure mounted and, on May 9, 1976, the *Sunday Times* published two letters, including the ill-fated "bunnies letter" which, while not conclusive, was certainly damaging. The following day Thorpe resigned as leader of the Liberal Party. He was subsequently charged with conspiracy to murder and, with a criminal prosecution looming, he lost his seat in the 1979 general election. The jury delivered a verdict of not guilty, but Thorpe's political career was in ruins.

24 The narrative structure of mediated scandals is discussed by Michael Schudson in his thoughtful book on Watergate and its legacy; see Michael Schudson, *Watergate in American Memory: How We Remember, Forget, and Reconstruct the Past* (New York: Basic Books, 1992), especially ch. 3.

25 On the distinction between lived experience and mediated experience, see Thompson, *The Media and Modernity*, pp. 227–34.

26 A number of laws were passed in the late 1970s which had a traceable connection to Watergate, most notably the Ethics in Government Act (1978); for a fuller account of post-Watergate legislation, see Garment, *Scandal*, pp. 38–42. Many commentators have noted how, in the aftermath of Watergate, the conduct of American presidential politics altered in various ways, as actual and aspiring presidents (and their teams of aides and advisors) struggled to avoid the kind of catastrophe that had engulfed the Nixon administration; see, for example, Mark Hertsgaard, *On Bended Knee: The Press and the Reagan Presidency* (New York: Farrar Straus Giroux, 1988); John Anthony Maltese, *Spin Control: The White House Office of Communications and the Management of Presidential News* (Chapel Hill, NC: University of North Carolina Press, 1992).

27 See, for example, Jeffrey C. Alexander, "Culture and political crisis: 'Watergate' and Durkheimian sociology," in his *Durkheimian Sociology: Cultural Studies* (Cambridge: Cambridge University Press, 1988), pp. 187–224.

28 See Anthony Giddens, *The Consequences of Modernity* (Cambridge: Polity Press, 1990); Diego Gambetta (ed.), *Trust: The Making and Breaking of Cooperative Relations* (Oxford: Blackwell, 1988).

29 See Garment, *Scandal*, pp. 288–9 and passim.

3 "And Besides, the Wench is Dead":

Media Scandals and the Globalization of Communication

John Tomlinson

> Fornication? But that was in another country: and besides,
> the wench is dead
>
> *Christopher Marlowe,* The Jew of Malta

D o scandals travel? Marlowe thought not. The eponymous Jew Barabas's rationalization of scandalous behavior is actually a far more cynical and dissembling one when taken in the context of this most ironical and "amoral" of Elizabethan plays.[1] But even out of its textual context the famous quotation suggests that, for Marlowe and his time, scandals were readily seen as context-bound, local affairs. The irony in the rationalization seems to acknowledge that, though moral standards are nominally universal (the moral content of a scandal *should* travel), in fact censure, disgrace, and moral indignation wane with time and distance.

Until relatively recently, in fact, there was a sense in which to go into another country was effectively to go into another moral and political universe. This sort of perception persisted right up to the present century: One way of dealing with or escaping from scandals was for those involved to go, or to be sent, "abroad" into other countries. The scandal of their conduct was dealt with by simply removing them from the cultural community of judgment. This is a very common theme in nineteenth-century English novels, where France often features as a convenient refuge/exile for miscreants – a sort of moral limbo.[2] And of course, there are real-life examples:

on his release from Reading Gaol in 1897 Oscar Wilde was immediately taken by his friends to Paris, where he lived in "moral
exile" until his death in 1900.

This sense of the separation of countries in terms of their moral
(and political) dispensations is also evident if we consider the context of international law. The notion of extradition, for example,
dates only from the nineteenth century. It could be argued then
that only in the context of "global modernity" – in this instance,
of the establishment of a reflexively operating nation-state system
(Giddens 1990): borders, passports, customs, immigration controls,
the very concept of international law – does the idea of handing
over a person from one moral–legal–political universe to another
have much force. Even today the extradition procedure is limited
to specific bilateral treaties between nation-states concerning specific criminal practices, and generally excluding anything deemed
to be a "political crime." This sort of limitation and compromise is
interesting in that it demonstrates how important it is to the reflexive idea of political sovereignty that nation-states continue mutually to regard themselves as separate legal–political universes. And
this is of course linked to the idea of them being distinct moral
universes. The derivation of the term "extradition" is interesting
here: *Ex* is Latin for "out of, from," and "tradition" is from *tradere*,
"to hand over, to hand on." Extradition is thus also partly cognate
with the idea of "tradition" as the "handing on" of a set of distinct
cultural practices that define separate moral universes from which
people may be "handed over." And if we want to pursue this sort
of etymological argument toward even more connotational complexities, both are connected with the idea of "betrayal" as a "handing over" to the enemy.

There is evidence then of a persistence into the modern world of
the idea of different national cultures as different moral universes.
However, against this we could argue that the process of globalization has defined for us, at the close of the twentieth century,
quite a different moral context. In some senses we live, as the title
of a recent United Nations report puts it, in a "global neighborhood" (Commission on Global Governance 1995). In such a context –
defined particularly by an increasingly technologically-sophisticated
global media system – we speak of international and even global
scandals. Watergate, the Iran–Contra affair, the Barings Bank debacle,
O.J. Simpson, Magic Johnson, the infidelities of Prince Charles and
Princess Diana, and so on are all international news stories, attract-
ing interest outside their country of origin. Do such scandals as

they are reported, watched on TV, read about and discussed around the world represent an expansion in people's cultural–moral horizons? Is globalization perhaps dissolving the sort of cultural barriers, the division of the world into a plurality of moral universes, that Marlowe's rationalization refers us to? Can we, indeed, infer from the "globalizing of media scandals" any more profound cultural–moral process – a movement toward a genuine "global neighborhood" as a single, unified, moral community with common values and so forth?

I do not think so. I want in fact to explore an intuition that, despite the cultural compression that comes (particularly) with the globalizing of media and communications, *scandals remain in some important senses essentially local affairs*. This does not mean that media scandals do not cross cultural borders: clearly in some senses, some do. But I am interested in the specific way in which this occurs, and of how this connects with the nature of scandals as moral–cultural events. Nor, it should be said, is the view of the essentially "locally-situated" nature of scandals that I shall develop necessarily a pessimistic one: it does not imply that human beings are incapable of a "cosmopolitan" cultural, moral, or political outlook. It directs us, rather, to an exploration of the nature of scandals as specific types of cultural–moral event, and to the implications of this for broader issues of global ethics, solidarity, and community.

Scandals as "middle-order moral events"

As the other chapters in this book show, there are several dimensions to media scandals that make them of interest to cultural analysis. The one that I want to focus on here is their significance as moral events. However they are approached, scandals obviously always have a certain moral content. In some approaches, the moral significance can be construed in terms of challenges to a dominant (ideological) moral code; in others – notably in the work of John Thompson (1990, 1995) – it is the increasing public visibility of formerly private practices produced by media scrutiny that shifts our moral frame of reference, our perceptions and expectations of public figures, and so on. My approach is slightly different from, though not, I think, incompatible with, these. I want to think of scandals as *middle-order moral events* which have a particular role in the cultural reproduction of modern societes.

What do I mean by a middle-order moral event? I think Anthony King is generally right to say that scandals "occupy a sort of middle ground of impropriety . . . On the one side, they shade into such petty misdemeanours as speeding or drinking too much at private parties; on the other, they shade into the realm of serious crime" (King 1986: 176). Of course it is difficult to be categorical, but King is right, I think, to locate the center of gravity of a scandal somewhere between the fairly trivial and the extremely serious. It is really the distinction at the upper limits that interests me. Scandals may range from mild sexual impropriety to serious crimes – murder (O.J. Simpson); high-level fraud (Barings). But the concept does not seem appropriate to the really major moral problems of our times: wars, genocide, starvation in the Third World, racism, the poisoning of the oceans and the atmosphere. These "high-order" moral issues may justly be described as "scandalous," but they are not the typical stuff of scandals.

One obvious reason for this, of course, is that most high-order moral issues are not easily personalized – connected to or instantiated in the behavior of symbolic individuals. But it seems also to be true that scandals connect with the mundane, lived experience of ordinary people in a way in which high-order moral issues often fail to. As Ulrich Beck has argued, the "long distance morality" demanded of modern people in respect, for example, of major environmental issues is difficult to engage with, and such problems are more likely to engender a response of fatalism – of "not listening, simplifying, apathy" (Beck 1992: 137) – in effect, a retreat from moral engagement. Scandals, by contrast, seem to engage people very successfully (if only transitorily), partly as a function of the way they are narrated by the media, partly since their moral content is concretized in the example of individual actions, but also partly because they often pose genuine moral issues that are recuperable to – that resonate with – the everyday experience of large numbers of people.

In this respect it is important not to fall into the trap of regarding media scandals as trivia, as the diversionary tactics of the tabloid media (the "bread and circuses" argument of some critics of ideology), or as merely appealing to prurient interest. Of course some scandals may have these elements. Nevertheless it seems to me there is something more interesting to say about them as moral–cultural events.

This is that scandals perform a specific role of "regulating" the tacit moral order of a community. They provide contexts for "communal" moral reflection and debate in modern secular societies where traditional sources of moral "authority" – the church and religious values, the state, the academy and the intelligentsia, the examples of the "great and the good" – are in serious decline. Scandals, as they appear in the media and are discussed in families, among friends, in workplace coffee breaks, in pubs, and so on, provide significant focuses for the informal, mundane, reflexive regulation of the communal moral order. They do this by providing moral challenges within narratives that catch people's attention and imagination (much, in fact, as the fictional narratives of the better soap operas do). When we respond to a scandal we do not just absorb the details, but inevitably engage in moral reflection: We typically debate with ourselves and with each other the circumstances, the motivations, and the complexities of the case. We argue over who is really right and wrong and (increasingly in knowing, mass-mediated communities) how the issues have been represented by the media. So when we are involved in such cultural events, we are not only exercising and refining our own personal moral judgments; we are simultaneously producing a reflexive review and readjustment of the overall moral order of the social formation.[3] In this sense the challenges to the moral order that scandals provide work to shift and re-form the common sense of what is permissible and what is transgressive in societies, and ultimately this impacts on our sense of our cultural identity – our distinctive understanding of "how we live here."

Now it seems to me that the success of scandals in fulfilling this sort of role depends to a large extent on their being what I have called "middle-order moral events." Too small-scale, commonplace moral infringements will fail to catch the public imagination, but so, in a sense, will too "high-order" ones. If we cannot grasp the morality of an issue in a fairly direct, personal way – if it cannot be narrativized so that we can empathize, recognize the moment of moral agency, imagine ourselves as involved and acting in one way or another within it – then people cannot be blamed for a failure to engage. For why should people be expected, in Beck's words (1992: 137), to provide "the biographical solution of systemic contradictions" which appear as abstract and beyond the compass of their moral "lifeworld"? Scandals may not pose the most urgent moral–political issues of our time, but they do generate significant amounts of popular moral discourse. And maybe, as I shall suggest in my conclusion, there is a lesson to be learned from their success for the way in which higher-order moral issues should be posed.

It may, however, be objected that the way in which I have construed the cultural significance of scandals is in some ways naive. For instance, it perhaps neglects the power of the mass media to construct and manipulate the moral agenda in the way the scandal is narrativized. My answer to this is that, though of course the various interests and strategies of the mass media must be recognized, they by no means entirely control the moral discourse that they distribute. The active, interpretive nature of media audiences is now so well demonstrated as to make a strong ideological manipulation thesis difficult to sustain (Ang 1996; Lull 1995; Morley 1992). But apart from this, it seems clear that, as I mentioned earlier, a critical awareness of the media's role in the framing of scandals is now part and parcel of the way people actually respond to scandals – an aspect of the routine cultural accomplishments of moral agents in mediated modern cultures.

A good example of this is to be found in a story that preoccupied the British media in mid-August, 1996. This is the case of Mandy Allwood, a woman who, as a result of fertility treatment, carried eight babies and declared very publicly her intention to attempt to give birth to them all, despite dire warnings of the probable consequences and medical advice to undergo "selective abortion" of most of the fetuses. This story was an excellent example of a middle-order moral event. It posed problems of the woman's actual intentions: Was her flying in the face of medical advice "scandalous" by involving a reckless risk of losing all her babies? Or was it rather a question of a woman's rights over her own body? It also posed questions of her motivation and sincerity: Did she really want to give birth to eight babies or was her declaration simply a cynical attempt to make money via publicity? But perhaps even more prominently, from the start the story posed as scandalous the involvement of the media in the construction of the event. For it soon emerged that Allwood was contracted by the *News of the World*, a Sunday newspaper with a long-standing reputation as a "scandal sheet," not only for her story but also to receive a large sum of money for each baby successfully delivered if the pregnancy was allowed to come to term. There are all sorts of extra dimension of moral controversy generated by this media "sponsorship." But the point is that this complex "scandal" is one which, from the outset, involved a high level of public awareness of the media's intrinsic framing role: of their potentially cynical interests and so on. Not only did this not prevent people from engaging imaginatively with the broader moral issues, but the media's dubious role became an important aspect of the scandal itself. We can conclude that sophisticated media audiences routinely reckon the factor of the "mediatization" of cultural events like scandals into their responses.

But even allowing all this, it might still be argued that the discourses constructed around media scandals are but poor vehicles for the moral regulation of modern societies: that they fall far short of the ideals of moral–political discourse proposed, for instance, in Habermas's notion of a radicalized public sphere (Habermas 1989). This is probably true, and I certainly do not want to overstate their significance, or to suggest that they provide any ideal of communal moral discourse. But on the other hand, media scandals do seem to offer real and recurrent opportunities for moral reflection in the mundane cultural context of what Roger Silverstone has called the "suburbanised" public sphere of everyday modern life (Silverstone 1994), organized particularly around television. And we have to search hard in modern societies to find other available – or at any rate flourishing – discursive spaces where moral issues can be widely aired.

Scandals, localities, and the "relevance structure" of cultural experience

So there are reasons to take media scandals seriously. But how do these relate to our main theme of the internationalizing of scandals? I want to argue that the moral–cultural nature of scandals as I have understood them suggests that, despite widespread distribution by a globalizing media, they remain local affairs. There are two possible reasons to think this, one fairly obvious, the other less so but, I think, more interesting.

The obvious answer is that media scandals, like all media representations, lose some interest, some "immediacy," as they cross cultural distance. This tendency can be understood in terms of what Hoskins and Mirus have referred to as the "cultural discount" that applies to cultural imports (in their specific example, television programs). As they put it, "a particular program, rooted in one culture, and thus attractive in that environment, will have a diminished appeal elsewhere, as viewers find it difficult to identify with the style, values, beliefs, institutions and behavioral patterns of the material in question" (Hoskins and Mirus 1988: 500). This quite obviously applies to media scandals. A British audience might raise some interest in the Clintons and the Whitewater affair (if the events could have been given a clear, more powerful narrativization!), but they would be far more engaged if it were Tony and Cherie Blair who were the protagonists. And on the other hand, British media audiences have been little moved, if at all, by recent corruption stories in Japanese political life. The cultural discount argument, then, is a powerful one, and there is indeed evidence that it has become structured into the way international news stories are actually framed for us by television journalists. In their study of the globalization of television news, for example, Gurevitch and his collaborators found that "Global events . . . are shaped and reshaped by television news reporters and producers in ways that make them comprehensible and palatable for domestic audiences" (Gurevitch et al. 1991: 214).

However, I do not think this argument gets to the quick of the issue. Scandals are local in a more specific sense than is grasped in the general recognition of the hermeneutically problematic nature of cross-cultural trade. They are local in respect of their nature as middle-order moral events. As I have implied, the success with which scandals engage our moral imagination depends on two factors. The first is the extent to which they pose for us novel, dramatic situations that simply catch and hold our attention. The second is the degree to which we can assimilate the moral content of the scandal to our cultural lifeworld.

The first factor is obviously related to locality in so far as a lower degree of drama or novelty will be required to catch the interest of very local communities. Thus, fairly mild, run-of-the-mill sexual indiscretions may have force as scandals in a small, face-to-face community, a local neighborhood, where people know the individuals involved. But as the relevant community of judgment becomes larger – up to the "imagined community" (Anderson 1983) of the nation-state and beyond – where relations are inevitably distanced, mediated, and symbolized, a greater degree of drama and originality will be necessary to engage us in the moral discourse. Like the cultural discount argument (which it in certain respects resembles), this argument about what we could call the relative "launch velocity" of a scandal seems to demonstrate a close connection between moral involvement and cultural proximity.

But it is the second factor that I think is the clinching one. We only fully engage with scandals insofar as they seem relevant to our ongoing, lived experience. We can put this proposal in terms of the concept of the "relevance structure" of lived experience. This

is a concept which John Thompson has retrieved from the phe-
nomenological theories of thinkers like Alfred Schutz and applied,
interestingly, to an understanding of the mediated experience of
modern cultures. It is a concept that connects the selective filtering
of the continuous stream of experiential data available to all human
beings with the ongoing constitution of the human self as a symbolic project. As Thompson explains:

> We do not relate to all experiences or potential experiences equally, but
> rather orient ourselves towards these experiences in terms of the prior-
> ities that are part of the project of the self. From the viewpoint of the
> individual, therefore, experiences and potential experiences are structured
> in terms of their relevance to the self. (Thompson 1995: 229)

What claims priority in our selective attention, then, is those experiences that speak most directly to the way in which we continuously
narrate our "selves" to ourselves. Those experiences that penetrate
deepest into our lifeworld are the ones that can be imaginatively
incorporated into this ongoing narrative of self-identity.

Now, as Thompson suggests, it is generally those experiences
that occur within the same spatiotemporal locale as the self that are
afforded greatest priority. Our routine daily interactions with our
significant others – family, friends, and colleagues – for example,
are the stuff out of which the self is basically formed. To this extent
it could be argued that "local, immediate" experiences generally
take priority over "distant, mediated" ones. Thompson thus argues
very plausibly that the experience we get from media like television, involving the representation of events which are at a distance
from us, are "more likely to bear a rather tenuous, intermittent and
selective relation to the self" (Thompson 1995: 230). However, in
modern societies it is clear that existentially relevant experiences
are not restricted to the world of physical proximity, but can be
gained from mediated cultural practices like television viewing as
these are more and more integrated into our everyday lives. The
way in which people become (sometimes heavily) involved in the
narratives of soap operas is a good example of this. As Thompson
goes on to argue, the precise "experience-mix" of mediated and
non-mediated experiences will differ in terms of its overall relevance between particular individuals. But the relevance structure
argument is equally applicable to the way in which we receive
mediated experiences. Those situations, be they in soap operas,
news stories, or media scandals, that get highest priority are likely
to be the ones which are most culturally proximate to our lived

experience. This can be illustrated by quoting the response of a woman interviewed by David Morley in his study of family viewing practices:

> Sometimes I like to watch the news, if it's something that's gone on – like where that little boy's gone and what's happened to him. Otherwise I don't, not unless its local, only when there's something that's happened local . . . I can't stand *World in Action* and *Panorama* and all that. It's wars all the time. You know, it gets on your nerves . . . I don't want to know about the Chancellor Somebody in Germany and all that. What's going on in the world? I don't understand it, and so I don't listen to that. I watch – like those little kids [an abduction] – that gets to me, I want to know about it. (Morley 1992: 251)[4]

This is, as Morley observes, a very cogent justification for a bias of interest towards the local. This woman is quite clear that her level of moral engagement is related to the cultural horizon of her immediate lifeworld, and she uses this selectivity explicitly in her viewing practices. Now it might be argued that this sort of response represents a low cultural horizon and even a sort of moral–experiential "nimby"-ism – a refusal to let the "outside world" penetrate into the immediate environment of the self. But I do not think this is the best way of reading it: for one thing, on what criteria could such a judgment about how people *should* order their personal experiences be made? It seems better to see this woman's self-insight as indicative of a general moral condition: the fact that, as Zygmunt Bauman puts it, our morality, even in a global–modern world, remains essentially the "morality of proximity" (Bauman 1993: 217) that we have inherited from pre-modern times. I shall return to this thought in the conclusion.

My general point, then, is that we mostly engage selectively with issues presented to us via the media in terms of their relevance to a lifeworld that is primarily locally situated. The implication from this is that the success with which a media scandal engages us is a function of this relevance, and this is basically why I believe we should think of scandals as essentially local events. What I mean by this is really two things. First, many scandals simply do not travel well because their existential–moral relevance is gained precisely by their particularity: their (real or imaginary) proximity to the lifeworlds of their audience. And, second, in those cases where we do relate to scandals originating in different cultural contexts, we generally do so by assimilating them to our own locally-situated lived experience. But it will be useful to flesh the argument out a little more, and so I want now to turn to two examples of recent media scandals, both of which have some claim to global currency. In both cases I hope to show that the widespread interest they have generated has not been due to their global scale as spectacularly scandalous affairs so much as to the way they have been successfully narrated to be relevant to local lifeworlds.

Global scandals, local lifeworlds

The first example is from an interesting sub-genre of media scandals: international market-trading ones. These are particularly well qualified to count as "global scandals," related as they are to the complexly interconnected, high-speed, high-stake, high-tech world of global capitalism. But the example I want to focus on – the collapse of the British merchant bank Barings in the spring of 1995 – demonstrates that it is neither the sheer scale of the fraudulent dealings, nor the breadth of their impact, that is the key to their "success" as scandals. Rather it is how they are narrated so as to "personalize" them. International financial scams are, of their nature, complicated technical matters which do not generally connect with the lived experience of the majority. In the case of the Barings debacle, the matter hung on complicated dealings in "derivatives," which are highly abstract financial instruments: meta-speculations on the future prices of commodities. It is unlikely that most people reading the newspaper accounts or watching the television coverage that unfolded the scandal would have grasped what precisely had happened in these dealings to bankrupt one of the oldest banks in the world – bankers to the British queen – so rapidly.

But none of this seemed to matter. From the outset the scandal was narrated in terms of the activities of a single individual: Nick Leeson, the "rogue trader" who was supposedly responsible for the loss of £869 million. This focus allowed the "abstract" scandal (a story really to do with the way international currency markets are insufficiently regulated) to be elaborated around a dramatized sequence of events: the discovery of the trading loss, Leeson and his wife's disappearance from Singapore, their discovery in Kuala Lumpur, their flight back to Europe, his detention in Germany and the long struggle over his extradition to Singapore, finally his trial and sentence to six-and-a-half years' imprisonment. Through this narrative were woven all sorts of theme to which people could relate on a "human-interest" level. Leeson was cast in the role of a new breed of working-class capitalist adventurer, a particular form of the "yuppie" culture that had emerged in the City of London's financial community during the boom years of the 1980s. He was young (only 28), from an "ordinary" working-class background (the son of a plasterer), not highly qualified (not a graduate) or well connected, but astute, a smart operator, and a risk taker. It was often implied that he was allowed free rein in his dubious trading activities by his shadowy patrician masters at Barings and then left to be the fall guy. Accompanying this was the theme of Leeson's struggle to avoid extradition, with the implications that he would receive less than fair treatment in Singapore and the stories of the grim conditions in the gaols there. Finally there was the drama of his separation from his young wife and of her predicament – the "riches-to-rags story" of her bewildered fall from the high life of the expatriate dealers' community in Singapore to living with her mom and having to find work as a waitress in a local tearoom; but, of course, also her determination to stand by her man and, later, even the story of her intention to train as an airline hostess in order to be able to travel to Singapore to visit him.

Now, compare all this wealth of "human interest" with a more recent international market-trading scandal: the case of the massive, complex fraud on the international copper market that emerged in the general news in June, 1996. Billed in a front-page headline in the British *Guardian* as the "world's biggest financial scandal," this story centered on the losses to the Japanese Sumitoma corporation of over $2.5 billion as a result of what was described as "the most ambitious global financial fraud: a systematic attempt to siphon off untold profits by controlling the entire world market in copper" (Donovan and Murphy 1996: 25). This was a labyrinthine story of market rigging spanning three continents, linking Sumitoma's losses with dealings on the London Metal Exchange, with the activities of offshore financial companies in Guernsey and the Cayman islands, and with the Chilean state-run Codelco copper corporation.

Despite Donovan and Murphy's (the *Guardian* reporters) description of the scandal as having "all the ingredients of a prime-time television thriller," it was in fact a difficult one to narrate. The story had a lot in common with the Barings one: essentially it concerned unauthorized dealings in an insufficiently regulated global market and the scope for corruption that this allows. It even contained a central character, a "rogue trader," on whom to focus: Sumitoma's chief copper trader, Yasuo Hamanaka. But the problem in "launching" the story out of the specialized interest of the financial pages in the "quality" press was that it simply did not have enough to personalize it. There was some feeble attempt to build the character of Hamanaka as a major international fixer "mainly interested in dice and girls," but clearly there simply was not enough available detail to sustain this. What is more, Hamanaka had not even been arrested at the time of the reports, but had merely been sacked by Sumitoma. So, despite the economic scale of the fraud – potentially much larger in its ramifications than the Barings affair – this was a story that never quite became constituted (in the UK at least) as a media scandal; indeed it was scarcely mentioned on British television news bulletins.

What does this comparison tell us? Most basically it illustrates the way in which news reporters strive to find human-interest angles to make a story appealing at the broadest level. Now this *may* be seen as the manipulation of the event, the deliberate construction of the scandal, by the media. And the most obvious critical response to this is probably to point to the way this manipulation extends to the story's moral content: the personalization involved is seen as a failure to confront the more important, "serious" issues. This is obviously, to a certain extent, true. However, we can read things in another way. We can see the construction of this sort of "abstract" scandal into a personalized narrative as providing an accessible context for the sort of moral–imaginative reflection that I have described. I would not want to argue that this is the ideal way in which these global issues should be discursively distributed, but, equally, it is a mistake to dismiss the genuine moment of moral engagement that they contain. And the broader point of the Barings–Leeson story, of course, is that people as a simple matter of fact are engaged in greater numbers where scandals can be narrated so as to bring them closer to their own life situations – in recognizable themes like destructive personal ambition, love relations, and so on. Personalization can be read here not as trivialization but as achieving greater imaginative proximity to the lifeworld of the audience.

However, as we have seen, proximity to the project of the self is not sufficient to make a successful media scandal: There has also to be the element of originality, of "extraordinariness" to catch the public imagination. The "ideal" of a media scandal, then, might be described as "extraordinary ordinariness," and this combination is particularly well illustrated in one of the most successful international media scandals of our time: the affairs (in both the general and the "scandalous" sense) leading up to the divorce of Prince Charles and Princess Diana in 1996. The "private lives" of the British royal family have been the focus of huge media attention for many years, but there had been particular fascination with the state of Charles and Diana's marriage. One register of this interest was in the spectacular audience figures recorded – indeed confidently anticipated – for the BBC *Panorama* interview with Princess Diana on November 20, 1995. *Panorama*, the BBC's "flagship" current affairs program, attracted a UK audience of 23.2 million for this edition, a virtually unprecedented figure for a current affairs show and exceeding the normal weekly "top-of-the-ratings" figure for the most popular prime-time shows. Although David Morley's respondent claimed to hate *Panorama*, it is a fair bet that she tuned in for this program, in which the princess told "her side of the story" of the troubled royal marriage. There is no doubting the human-interest angle here. Diana spoke of her love for Charles, of her struggles to live up to the demands of a life lived in the public gaze, of the oppressive nature of the royal clan, of her growing entrapment in an unhappy and "crowded" marriage (a reference to Charles's affair with Camilla Parker-Bowles), of the collapse in her sense of self-worth – her bulimia, her attempted suicide – of her own infidelities, and finally of her survival, her personal growth, and her determination to make an independent life for herself and her children. This was, on any account, compulsive viewing. And it is fairly easy to understand why interest should be high in the UK, where the royal family is obviously in some ways central to the elaboration of British national culture. But why does the story have such global reach? The *Panorama* program was simultaneously broadcast on the BBC's World Service to eager audiences in Europe, Africa, Asia, and the Middle East. It was eventually shown in 112 countries around the world. In Australia it was watched by two in three of the population. Why should this be? Why should so many people around the world share an interest in the doings of the rather anachronistic symbolic elite of a small European country?

No doubt the reasons for this are complex, but principal among them must be the way that the generalized category of "royalty" signifies a special social–cultural type, a "breed apart" from ordinary people. The "extraordinary ordinariness" of royal scandals thus arises out of the simultaneous presentation of royals as categorically different from us, yet as flesh-and-blood human beings, sharing our mundane practices, our temptations, weaknesses, and emotional and relational problems. This dual nature of the media presentation of royalty was nicely grasped by Roland Barthes in the much more decorous period of the early 1950s. In one of his short *Mythologies* essays, "The 'Blue Blood' Cruise," Barthes reflects on the French press reporting of a cruise holiday enjoyed by various assorted European royals aboard the Greek yacht, the *Agamemnon*:

> Ever since the Coronation, the French have been pining for fresh news about royal activities, of which they are very fond . . . The Coronation of Elizabeth was a theme which appealed to the emotions and senti-mentalities; the "Blue Blood" Cruise is a humorous episode in which kings played at being men . . . there followed a thousand situations, droll because of the Marie-Antoinette-playing-the-milkmaid type. . . . Thus the neutral gestures of daily life have taken, on the *Agamemnon*, an exorbit-antly bold character . . . kings shave themselves! This touch was reported by our national press as an act of incredible singularity . . . King Paul was wearing an open neck shirt and short sleeves, Queen Frederika a *print* dress, that is to say one no longer unique but whose pattern can also be seen on the bodies of mere mortals. (Barthes 1973: 32)

Barthes uses this episode to point out how the representations of "monarchy at play" by generally conservative and sycophantic media serve to maintain their anachronistic status, privilege, and even political power in a democratic society: "to flaunt the fact that kings are capable of prosaic actions . . . is to acknowledge that the king is still king by divine right" (Barthes 1973: 32). But the cul-tural politics of the 1950s which Barthes demystifies are not iden-tical to those of the 1990s. No doubt the media still act to maintain some of the myth of "quasi-divine" royalty, but in a much more problematic way. The sheer increase in the media visibility of roy-alty in the 1990s has meant a loss in their power to manage their image.[5] Where Barthes could describe a smoothly finessed presenta-tion of the delicate balance between the divine and the mortal, today the "ordinariness" of royals bursts through in an uncon-trolled way. As John Thompson argues, in a world of intense media scrutiny, "it is difficult for the temporal representatives of the mon-archy to avoid appearing as ordinary individuals, as men and women who are little different from other individuals apart from the accident of their birth" (Thompson 1995: 201). So whereas for Barthes the issue was how the dual nature of royalty was compla-cently presented by the media, feeding a public fascination which depended ultimately on the successful maintenance of distance, for

Thompson it is the tensions in this duality, as they are increasingly revealed by the media, that constitute the essence of royal scandals which may ultimately threaten the reproduction of the institution.

The common factor in both these accounts, however, is that of the "extraordinary ordinariness" that is central to the cultural significance of the category of royalty. This, it might be argued, is what allows royal scandals to cross national–cultural boundaries so easily. It is unlikely that people in other cultures are particularly interested in the moral climate of British elite public life, or concerned with the possible degradation of one of the UK's cultural–political institutions and the constitutional threat this portends. They are more probably interested in the doings of British royals insofar as these offer a dramatization of the moral and emotional problems they recognize in their own lives. In this sense royal scandals are culturally generalizable (hence mobile) because they can act as vehicles for reflection on the everyday moral–relational problems generated by social–cultural modernity: How does one cope with infidelity? Should one stay in an unhappy marriage for the sake of the children? Does individual self-fulfillment come before family responsibilities? What rights do people have to privacy in their relationships?

Conclusion: Long-distance morality and cultural re-embedding

What I have mainly tried to argue is that, when we engage with scandals that have their origin in other countries, we do so largely by assimilating them to the relevances of our everyday life-world. The aspects of a scandal that resonate with our own moral–existential concerns are the ones that best capture our imagination, and these concerns are, of their nature, locally situated – formed out of the day-to-day, culturally specific experiences through which we elaborate our sense of self. Thus a successful "global scandal" is one that can be, to borrow Giddens's terms (Giddens 1990), "disembedded" from its local context and "re-embedded" into a multitude of other culturally distinct contexts. To put this proposal in its most challenging form would, indeed, be to say that there are no global scandals but only re-embedded local ones. This does not mean that scandals never achieve global scale or have global moral–political implications. But it would be a defensible claim in respect of the way we have defined scandals, as "middle-order moral events" which lend themselves to narration at a level at which people can imaginatively and empathetically engage with them.

What implications does this view hold for the "higher-level" moral issues – environmental damage, racism, the poverty, illiteracy, and immiseration of Third World populations, war, and so forth – that, it might be argued, are the really "scandalous" issues of our age? The context of globalization, of the increasingly complex interconnection between spatially-spread social–cultural formations, suggests that we can no longer maintain the sort of moral–cultural particularism that might have been possible in Marlowe's age. In all sorts of ways, we now live in a "global neighborhood" that forces these moral issues upon us.

Extrapolating from the arguments I have advanced in relation to scandals might, however, suggest a pessimistic view of the possibilities of constructing a moral–political order at the global level. Thinking of moral imagination as essentially local suggests a point at which involvement vanishes, just where it might most be needed. As Zygmunt Bauman argues, "we do not 'naturally' feel responsibility for . . . far away events, however closely they may intertwine with what we do or abstain from doing. . . . Morality which always guided us and still guides us today has powerful, but short hands" (Bauman 1993: 218). The pessimistic view, then, is that our social–communicational–technological development has outstripped our moral development: The globalized social world and our moral worlds have simply become out of kilter.

Perhaps the first thing to say in this respect is that the analysis of scandals alone should not push us toward such a bleak conclusion. For scandals are, after all, rather specific contexts for the exercise of the moral faculties. Although I have argued that they do generally contain a moral element – they are not merely excuses for idle curiosity, prurience, or, worse, *schadenfreude* – scandals are obviously not the only (and certainly not the ideal) form in which moral discourse can be conducted in modern societies. Furthermore, it does not follow that because people so readily involve themselves in the "personalized" morality of scandals, they therefore lack the capacity or the innate motivation to engage with more "serious" moral issues: It may be a question of how these issues are presented to them.

However, I do think that the analysis of scandals may have a lesson for us about this broader moral discourse. It is this: We should not struggle to extend the "short hands" of "localized" morality up to the level of global abstractions. Rather we should try to pose the moral issues that globalization presents within the context of local experience. This is a lesson in moral engagement we can learn by paying attention to the moral–cultural proclivities that people actually demonstrate in their lives, rather than by expecting people to "rise to the challenge" of remote events.

The media have a clear and crucial narrational role, and perhaps even a peculiar responsibility, in this respect. For global scandals typify broader issues of global morality in being essentially – for most of us, exclusively – mediated experiences. It is overwhelmingly as a result of our use of globalizing media technologies, particularly television, that the wider world opens up to us as "our world." The global media make events in distant places proximate to our local lives by bringing representations of them into our living rooms. The issue then becomes that of how these images and narratives can be made morally significant; how they can pass from the world "out there" into our own moral lifeworlds.

As we have seen in the case of media scandals, the "popular" media are actually rather good at framing certain events so as to make them engaging at a personal level. But often, as we have also noted, they are criticized for making issues *too* personalized – for trivializing them, for obscuring their more challenging aspects in a blur of sentimentality or (worse) by framing them in terms of crude and ideological moral stereotypes. Often this criticism is justified. However, it seems to me that the answer is not to insist that "serious" issues should be entirely "depersonalized." Of course a lot of the problems that confront us in a globalized world are large, complex, and abstract – simply not of the same moral order as those of media scandals. But if people are to engage with these issues at all, to exercise any degree of moral agency, then ways need to be found to narrate them so that they become congruent with individual, locally-situated lifeworlds. A certain degree of personalization may thus be considered an essential entry-level qualification into a moral discourse. If this is so, then the "popular framing" of high-order moral–political issues, judiciously exercised, should be regarded as not only a legitimate media practice, but an essential one. Media scandals may not be the perfect models for global moral discourse, but they do in this respect offer some clues as to how the more difficult and "remote" problems of our time can be "brought home to us" as moral concerns.

Notes

1 Barabas in fact "admits" to the moral offense of fornication only in the context of concealing the greater one of multiple murder.
2 Of the many that could be cited, see Mrs Henry Wood's wonderful melodrama, *East Lynne* (1861), or for a much later example of the theme, Arnold Bennett's *The Old Wives' Tale* (1908).
3 For a discussion of the reflexive nature of institutions of modernity, see Giddens (1994) and Beck et al. (1994). For an argument about the significance of reflexivity to cultural experience and practice, see Tomlinson (1998).
4 Morley originally relates this response to a discussion of gender differences in the perception of news, and to the distinction between the public and private spheres. This gender dimension of the local reception of media scandals potentially complicates the analysis I offer here, but not, I think, in ways that undermine the central argument.
5 This can be seen in the increasingly difficult relations between the British royal family and, particularly, the tabloid press. In August, 1996, Princess Diana was obliged to apply for a legal injunction against a press photographer to prevent him from "stalking" her. Relations with the broadcast media have also deteriorated. At about the same time it was disclosed that the queen was to end her tradition of broadcasting a Christmas message exclusively on the BBC. This was rumored to be out of resentment against the broadcasting of the 1995 *Panorama* interview with Diana.

References

Anderson, B. (1983). *Imagined Communities*. London: Verso.
Ang, I. (1996). *Living Room Wars: Rethinking Media Audiences for a Postmodern World*. London: Routledge.
Barthes, R. (1973). *Mythologies*. London: Paladin.
Bauman, Z. (1993). *Postmodern Ethics*. Oxford: Blackwell.
Beck, U. (1992). *Risk Society: Towards a New Modernity*. London: Sage.
Beck, U., Giddens, A., and Lash, S. (eds) (1994). *Reflexive Modernization*. Cambridge: Polity Press.
Commission on Global Governance (1995). *Our Global Neighbourhood: The Report of the Commission on Global Governance*. Oxford: Oxford University Press.
Donovan, P. and Murphy, P. (1996). The copper and the robbers riddle. *Guardian*, June 25.
Giddens, A. (1990). *The Consequences of Modernity*. Cambridge: Polity Press.
Giddens, A. (1994). *Beyond Left and Right*. Cambridge: Polity Press.
Gurevitch, M., Levy, M.R., and Roeh, I. (1991). The global newsroom: Convergences and diversities in the globalization of television news. In Dahlgren, P. and Sparks, C. (eds), *Communication and Citizenship*. London: Routledge.
Habermas, J. (1989). *The Structural Transformation of the Public Sphere*. Cambridge: Polity Press.
Hoskins, C. and Mirus, R. (1988). Reasons for the US dominance of the international trade in television programs. *Media Culture and Society* 10: 499–515.

King, A. (1986). Sex, money and power. In Hodder-Williams, R. and Ceaser, J. (eds), *Politics in Britain and the United States: Comparative Perspectives*. Durham, NC: Duke University Press.

Lull, J. (1995). *Media, Communication, Culture: A Global Approach*. Cambridge: Polity Press.

Marlowe, C. (1994). *The Jew of Malta*. London: A. & C. Black.

Morley, D. (1992). *Television Audiences and Cultural Studies*. London: Routledge.

Silverstone, R. (1994). *Television and Everyday Life*. London: Routledge.

Thompson, J.B. (1990). *Ideology and Modern Culture*. Cambridge: Polity Press.

Thompson, J.B. (1995). *The Media and Modernity: A Social Theory of the Media*. Cambridge: Polity Press.

Tomlinson, J. (1998). *Global Modernity: The Cultural Implications of Globalization*. Cambridge: Polity Press.

4 Anxiety, Desire, and Conflict in the American Racial Imagination

Herman Gray

> In the Simi Valley courtroom, what many took to be incon-
> trovertible evidence *against* the police was presented instead
> to establish police vulnerability, that is, to support the con-
> tention that Rodney King was endangering the police.
> *Judith Butler, "Endangered/endangering," (original emphasis)*

Separated by some eighty years, at first glance, it appears that a film like *Birth of a Nation* and the videotaped beating of Los Angeles motorist Rodney King have little in common. On closer inspection there is much that the two representations share, despite the fact that one is, in John Fiske's terms, a high-tech fictional film and the other a low-tech home video (Fiske 1994). *Birth of a Nation* inaugurates and organizes visually a discursive field where black-ness serves as the marker of downfall, moral transgression, and the crisis of white southern identity. The videotaped beating of Rodney King, on the other hand, reiterates and re-enacts the contemporary scene of similar anxieties expressed as crisis in the conservative environment of America in the 1980s. Both representations render as "scandalous"* the real and potential transgressions of the black

---

* *Editors' note:* In this chapter, the author places "scandal" and "scandalous" in quotations when he wishes to illustrate how the term is used in normal journalistic practice.
He italicizes the same two words when he wants to emphasize what he believes is truly
scandalous.

corporal body, which, when seen from the perspective of white workers and former plantation owners, appears as threatening and out of control.

I recognize, of course, that the notion of scandal is usually applied to personal, often moral acts of transgression and behavioral lapses of the normative boundaries of the collective. I, however, want to extend and broaden this understanding of scandal by proposing that we consider it as a political and cultural construct which hides and glosses as much as it reveals about the terms of the American moral and social order. Consequently, I apply the notion of scandal to a discursive regime that has invested in representing social, cultural, and political struggles over power in racial terms, framing such struggles to the racial and economic order in moral terms. I want to suggest, moreover, that such racialized discourse works, by naming and rendering as "scandalous" transgressions and oppositions to the dominant order of things. Thus within the discourse which *Birth of a Nation* visualizes, the film constructs as "scandalous" the rise of Reconstruction and the fall of the southern plantation economy. In the case of the Rodney King video it is the Los Angeles Police Department (LAPD) officers who regard King's behavior as "scandalous" because, from their vantage point, he refused to submit to their power.

But I also want to go further and suggest, as the civil rights movement demonstrated, that the notion of scandal is sometimes an illuminating critical construct when viewed from the perspective of those who are marked and discursively positioned outside the dominant social and moral order. Because Martin Luther King and the leaders of the civil rights movement framed the question of black equality and civil rights in moral and religious terms, they were able to effectively define and reveal as *scandalous* the inhuman and brutal treatment which blacks suffered at the hands of a racist social system. Thus, one need only step outside the terms of racist discourse to see that the historic treatment of black victims at the hands of LAPD violence and abuse is no less *scandalous* than the depiction of blacks found in *Birth of a Nation*.

Race continues to quietly organize the discursive terms through which the boundaries of the American social, cultural, and moral order are made visible and maintained. In the age of media saturation and celebrity, race as a signifier helps to make such boundaries and those who transgress them visible and representable; thus black social visibility, in contrast to white social locations and discursive positions, and the racist cultural discourse through which blackness is assigned negative value, also helps to subject such transgression to intense policing, mythical representation, and, where necessary, brutal enforcement.[1] As late as the 1980s blackness as a negative signifier of moral transgression appeared in the media representations in the form of the black welfare queen, black teen parents, female-headed households, male youth, and black gays and lesbians. This framing function, this marking of limits and assignment of a devalued social status to black subjects as symbols of transgression, is, to be sure, a cultural and historical process and therefore involves issues of discourse, power, judgments, and contestation. As a social construct in the American moral and social economy, blackness is constructed and marked as the sign of excess where such excess functions to maintain the boundaries of permissibility, stability, and coherence. Symbolically, these *scandalous* constructions and representations of the social breakdown and moral decay which they signify have worked effectively to mobilize and consolidate a conservative, largely white, rightwing hegemony.

Scandal as epistemology

As a discursive and epistemological matter, the framing function which blackness serves in the American cultural imagination (especially in its construction and racialization within media of representation such as television, news, and cinema) I believe has its paradigmatic origins in the classic American film, *Birth of a Nation*. This film both constructs and stages as "scandalous" perhaps the most traumatic event – as it concerns national character, whiteness, and citizenship – in the nation's history: slavery, the civil war, and the entry of former slaves as political subjects (as opposed to chattel) into the cultural and civic life of the nation. In short, *Birth of a Nation* established the terms of the representational (visual and narrative) paradigm within which and through which the national culture has managed its own "scandalous" history of terror and violence against blacks. If slavery can be seen as a system built on terror and intimidation, then what better way to cover and re-stage such terror than through the metaphor of "scandal."

Birth of a Nation frames the question of black freedom as "scandalous" at a number of different levels. The film constructs as "scandalous" the fact that the plantation south has fallen; that former black slaves should be regarded as citizen subjects; that they should be given responsibility of governance (over themselves as well as whites); that whiteness (especially white womanhood and sexuality) is threatened by blackness; and that white masculinity and sexuality virility are challenged.

Birth of a Nation stages this "scandalous" representation of the fall of the slave south by resorting to a romantic construction of the old south. Blacks appear as happy, helpful, and loyal to the plantation economy. This representation is achieved by repressing and erasing any hint of that economy as a brutal and dehumanizing system which was dependent on the exploitation of black slave labor. Nor is there any hint of resistance and challenge to this system by blacks. In this romantic fantasy, the old slave south is displaced and eventually destroyed by a Reconstructed system where inhuman, oversexed, dangerous, and lazy black brutes are installed (by cunning northerners) to run things.

But *Birth of a Nation* is itself "scandalous," for it constructs a "scandalous" rewriting of social history, in effect enacting a "scandalous" representation of blackness and blacks as untutored, inhuman, greedy, and incompetent. This "scandalous" representation of blacks and the lament about the horrors of black liberation from slavery is poignantly described by film scholar Ed Guerrero:

> In contrast with Griffith's depiction of a genteel South and its loyal black slaves, the film counter-poses the chaos of the Reconstruction South and its "insolent" free blacks. With depictions of a totally *fantasized* black legislature in Reconstruction South Carolina and the "renegade negro" and would-be rapist Gus, *Birth* offers blunt and unique racial deformations. The incredible mis-en-scene of the Reconstruction legislature is an elaborate and detailed lie showing black members, while in session, eating chicken, sipping whiskey from flasks, ogling white women, and passing a motion that all legislators must wear shoes in the legislative chamber. Playing on the much-incited white fear of interracial sex, *Birth* [sic] claims that the black legislature's first law is one permitting marriage between blacks and whites. Carrying this anxiety to its white supremist extreme, the film depicts Colonel Cameron's little sister jumping off a cliff to preserve her purity, rather than submit to the amorous advances of Gus, who is obviously and ironically played by a white man in black face. (Guerrero 1993: 16, my emphasis)

One need only qualify the term "fantasy" with the adjective "scandalous" to appreciate, from an African American perspective anyway, the way in which blacks in *Birth of a Nation* come to embody the acts of transgression as well as the boundaries which give coherence and meaning to this fantastic view of the decline of the plantation economy and the slave system. Indeed, in *Birth of a Nation* one can see the process of social construction and labeling laid bare through its cinematic language and the racist discourse in which it is embedded. Furthermore, the white moral outrage articulated by the film is present in contemporary representations like those revealed in the infamous tape of the Rodney King beating, the news footage of black anger and rebellion during the 1992 Los Angeles riots, the national outrage expressed at black responses to the "not guilty" verdict in the O.J. Simpson trial, and the "wanna-be" news packages of gang warfare and drug busts depicted in reality-TV genre shows like *Cops*. As with *Birth of a Nation*, the cultural construct "blackness" marks the limits of social transgression and African American people appear as the transgressors, hence the source of moral and social threat to the national life.[2]

The inaugural framework established by *Birth of a Nation* semiologically implicated the new mass media of representation in the overt assignment to blackness of the signs of danger, excess, and social decay. When applied to contemporary media coverage of social and moral transgression, this framework has become more subtle and sophisticated as a result of significant historical changes and political challenges in media, politics, and culture over the last eighty or so years. These transformations and challenges include the notable proliferation of black image makers in television, film, and the press, as well as the emergence and formation of explicitly oppositional black political and cultural voices. Significant twentieth-century social movements for civil rights, gender equality, and the recognition of sexual orientation have, in important respects, expanded the boundaries of moral and social possibility. These expansions and the political challenges which produced them have generated new social frontiers of permissibility and recognition. They have also produced more vehement contestations at those frontiers, as well as new candidates for labeling and policing based on new perceptions and definitions of their potential transgressions. These contemporary representatives of "scandalous" social and moral social transgression include immigrants, youth, female-headed households, and teen mothers. Unequal power relations, social inequality, racism, sexism, and homophobia based on various forms of racial and cultural difference continue to nurture the framework established by *Birth of a Nation*. Blackness and difference continue to function as the markers of "scandalous" threats to the moral and social boundaries. Hence, while the overt strategies through which the demonization of African Americans within media representations have certainly become more subtle, the psychological and cultural role which blackness plays in the national life and cultural imagination of American remains, in many respects, fundamentally the same. The dominant epistemological and cultural framework through which blackness (and other expressions of difference) is rendered visible and thus made to shore up the social and moral boundaries of the national culture has remained resilient. The power of this epistemology has never been more subtle, yet consequential.

Anxiety and desire

Because we live in an age in which corporately-produced, mass-media images circulate at such a rapid pace, they are literally rendered obsolete before they reach their intended audiences. Along with this structured obsolescence, in the West ours is a media environment where fame and celebrity, no matter how momentary, are the currency which stimulates desire and fantasy. So combustible is celebrity when combined with media that it transforms even the most mundane events and ordinary lives into fuel for television news, talk shows, and gossip magazines. New television shows and print publications regularly appear whose sole purpose is to cover fame and celebrity and report on social and personal transgression.[3] In print media, tabloid publications specializing in matters from the bizarre to the unimaginable clutter the American imagination, competing for attention with news stories of war, famine, and the economy. On television, talk shows, entertainment shows, and special feature programs like *Geraldo*, *Oprah*, the *Barbara Walters Special*, *Hard Copy*, and *Inside Edition* have become acceptable venues for breaking and circulating stories about personal, political, and social transgression. It was, of course, a national tabloid which broke the 1996 Richard Morris story of prostitution and the disclosure of White House secrets, while the *National Inquirer* and *Geraldo* led the way in reporting developments in the O.J. Simpson murder trial. Tabloid news outlets which focus exclusively on tantalizing stories about the personal excesses and lapses of public figures, entertainers, athletes, and politicians regularly blur the line (at least in the public mind and increasingly in academic discourse and journalism) between so-called legitimate news and sensationalist journalism.

Of course all epochs, cultures, and societies operate with explicit and implicit understandings of scandalous activity. So we might ask what the social and cultural meaning of transgressive behavior is in an age of racial and ethnic domination, mass media, cinematic representation, and instantaneous if only momentary fame. What does it mean, for example, when Rodney King (who gained notoriety as the victim of a malicious and scandalous beating at the hands of the Los Angeles Police Department) is repeatedly arrested for approaching prostitutes and for abusing his wife, while Hugh Grant, the boyish British actor who is arrested for using the sexual services of a black prostitute, appears on a national television talk show to dismiss the entire episode as simply a harmless case of bad judgment? And what are we to make of the reactions to Washington DC Mayor Marion Barry, who was caught by a low-tech undercover FBI surveillance tape (which was in turn played on high-tech network television newscasts) smoking crack cocaine, convicted, and sent to prison; or Mel Reynolds, the former Illinois Congressman who was convicted of having sex with a 16-year-old and removed from Congress, while white Congressmen like Donald Lukens, Gerry Studds, and Dan Crane, who all admitted similar transgressions, were permitted to remain in the US Congress? How do we sort through the metaphors of heroism and courage that were employed by the sports press to characterize the revelation of white Green Bay Packer quarterback Bret Favre, who publicly admitted addiction to painkillers, and the disappointment and narratives of collapse which accompanied revelations of drug use by highly-visible and well-paid black athletes like Michael Irvin, Darryl Strawberry, and Dwight Gooden?[4] And what of the ugly demonization, character assassination, and public humiliation which accompanied and framed the public ordeals of professional black women like Lani Guiner, Anita Hill, and Joycelyn Elders, while similarly visible and influential white woman like Zoe Baird and Susan McDougal suffered public embarrassment, to be sure, but largely avoided the vituperous and bitter attacks on their character?[5]

All the public figures in these examples share some measure of notoriety, fame, and celebrity generated by widespread news coverage and media exposure. Each of their situations involves perceived transgression of the social and moral boundaries of family and individual responsibility, particularly in terms of sex, drugs, and trust. The power of such transgressions depends on a stable discourse of meaning which is available (largely through common sense) to be mobilized and placed in the service of social control and moral judgment. I want to suggest that in each of the examples, blackness, especially in relationship to sexuality, is the cultural trope which mobilizes and organizes such meanings. In other words, as is obvious, race and sexuality operate as crucial markers of the boundaries of cultural and social propriety. Even at the personal level, where common sense is organized and its social meanings circulated, blackness and the already racialized discourse in which it is embedded continue to mark the social boundaries of moral transgression.

Birth of a Nation helps to illuminate, historically and culturally, the process by which cultural, social, aesthetic, and moral discourses about white superiority, anxieties over the loss of tradition, and the erosion of economic and social hegemony underwrite perhaps the crucial media and cinematic moment in American society. These cultural, social, political, and moral discourses continue to have purchase in the collective common sense, for they continue to frame, reiterate, and make available a storehouse of meanings. These meanings are still sharply focused on, and animated in popular culture and media around, race and sexuality. In particular I want to argue that blackness, through its sheer historicity and ontological presence – what Fanon calls the fact of blackness – exposes and activates the limits of the national cultural imaginary. Just as it did in *Birth of a Nation* some eighty years ago, when linked to scandal, in matters of citizenship, morality, and acceptable behavior, blackness profoundly unsettles commonsense understanding – so much so that it has periodically been used by conservative political forces to mobilize, reconsolidate, and re-install racist and nationalist formations.

The influence of tabloids on legitimate news, and its obverse, the legitimization of tabloid journalism, have helped make more visible and unstable the frontiers of transgressive disputes. Indeed one could reasonably argue that while these processes – producing, marking, policing, and enforcing – are a more routine feature of news-work and a more visible staple of programming, they are also more insidious.[6] So although the "scandalous" discourse inaugurated by *Birth of a Nation* some eighty years ago has no doubt become more subtle, its continuing purchase as a discursive regime, and the dependence on blackness on which it relied, are also more entrenched (but no less contested).

Scandal and black popular culture

From a longer historical vantage point – that of collective American culture as opposed to the purely personal and individual – the centrality of blackness, especially its expression as black popular culture, for exposing and maintaining the social and moral boundaries of the national culture can be brought into sharper relief. For example, the social, moral, and cultural response to black popular music illustrates the attempt both to expose and to consolidate social boundaries and definitions of family, motherhood, and children, especially as existing definitions were perceived to be unsettled by expressions of black pleasure and sexuality articulated by popular music. In the decades of the 1920s and 1950s, and again in the 1980s and 1990s, black popular music and black dancing bodies appeared as visible objects of close cultural scrutiny and moral policing for their presumed threats to the civility of American national culture. Whether it was jazz, rhythm and blues, or rap, each genre of black popular music has been met at one time or another with a curious mix of popular acceptance and moral suspicion. Black musical forms significantly stretched the boundaries of sound and imagination by the sheer force of their energy and creativity. As is well acknowledged by historians and critics of popular music, these genres also invigorated a national culture weighed down by the sluggishness and prudishness of moral and social propriety. Furthermore, in one form or another, they have all consistently contributed to the vitality of popular cultures throughout the world.

And yet, these musics have, at one time or another, all been the objects of aesthetic surveillance, social censorship, and moral outrage because of their supposed contamination of cultural standards and threats to social civility. In the 1920s, jazz and the secular music of black Americans from which it was derived expressed (at least in the popular imagination of white, middle-class cultural gatekeepers) an infectious primitivism and rhythmic power from which white woman and children had to be protected. Police, clergy, educators, parents, civic leaders, and politicians created an alliance of cultural guardianship, erecting moral and social boundaries to keep the offensive music at bay. Similarly, rhythm and blues, jazz, and related forms like rock and roll were publicly associated with drugs, sexual promiscuity, and youth rebellion – all of which were thought to contribute to the social and moral erosion of a culture and society undergoing rapid political and social change. More recently rap and hip-hop styles have received heavy scrutiny and condemnation for violent lyrics, drug imagery, and offensive language. Rap has been subjected to a ratings system led by groups such as the Parents Music Resource Center (PMRC), a US Congressional committee, and public officials like William Bennett, again in the name of protecting women, family, and especially children. Attacks on black popular music are, to be sure, part of a broader campaign waged by conservative political and religious groups to discipline the so-called permissive culture of liberalism, including vendettas against student protests and white youth cultures. For its detractors, black popular forms like rap music constitute the most visible and offensive expressions of the presumed assault on and subsequent erosion of American cultural standards and moral values (see Gray 1989a, 1989b; Grossberg 1992; Rose 1993; Walser 1993). As the historical pattern of these assaults on black popular culture suggests, blackness periodically (but consistently) serves as the highly-visible cultural repository of struggle over the central values and life-ways of American culture. Although these contentions are seldom framed in the explicit language of scandal, the purported transgressions which they signify and enact are read from one perspective (i.e. the dominant) as "scandalous."[7]

In the case of black documentary film, one contemporary assault on black cultural practices which both revealed the anxiety over race and sexuality and made little attempt to conceal its moral outrage and social anxiety about such presumed transgressions was the public controversy surrounding the film *Tongues Untied*, by the late Marlon Riggs. *Tongues* is singularly significant for enabling the voices and representing the humanity of black gay men. The documentary film so outraged reactionary conservatives that Jesse Helms, a right-wing senator from North Carolina, led a scathing (*scandalous* really) attack on the film and the collective character of black gay men. Neither diplomatic nor gracious in his hyperbole, Helms clearly saw both the film and financial support of it by the National Endowment of the Arts as offensive to the moral sensibilities of his conservative constituents, thus "scandalous." From the floor of the US Senate, Helms railed against what he regarded as explicit sexual references, displays of affection, and sexual intimacy.[8] For Helms and other conservative critics, Riggs's film explicitly violated the moral boundaries of heterosexuality, nuclear family, racial separation and "purity," masculinity, and womanhood – all in the short space of a one-hour documentary. Footage from Riggs's

film even turned up in negative campaign ads designed to mobilize right-wing outrage and elect "moral majority" conservatives.[9]
Because this attack was also aimed at the federal agency which
used public tax moneys to fund and broadcast the film, Helms (like
D.W. Griffith) attempted to construct the liberal welfare state as
immoral and scandalous.

As both examples indicate, blackness – along with the attendant histories, experiences, and life-ways which are expressed in
popular practices and cultural representations – is squarely at the
center of larger national debates about morality, transgression, and
social decline. While it is tempting, even plausible, to regard these
debates as a simple conflict of values generated by different social
positions, such an explanation seems limited because it seriously
misreads and marginalizes the centrality of African Americans to
the cultural history and life of America. Because the African American presence is tied so fundamentally to the historical experience
and cultural imagination of the American experience (despite continuing class and racial marginalization), it is not at all surprising
that it subsequently provides the most poignant, immediate, and
contentious site through which the national culture grapples with
its most deep-seated and persistent social and moral anxieties.

Scandal as rupture and contestation

> As the court prepared for a new trial last week, [Michael]
> Irvin [a successful black American athlete arrested on a drug
> charge] showed up in a lavender coat and pants, with two-
> toned lavender-and-dark-red alligator loafers. Generally this
> is not the image that defense attorneys like to showcase for
> a jury.
>
> R. Hoffer, "The party's over"

The mediated anxiety first expressed cinematically in *Birth of a
Nation* and articulated through the *scandalous* representation of
blackness as the source of social dis-organization, civic chaos, and
moral transgression is of a piece with the very same anxiety reiterated and re-enacted in the *scandalous* demonization of black youth,
welfare mothers, gay men, and lesbian woman articulated by Helms,
the PMRC, Reaganism, and neo-conservatives. *Birth of a Nation*
helped establish a social and aesthetic framework through which a
racialized American order narrated its collective outrage about the

trauma of decline and loss of an idealized way of life (Taylor 1991). And to this day, race continues to help establish the discursive territory wherein the moral boundaries are drawn. The paradigm established by the film provides the *symbolic hook* on which to make these anxieties representable, the *moral angle* from which to stake out the limits of transgression, and the *political framework* within which to ponder collective solutions – which often take the form of social and cultural policing of the most marginal. In our time, anxieties about the stability of the nuclear family (single-parent families), social equality (affirmative action), social responsibility (the welfare state and crime), and bodily pleasures (drugs and sexuality) take the form of symbolic representation and moral surveillance.

Birth of a Nation and subsequent representations of scandalous behavior, structured as they are by a racial discourse, are produced by their own epistemology, their own way of seeing. In other words, this paradigm establishes not just *what* can be seen as scandalous, but *how*. It makes visible, at a collective and cultural level, what from the angle of whiteness counts as transgressive. As Guerrero notes, so long as blacks are happy and contented slaves who remain loyal to the plantation economy, there is no crisis of representation; they remain invisible. As long as Rodney King is compliant and accepts the beating, which literally marks on his black body his place in a racial hierarchy, there is no problem (Butler 1993). And as long as Michael Irvin is contrite and humble with respect to his image as a sports superstar who confirms the American mobility myth, there is no problem. It is only when, in each case, the figure of blackness (and especially black masculinity) fails to conform to the paradigmatic representation that the discourse works to make blackness visible, marking it as transgressive and therefore "scandalous." African Americans are constructed as invisible and hence ordinary as long as they conform. They become "black" and thus dangerous when they transgress.

When fused with race, scandals use blackness (and other forms of difference) to mark the boundaries of a national state and culture in crisis, struggling with the privileges and attendant inequalities of whiteness, heterosexuality, and the hegemony of neo-conservative claims on the nuclear family and patriarchy. If the representational paradigm established by *Birth of a Nation* conditioned how to see blackness as scandalous, it is repeatedly re-enacted and reiterated through contemporary media framing and coverage of America's "big" events such as the 1992 Los Angeles riots or the O.J. Simpson trial. In key moments such coverage organizes and enlists a gener-alized consensus about moral transgression. Crime, drugs, and the taped behavior of the LAPD in the Rodney King case are obvious examples. But at other times such coverage and the inter-pretive frameworks which organize them come to be seen, espe-cially by African Americans, as *scandalous*. The reaction of African American students at Howard University who cheered the "not guilty" verdict of Simpson was framed by the press as "scandal-ous" – the surprise and outrage at this reaction were especially troubling for white women (and many black women, though this dimension of gender was subordinate to the racialized dimension). Many African Americans regarded the acquittal as a deserved and long-overdue expression of justice in a racist criminal justice system that disproportionately imprisons black men. This crack in the frame, this contestation of meaning, was the reason that the response to both the trial and the LA riots were for a time literally incomprehensible to the largely white press which covered the story, as well as white audiences who saw the televised reactions.

The reaction of the Howard University students is perhaps not so far-fetched and incomprehensible. Ironically enough their reac-tion – as an expression of the slippery and contested meanings of scandal – inverts the representation of blackness in *Birth of a Nation*. When read through the more contested and disputed lens of scandal which I have offered here, coverage of the riots and the black reactions to the Simpson verdict laid bare the long and tortured history, conflict, and struggle over meaning and representation in American society.

Notes

1 Ironically in a society where black popular culture has been critical to stretch-ing the frontiers of American cultural imagination and possibility, blackness has also functioned historically as a negative symbol, marking the limits of the American moral frontier.
2 As I insist throughout, there is another way of seeing, another reading of these activities and behaviors as black rejection and refusal of dominant and racialized codes of containment, dehumanization, and derision.
3 Television talk shows are the most obvious such venues; I would add to them shows like the Fox network's *America's Funniest Home Videos* and Entertainment! Television's *Talk Soup*. In terms of print, *People* and *US* are the most obvious examples.
4 See Neff (1996) for an interesting inventory and comparison of the number of prominent black politicians who have been investigated or indicted for various alleged acts of social and moral transgression.

5 Perhaps the significant exception, at least in the case of women, is Hillary Clinton, who had her character maligned during the 1996 campaign season. See also Williams (1995).

6 See Campbell (1991) for an excellent discussion of the impact of such conventions on legitimate news, and of the centrality of scandals and their revelation for other shows that fall into the genre of the newsmagazine.

7 This process of reiteration is illustrated in the events surrounding the beating of Rodney King and its aftermath. For insightful discussions see Gooding-Williams (1993) and Fiske (1994).

8 For a particularly useful treatment of the controversy, including excerpts of Helm's attack on the film, see the documentary film by DiFeliciantonio and Wagner (1995).

9 *Tongues Untied* was not the only NEA-funded project which came in for Helm's wrath; he also attacked a photographic exhibition by the late photographer Robert Mapplethorpe which explored themes of homosexuality using the images of black gay men.

References

Butler, J. (1993). Endangered/endangering: Schematic racism and white paranoia. In R. Gooding-Williams (ed.), *Reading Rodney King, Reading Urban Uprising*. New York: Routledge.

Campbell, R. (1991). *60 Minutes and the News: A Mythology for Middle America*. Urbana, IL: University of Illinois Press.

DiFeliciantonio, T. and Wagner, J.C. (1995). *The Question of Equality: Culture Wars*. San Francisco: California News Reel film.

Fiske, J. (1994). *Media Matters*. New York: Routledge.

Gooding-Williams, R. (ed.) (1993). *Reading Rodney King, Reading Urban Uprising*. New York: Routledge.

Gray, H. (1989a). Rate the record: Symbolic conflict, popular music and social problems. *Popular Music and Society* 13(3): 5–16.

Gray, H. (1989b). Popular music as a social problem: A social history of claims against popular music. In J. Best (ed.), *Images of Issues*. New York: Aldine de Gruyter.

Grossberg, L. (1992). *We Gotta Get Out Of This Place*. New York: Routledge.

Guerrero, E. (1993). *Framing Blackness: The African American Image in Film*. Philadelphia: Temple University Press.

Hoffer, R. (1996). The party's over. *Sports Illustrated*, July 8: 30–3.

Neff, J. (1996). Is justice blind? *George*, October: 126–30.

Rose, T. (1993). *Black Noise*. Middletown, CT: Weslyan University Press.

Taylor, C. (1991). The re-birth of the aesthetic in cinema. *Wide Angle*, 13(3/4): 12–20.

Walser, R. (1993). *Runnin' With the Devil*. Middletown, CT: Weslyan University Press.

Williams, P. (1995). *The Rooster's Egg: On the Persistence of Prejudice*. Cambridge, MA: Harvard University Press.

5 | What a Story!

Understanding the Audience for Scandal

S. Elizabeth Bird

No matter how often media scholars and columnists scold them for it, people *like* scandal. Scandal sells newspapers and tabloids, keeps people in front of their televisions, and provides endless opportunities for conversation. Of all the news stories current in 1989, the "top two" in terms of audience recognition were the conviction of Oliver North and the trial of the Rev. Jim Bakker, while the major story with least recognition was catastrophic health-care coverage, which surely touches the lives of many more of the news-watching public (Price and Czilli 1996). Two of the highest-rated news interviews ever, at least before the O.J. Simpson trial, were Barbara Walters's conversation with Donna Rice in 1987, and Diane Sawyer's with Marla Maples in 1990 (Mellencamp 1992).[1]

Why is this so? While the popular appeal of "scandalous" news is widely acknowledged, there has been little serious attempt to understand that appeal from the point of view of the audience. In this chapter, I apply data from two small, empirical studies to offer some observations about how people interpret and use scandals in their everyday lives, as a step toward understanding the pleasures they derive from such disreputable stories.

John Langer efficiently documents what he calls the pervasive "lament" among media critics about the state of contemporary news, especially television news: "In its unease, the impulse of the lament is to act, to 'clean up' television news in order to get rid of the unworthy elements, relegating them to the dustbin of journalistic history" (1992: 114). The "unworthy elements" that are commonly decried are those that are defined as "sensational" – personality-driven stories focusing on people who flout society's norms, whether these are celebrities or "ordinary people" thrust into the limelight by remarkable events. The supermarket tabloids, often called "scandal sheets," have come to epitomize the worst of the unworthy.

What is often lacking in the "lament" about news is any real understanding of why scandalous or sensational news is appealing. Some critics apply psychological explanations, defining the audience as "sensation seekers" who need increasing doses of exposure (Zuckerman 1984), or as the "morbidly curious" (Haskins 1984). These explanations tend to have the effect of neuroticizing the audience, suggesting that there is something sick or abnormal about being attracted to unwholesome news. If the audience is considered at all, it is often to be condemned as lacking in taste and judgment, as Langer discusses. In a more recent development, cultural studies scholars have discovered the "active" audience for scandalous or sensational news. Thus Fiske (1992) and Glynn (1990) celebrate the tabloid style in print and television, arguing that audiences may epitomize de Certeau's "textual poachers" (1984). The "excess" in this kind of news can be "transgressive" and "calls up skeptical reading competencies that are equivalent of the social competencies by which the people control the immediate conditions of their everyday lives" (Fiske 1992: 54).

Studying the reception of scandal

As I have written elsewhere (Bird 1992a), I am not convinced that the skeptical, carnivalesque reading of tabloid style is actually typical of most consumers of this kind of news, although it is definitely one way to read these texts. Rather, I am more inclined to see audiences as active, selective readers, who approach all kinds of news from an unstated perspective that essentially asks: "What can I get from this information, or this story? How does it apply to my life, and why should I pay attention?" Thus, following from my earlier study of supermarket tabloids (Bird 1992a), my goal has been to explore audience responses to news of all kinds. An initial, pilot phase of this research did not focus on "scandal" as such, but rather was an attempt to throw some light on the role that news stories play in everyday life. What kinds of story do people find memorable? What do they do with them? Drawing on qualitative data from this project and from my earlier work on tabloids, my aim is to place "scandalous" news in a larger cultural context.

My data collection for the tabloid project is described in detail elsewhere (Bird 1992a); it involved soliciting letters from tabloid readers, followed by in-depth telephone interviews with a smaller sub-group. In the more recent study, I used a two-phase, somewhat experimental technique, aimed at eliciting data that more closely paralleled everyday experience.[2] In the spring of 1993, I prepared a videotape made up of excerpts from the "tabloid" TV show *A Current Affair*, the "reality-based" show *Unsolved Mysteries*, and an episode of ABC's *News with Peter Jennings*. Copies were lent to a small sample of people (20), who watched the tapes in their homes with a family member or friend, and then discussed the tapes, recording the conversation with a small audiotape recorder left with them. Some guiding questions were included, asking, for example, which stories they found most memorable and why. Later, I interviewed the same people by phone, asking them a range of similar questions, such as what the idea of "news" meant to them, which kind of news stories they paid attention to, and so on. Through all of this, I was trying to get a sense of how news fits into people's lives on an ongoing basis.

News and storytelling

The first step toward understanding the role of "scandal" is to recognize that this kind of news is invariably in the form of the "story," rather than the terse, inverted-pyramid, "news" style. I have discussed elsewhere the difference between these two, and reviewed some of the literature regarding audience preference for "story" news (Bird and Dardenne 1988). Media scandals may begin with a short news item – Hugh Grant has been arrested following an "encounter" with a prostitute – but the full-blown media scandal only develops with the follow-up stories: How could this clean-cut actor do such a thing? Does he have a dark side? How does his girlfriend feel? If you cannot even believe in a nice guy like this, whom can you trust? Not all potential media scandals develop like this; but there do seem to be certain characteristics of the media scandal that need to be present, a point to which I will return. For now, I will focus on the story dimension of news, because there is a larger set of narratives to which scandals belong: All media scandals are stories, but not all stories are scandals. I believe that this is the key to the enduring appeal of scandal – that it is *one* type of narrative that helps people structure their view of what the world is and how it should be.

But are stories actually important to people? Do people care how they get their news, or do they just want to be informed? Conventional journalistic wisdom suggests the former – all journalistic textbooks encourage student writers to "find the story," to humanize it and so on. Price and Czilli (1996) point to a substantial literature that confirms this, and they provide their own data demonstrating the memorability of human-interest stories. Participants in my 1993 study consistently reported that the news items they remembered from the tape, and those they wished to talk about, were human-interest stories.[3] Thus, a 39-year-old woman says that she likes such stories because, "life without emotion is life without feeling, life without forethought, and life without good results. You've got to feel in order to react." She continues, "There's lot of reasons why things happen, a lot of reasons why people do the things they do, and if a person understands the story behind it, they can have a better idea and a better awareness to avoid being in that situation themselves." These comments point to the way that news stories are applied to a person's life, an issue to which I will return.

A younger woman, a student in her early twenties who enjoys *A Current Affair*, explains what kinds of stories catch her attention:

> Usually things about people being in trouble, as far as, you know, like getting involved in a murder or like a big sex triangle, or like, I read the *Wall Street Journal* lately, and like people making a bad choice, and then all of a sudden they're involved in a fraud . . . and how their whole life now is a shambles.

She continues, explaining the importance of the story:

> With that storytelling, they seem to, they start from the beginning, like if they do have a person there who is in this big news event or whatever, they'll like start from them when they were real little, and them growing up, and them getting married, and you find out stuff from their background, and they just make the whole ordeal sound like something that could happen to anybody. . . . and on *Current Affair*, they give every little news item, they give it like a little name . . . That kind of makes it seem more of a good story.

Her comments point to one of the key elements of the satisfying story – that it is a coherent narrative that has a point to it. She notes that *A Current Affair* titles its stories, as do newsmagazine shows; the title functions to sum up the story and package it. Media scandals tend to gradually cohere into "a story" as they develop, so that after a while, the public recognizes the central narrative associated with "the PTL scandal" (see Soukup, this volume) or "the Amy Fisher case" (see Lull and Hinerman, this volume).

A college student in his early twenties also explains the way certain news shows are able to direct the unordered flow of a narrative into a "story":

> For example, I was watching *Rescue 911* one time, and an ambulance was following a car, and the car they were following, the mother had a seizure and she fell asleep at the wheel, and there was a baby in the front seat, and they totally recapped this, the story, and the thing was, she was like bouncing off curbs, and swerving, and one of the ambulance drivers got out and tried to run and catch the car, well he couldn't – it was going too fast – so what they did is, you know, the story went on and on and on, and just how they showed it, I mean you're like, wow, that really can happen. And I'd say something like that was really beneficial to understand the story . . . You're kinda . . . you kinda get involved in the story. Kind of like a movie.

This young man was describing a show he had seen some time ago, while being unable to recall stories from the previous night's evening news. As he commented:

> I mean people want to see what happened and how it happened, and when you're watching the regular news, I mean, they just tell you what happened, and not how it happened. I mean, they might show you a couple scenes, for example, like Waco, but they won't recap on what David Koresh was thinking, or what happened to him . . . I mean I don't even know if they found the guy!

A woman in her thirties referred quite specifically to the value of "storytelling" in news, pointing to her preference for talk shows and magazine programs like *20/20*:

> It's different than the basic news that you receive, you know, at 5 or 6 o'clock. Storytelling would be just people living their lives, and what's happening in their lives, and how they're bettering their lives, or how they're screwing up their lives, or whatever, and I guess that I'm just more interested in that type of thing, and what's happening more on a personal level . . . I guess I just find it more interesting to listen about something someone personally has achieved, or whatever.

Others, while dismissing shows like *A Current Affair* as being "trashy" or "sleazy," admire magazines like *60 Minutes* because they are "more dramatic" or "more personal."

Thus while many people feel an obligation to be "well informed" and listen to "important" news, their emotions and their attention are caught by dramatic, exciting stories. These do not have to be scandals – they might be any story with special human appeal. Tabloids are full of heartwarming stories about ordinary people who become heroes for a day, or about beloved celebrities who overcome drug problems or obesity. News magazines and "tabloid" TV shows mix scandal and "upper" stories comfortably. Sagas like the heroic, subterranean rescue of Baby Jessica McClure are as big ratings boosters as the scandal of Amy Fisher.

Thus to put scandal in context, we need to consider it as one element in a mesh of stories through which people construct and interpret their lives. Indeed, as I see it, a barrier that stands in the way of our understanding of media scandals is that too often we tend to separate out types of media narrative both from the array of other types of narrative and more broadly from the culture of which they are part. We look at the text of the news story or the TV show, analyzing what it says, and what it might mean for the audience. Instead, we need to think of these stories as emerging out of the culture, and as then sparking a broader set of interrogative narratives and discussions among the people.[4] For as Richard Johnson (1983) writes, in describing "cultural studies," a full understanding of any text must take into account the complexity of the relationship between the three components of producer, text, and audience. He argues that this relationship should be seen as circular rather than linear, in that producers incorporate readers in their production of texts; texts in turn may have an impact on readers, whose response then feeds back into the text.

I have argued elsewhere (Bird 1992a) that media and oral storytelling are comparable, though not identical, communication processes, during which narratives are constructed from familiar themes that repeat themselves over time. And if audience members are seen as active in helping to shape the way popular media are created, they become much more comparable with folk "audiences." Even in an oral culture, not every individual is a storyteller or an active, performing bearer of all traditions. Rather, the role of people in many contexts is to respond to the storyteller, helping her or him shape future versions of the tale. The popular media audience can play an analogous role.

In certain media genres, the kinship with folk traditions is absolutely clear. The most sensational of the supermarket tabloids, for example, draw deliberately on folklore, and the beliefs and concerns they know their readers already have. According to a tabloid reporter, "When looking for ideas for stories, it's good to look at fears, and it's good to look at real desires. That's why a lot of people win lotteries in the stories, and why people get buried alive all the time" (Hogshire 1992). Tabloid writers rely quite heavily on tips from their readers in developing stories, some of which can grow into long-running narratives fed by reader interest and participation, such as the "Elvis is Alive" narrative that has extended over years. The more "respectable" tabloids, which focus on celebrity gossip, borrow less directly from folk narratives, but nevertheless clearly shape their stories according to the standard themes that work for audiences, such that the specific stories change, but the overarching narratives recur. The lives of individual stars become molded to the established repertoire of celebrity sagas, retelling the folk tales that preach the dangers of hubris and the lesson that money and power cannot buy happiness. While more mainstream news practitioners like to maintain a distance between themselves and tabloid styles, clearly their human-interest stories adhere to many of the same narrative conventions (see essays in Carey 1988).

Media scholars, then, have learned from folklorists and anthropologists that culture is participatory, rather than coercive. In a classic article, William Bascom (1954) argued that folklore serves to educate audiences in the values of a culture, validate norms, and also allow an outlet for fantasy and wish fulfillment. I would argue that news, especially "story" news, does the same things, involving and drawing in its readers and viewers. Different types of story perform any one or more of the same kinds of function as folk stories do.

Scandal and the audience

Indeed, in many ways the notion of "scandal" is more firmly embedded in the oral, interpersonal dimension of our lives than in the media dimension (although these are closely intertwined). The media play the role of the storyteller or town crier, but the scandal gains its momentum from the audiences. Anthropologist Max

Gluckman, in a classic discussion of gossip and scandal, describes the role of individuals known as *simidors* (leaders) in Haitian villages, who lead "scandal" songs sung at working bees, in which the indiscretions or failures of people in the community are lampooned. People fear their power; as one Haitian put it, "The *simidor* is a journalist, and every *simidor* is a Judas!" (Gluckman 1963: 308). It is not so much the song itself that is feared, but rather the way the story now becomes the public property of the village, and source for endless speculation. Some songs tend to die, while the subjects of others may fuel gossip and discussion for weeks. Likewise, many news stories could potentially spark larger "media scandals," but not all do. To become a real scandal, the media accounts must spark the imagination of the public.

Price and Czilli (1996) suggest that one reason people remembered stories like those about Oliver North and Jim Bakker is that they simply received a great deal of coverage. This explanation comes from a linear perspective on media communication – that the media produce a text, and the audience responds. If instead we see the relationship between media and audience as more circular, then we would note that increased coverage certainly would have raised awareness of the stories, but was also a direct result of the high level of interest and speculation that was being generated among audience members.

In fact, as Mellencamp begins to suggest, the initial media coverage may actually emerge from gossip and speculation among the community, as in the case of Jim and Tammy Faye Bakker: "The gossip about their private lives, initiated by Jim's illicit sex with Jessica Hahn and Tammy Faye's drug addiction, fueled the story and the legal machinery" (1992: 222). Media stories then led to more gossip, spin-offs into other scandal forums, and so on: "The Bakkers were tabloid fare which made it to the nightly news; a personal catastrophe was transformed into a media scandal, created and uncovered by gossip" (1992: 222). Mellencamp then chronicles the rise and fall of the Bakker media scandal in television, tabloids, newspapers, and newsmagazines, until, "The end had come for Jim and Tammy Faye Bakker – that is, until the made-for-TV movie" (1992: 229).

Dramatizing morality

And why do some stories turn into major scandals, while others do not? Compelling stories must have a point – they must mean something. Folklorists and anthropologists who study oral narrative assume this without question, even if the narrative concerned is primarily told for entertainment rather than for moral edification. Of the many thousands of stories that are told in any culture, only some catch the people's imagination and enter the tradition. Since the oral process is selective, scholars assume that those stories with a long "shelf life" are significant in some larger sense: They speak to the moral values, fears, or fantasies of the people. Media scandals, or any media story that has staying power, should be explored in the same way, for the values and boundaries they are expressing.

The scandal story, above all, interrogates morality, as Gluckman suggests. Other anthropologists also document the role of gossip and scandal in drawing moral boundaries. Antoun (1968), for example, describes the complex system of satire and gossip that punishes unacceptable behavior in a Jordanian Arab village, while Gilmore (1987) shows how conformity is enforced in a small town in Andalusia, Spain, by an informal mechanism of gossip and backbiting that aggressively attacks people who violate the status quo. Jesus Martin-Barbero points to the way media texts have long been incorporated into oral culture in Latin America, with people commenting on the stories, and applying social values to them:

> It is a listening marked with applause and whistles, sighs and laughter, a reading whose rhythm is not established by the text but by the group. What was read was not an end in itself but the beginning of a mutual acknowledgement of meaning and an awakening of collective memories that might set in motion a conversation. Thus, reading might end up redoing the text in function of the context, in a sense, *rewriting* the text in order to talk about what the group is living. (Martin-Barbero 1993: 120)

In particular, Martin-Barbero underlines the need to comprehend the oral roots of the tradition of melodrama: "The stubborn persistence of the melodrama genre long after the conditions of its genesis have disappeared and its capacity to adapt to different technological formats cannot be explained simply in terms of commercial or ideological manipulations." Popular media narratives, he argues, are essentially melodramatic, emphasizing morality and excess:

> Everything must be extravagantly stated, from the staging which exaggerates the audio and visual contrasts to the dramatic structure which openly exploits the bathos of quick and sentimental emotional reactions.

. . . Cultured people might consider all this degrading, but it nevertheless represents a victory over repression, a form of resistance against a particular "economy" of order, saving and polite restraint. (1993: 119)

Scandal stories, indeed, are not "polite," and as they gather momentum, they become increasingly unrestrained. Ian Connell points to the importance of the scandal story in drawing moral boundaries between what is acceptable and what is not, with celebrities acting as larger-than-life, melodramatic personifications of correct or illicit behavior. He discusses a British scandal in which Jimmy Tarbuck, a popular comedian with a wholesome family image, was exposed as an adulterer, and suggests that the public views celebrities as a privileged class: "It is status which grants rewards, but it also grants responsibilities . . . Tarbuck's affair has been disclosed because he has chosen to ignore these responsibilities" (1992: 81).

Regular tabloid readers clearly agree. Thus a 60-year-old woman argues that celebrities should not expect privacy, and deserve scandalous exposure if they behave immorally:

I think if you're a celebrity you have to expect this . . . listen, once you're celebrity you don't have anything to yourself, you belong to the public . . . and I think a lot of them, they're a little out of line as far as the ways they live . . . I think they should live a life that will be respectable. So I think if you want privacy, go lock yourself up somewhere.

Others agree: "I think once you're in the public eye, in any capacity, whether you're a politician or a movie star or a TV star . . . You're fair game . . . they'd better be clean or they'd better stay out of it." Yet another woman talks about Prince Charles and Princess Diana: "They make too much of it, and it's sickening . . . we need something to look up to . . . they're not it, and they don't deserve what they have." Stories are clearly seen as comprising useful checks on public excess, much like the licensed gossips of oral cultures: "If people know they're going to be spread across the front page of the *National Enquirer*, I really do think it may not give them pause to think at the time, but it certainly gives them cause to think later."

So the stories as they appear in the press, particularly in tabloids and tabloid-style TV shows, make the point about morality clearly and often melodramatically. Yet these melodramatic tales also leave plenty of room for discussion and comment: While melodrama often places good and evil in stark contrast, the audience becomes involved in the speculation of how and why such shocking and exciting things came to happen. Actual "applause and whistles, sighs and laughter" may not accompany the watching of *Current Affair*, but the discussion afterward may incorporate many of the emotions these suggest. Media scandals, at least the ones that have the longest staying power, often are making an overarching statement about right and wrong. Jimmy Tarbuck is an adulterer, and that is wrong, especially given his image. Jim Bakker is licentious and immoral, and that is wrong, since he should stand for Christian morality. Oliver North is a liar . . . but wait, one hears a reader say: Didn't Ollie lie for the very best of motives? And wasn't Bakker driven to adultery by his freakish wife's drug habit? And he did repent, didn't he?

Speculation

Thus, a scandal that is relatively long-lived must enter the public conversation. In doing so, it tends to follow a fairly standard pattern. First, there is *speculation*: Yes, something is wrong, but why did it happen? If a rock star known for dissolute ways were caught with a prostitute, as Hugh Grant was, there would be little public interest – it is what we might expect. The Hugh Grant story was so huge because it was both excessive and incongruous. The incongruity surrounded the lack of fit between the public image of the clean-cut, gentlemanly British movie star, who maintains a stable relationship with a well-known model, and the man who turns to a prostitute for sex. And this is compounded by excess – he does not call a high-class escort service for "regular" sex, but is caught in the back of his car with a "cheap" hooker fellating him. The Lorena Bobbitt stories has the same elements, in that we see the incongruity of a young, apparently mild-mannered married woman not merely hitting back at or even shooting a possibly abusive husband, but actually cutting off his penis. Not stopping there, she throws the offending member in the street – melodramatic excess *par excellence*. These stories invite speculation and moral judgment, as well as the laughter, jeers, and ribald commentary of the melodrama audience. As it grows, the saga takes on the quality of a dialogue among members of the public, and between them and the media. The scandal story, then, is not clear and closed, but "open," allowing for many competing versions and interpretations.

As people speculate, they tend to look for answers from within their own experience. People's level of interest is often connected to how closely they can relate the scandalous events to their own lives: What would I do if this happened to me? How can I prevent this happening to someone I know? During the period of several of my interviews, the Amy Fisher–Joey Buttafuoco scandal was at its height, after months of news stories, with two competing made-for-TV movies airing. Although the story was not included in the tapes my subjects watched, several participants raised it as an example of distasteful sensationalism, yet were almost irresistibly drawn to discuss it. Their varied opinions point to the openness of the Amy Fisher story, and the many questions it raised. In particular, people of different ages and backgrounds applied the story differently in their lives. Thus, a 67-year-old woman said:

> Oh, I think it's rather creepy. Let me tell you, I'm retired now, but I was a social worker. And I guess that I worked with a lot of people . . . People . . . a little bit lower in morals, and so forth . . . and I guess at this point I'm kind of hoping he gets his, too . . . I think we all know things like that go on, and again you can look at it from several standpoints as the woman is blamed, although certainly she was wrong, and I just have an idea that he probably egged her on . . . so I think he's equally guilty. And I think she was, oh, you know, just a young gal who thought everything would be OK if she just got rid of the wife. Naive. Even though she was well-versed in sexual matters.

A second woman, age 39, stresses different elements in the story:

> It was just an amazingly huge story, and it was this young girl, older man, and I think what made it kind of interesting was the wife being so strong behind her husband, and I found that kind of fascinating myself, because everything just seemed to stack against him. But yet, this woman just really steadfastly, you know, stands behind him. And Amy steadfastly stands behind her story, too, they all do. And it's, I guess it's whatever you want to believe, and everybody takes it their own way . . . And to think that a young girl would actually, you know, shoot another woman in a love affair, I guess.

A 21-year-old woman perhaps reflects her closer sense of identification with the teenage Amy Fisher:

> It's a thing I could never imagine happening to me, being involved in a murder, or having this big love triangle or something . . . I mean, how did Amy get into that situation, that she had to shoot that sleazy guy's wife, I mean you'd have to be desperate, and he must have had some kind of hold on her – he was just slime, don't you think? I mean really, his wife didn't deserve that . . . If I ever thought my life was bad, at least I'm not this person.

Finally, a woman in her forties saw the story as a vehicle for speculation that led into a consideration of how people allow this to happen, and what sorts of circumstances throw ordinary people into these extraordinary events:

> You know we watched a couple of 'em here, my kids and I. Because, I don't know why we did, I think because we had read so much about it, and then they had the different sides, and it was sort of like, we watched it and then we decided who we really thought was the guilty person, and who gave us the facts and who didn't, and . . . but it's garbage, I mean, really, it's garbage.

When asked why this story was so interesting, she continued:

> Just maybe human nature, I guess . . . like when I hear about stuff like that, what I always ask myself is how, you know, how could they get to that point . . . show me why this person got to this point . . . it's, you know, you cannot relate at all to what this person has done or why they've done it, and so you want this explanation . . . And maybe that's because you're afraid that your neighbor could end up like that, you know.

Personalization and participation

Scandals, like other kinds of news stories, are clearly integrated into this last woman's life, allowing her to interrogate boundaries, aspects of motivation, and issues that seem much more relevant to her life than, say, economic news does. She describes how she discussed with her family the "Spur Posse" scandal, in which the media focused on a group of white youths from "respectable" homes, who awarded each other points for having sex with as many girls as possible:

> Oh, it made me sick . . . I've got high school aged kids, and then a daughter that's in college, and especially the high school age, they talk about things like that in their classes . . . She reads everything she can, and that really interested them, so it's kind of fun to sit down and watch something with them . . . They may be able to relate that to certain guys or girls . . . it's like, tell me this isn't happening in your school.

This personalizing of "story" news is crucial to understanding people's enjoyment: An important aspect of this process of personalization is that it is participatory. As we struggle to make sense of a story, we involve others in the negotiation of meaning. Thus a

21-year-old man says: "When you watch by yourself, a lot of times you have ideas that you have unsolved because you can't converse with other individuals." A 37-year-old woman agrees: "I feel that in order to really be a good conversationalist, you can't be self-centered, and I want to hear everyone's opinion about what's going on in the news. There's something in their view that I can use, and hopefully there's something in my view that can contribute to making theirs better." She considers *Unsolved Mysteries* to be important news because, "it helps others in the community feel a part of the news world ... The community or the listeners get to contribute to the story and make the news effective and be part of the results."

A pair of short excerpts from the taped conversations between participants give a flavor of how people explore the meaning of scandalous stories together. The first gives a snippet of conversation between a 29-year-old male office manager and his male friend, discussing a *Current Affair* story on the videotape, about a woman who persuaded a teenage boy to murder her husband:

PARTICIPANT: I mean how can you, in a normal fashion, walk up to someone and even hit him? Let alone shoot him four times in the head?

FRIEND: I guess that's maybe its value to anyone of us knowing ... I mean ... here's this woman that appears to the neighbors to be great with all the kids ... everybody's pal, then she doesn't get along with her husband ... I mean ...

PARTICIPANT: Yeah, there's a lot of non-related things to bring up, so you could suspect everyone in the world, and that's like, wow, you know, our neighbor, she sure seems nice – could she kill her husband, and what would make her do that?

A husband and wife in their early forties discuss the same story:

WIFE: We're just noticing how, the progression of how the seed was planted in the kid's head, and by this woman, and how it just grew, and she kept feeding and encouraging it ... But the saddest part is that this kid, he's kind of backed in a corner by these three girls saying hey, let's do it. And the next thing you know, he shoots this guy ...

HUSBAND: Yeah, one of the things that struck me as they were interviewing the kid in prison was that he didn't show any remorse or sorrow other than the fact he couldn't have children. He never once said how bad he felt about killing the guy . . .

WIFE: Yeah. My own, like, my biggest thought was, you know, what kind of family life did he come from, what would put a person, a teenager in this kind of position . . . to be so bland of caring and emotion . . . ?

The stories that become larger scandals are often not simple, in that they do not have closure, and there could be more than one answer. The Oliver North story, for example, was so big not because it was a simple morality tale, but because people disagreed on what the story really was, and so many questions remained unanswered. In large part, it played out as a "misunderstood hero" story (Andersen 1992). But not everyone thought North was a hero; some saw him as a liar and a cheat. Speculation ran rife about why he did what he did; which powerful politician knew what, and when; where his glamorous secretary Fawn Hall fit in; and so on.

Likewise, the Gary Hart scandal was a story that invited participation from the public. The spin-off from the story was not just a simple lesson that politicians should not have affairs. After all, many had done so in the past, and their reputation was unsullied. Hart's scandal was not just about morality, but about whether personal morality or lack of it was an issue in a political campaign. Gripsrud writes that morality scandals around politicians are clearly understandable: "for one thing, it is not without public interest if the minister of defense is a paranoid junkie" (1992: 92). That view certainly seems accepted now; yet not so long ago, people were not so sure that personal moral failings were relevant to political achievement. John F. Kennedy was actually protected by the press corps, who knew all about his adulterous affairs, but did not consider them relevant to his abilities as a president (Gans 1979). Hart's story involved extensive interrogation, both in the media and among the public, about the importance of marital fidelity as a qualification for political office – the "character issue" and so on. In some ways, the story marked a watershed, in both public opinion and media coverage of politicians' personal lives.

A few years later, Sen. Bob Packwood became the focus of another watershed scandal, as the media *and* the public rejected the notion that sexual harassment was normal and acceptable. Yet Packwood's behavior was not that different from the way other politicians had behaved in the past, without censure, and certainly not everyone agreed that the moral lessons of the story were cut and dried. In my study, Packwood's case was mentioned in a brief *World News Tonight* item, and while most participants passed over the story as unmemorable, a 22-year-old man discussed what he saw as the implications of cases like these:

> I mean right now, the way things are going, men are, white males are becoming a minority more than anything with saying things and pretty soon we're going to be doing the same thing women are doing. I mean it's getting to the point where you have to sit down and state what actually is prejudice and what is slurring and so forth.

The pleasure of the story

The point here is that scandal stories, like other tales, bring changing mores into sharp focus through media narratives and the popular discussion that takes off from those narratives, whether that be in homes, in workplaces, or on *Oprah*. Media scandals help set the agenda for discussion, but they do not exist as some definable text separate from the wider cultural conversation. Thus the biggest media scandals are open texts: They draw some lines about morality, but they do not answer all the questions. Often indeed, the most popular scandalous stories are those where there is debate: Who is worse, Amy Fisher or Joey? Who is the victim, Charles or Diana? Was Lorena Bobbitt an avenging angel or a crazy devil?

John Langer analyzes the appeal of "victim" stories – the human-interest tales about ordinary people who are caught up in accidents, crimes, and so on, rather than scandals. He argues that these stories provide three kinds of pleasure. The first pleasure is seeing "the social and psychological mess when the orderly arrangements of everyday life collapse" (1992: 126). Coupled with this is the "pleasure of uncertainty" (1992: 127), in which people enjoy the vicarious awareness of random danger in the world. Finally there is "narrative pleasure," as sensational news "can more readily foreground its story-like constructedness by positioning its reader/viewer into a kind of mutually confirming declaration with the response: that was a good one!" (1992: 127). Scandal stories evoke the same kinds of pleasure, as audiences both revel in and are repelled by the social mess that is created when the famous transgress moral norms, like Hugh Grant or Jim Bakker, or when an "ordinary" person like Lorena Bobbitt does something so bizarre.

This kind of pleasure is analogous to the way people listen to personal tales, urban legends, and so on. Bill Ellis describes the questioning and playing with belief that often accompany the telling of such tales, as the story demands "that the teller and listener take a stand on the legend: 'Yes, this sort of thing could happen'; 'No, it couldn't'; 'Well, maybe it could' . . . a legend is a narrative that challenges accepted definitions of the real world and leaves itself suspended, relying for closure on each individual's response" (1989: 34). A 69-year-old male tabloid reader describes much the same kind of response: "We do hand 'em round each other and then we get to talk about the stories and then we'll say, did you read about that thing in there! And of course it makes a little conversation and then we'll say, Oh, you don't believe that, do you!"

The enthusiasm with which audiences participate points to another dimension of the news story in general and the scandal story in particular. People say they like human-interest stories because they identify with the people in the stories, whose plights engage their emotions. This does seem to be true, and this emotional engagement continues in certain "big," human-interest stories, such as the Baby Jessica McClure rescue, or the ongoing story of the recovery of Oklahoma City from a 1995 terrorist bomb.

Distancing

This level of engagement clearly entails a personalization of the story, and a sense of empathy with the subjects. However, many scandal stories move past a sense of personal empathy, creating a distance between the audience and the story. This seems to happen at a point at which a general consensus has been reached about what the "end" or the "meaning" of the story was – what the moral lessons actually were. Langer raises this question: "We might speculate then, that at the ideological level, the recognition of storyness may act, not to engage the viewer/reader in the victim story's premises and potential outcomes, but to produce distantiation: these are real people, here is misadventure, but after all, it's only a story" (1992: 127–8). This is an important insight that has relevance to the media scandal, and to its reception as melodrama. Melodrama, as we have noted, is about excess – the "I can't believe it!" dimension of life – just as are urban legends and jokes. Once something becomes seen as an over-the-top melodrama, the people caught up in it begin to seem less like real human beings, and more like cartoons or symbols. Scandalous celebrities, already larger than life through their status, become even more the property of the public. People feel free to speculate about the most personal aspects of their lives, using them as props to work out their own moral codes.

This distancing becomes most apparent in the way media scandals evolve so easily into jokes. Even though the news media tend steadfastly to ignore the jokes that cluster around the stories, disdaining them as tasteless, these joke cycles become an integral part of the public discourse on major news events, whether disasters or scandals (see, for example, Goodwin 1989; Oring 1987). Almost everyone has heard jokes about Ted Kennedy and Chappaquiddick, Gary Hart, Tonya Harding–Nancy Kerrigan, Michael Jackson, O.J. Simpson, and so on.[5] The existence of the jokes presupposes a wide knowledge of the particular story; the jokes then contribute to the firming up of the story in particular ways, confirming Gary Hart as a lying philanderer, Michael Jackson as a pathetic pedophile, or O.J. Simpson as a man who got away with murder. As Davies writes, "jokes are ambiguous forms of discourse that are created in circumstances and around issues where there is a good deal of uncertainty" (1990: 8), just as media scandals surround events that provoke speculation. But as he also points out, as they develop, jokes tend to reflect the prevailing moral judgment of the public: "the sense of sudden vicarious superiority felt by those who devise, tell, or share a joke" (1990: 7). There is an exhilarating satisfaction to be gained from transforming Hugh Grant from the envied guy who has it all to "the Englishman who went up Divine and came down his pants." With the widespread circulation of jokes, the scandal reaches a kind of resolution, with the subjects of the joke/scandal becoming caricatures with whom we have little sense of identification as people. Significantly, when people still feel pain about a major event, such as the Oklahoma City bombing, few if any jokes emerge.

Conclusion

The term "media scandal" is in some ways a misnomer. Certain news stories become true scandals only with the participation of the media audience and the public at large: People know about major scandals even if they have never read or seen a single news story about the event. Certainly the media are now the major tellers of scandalous tales, but the narratives cannot be sustained by the news media alone. The narratives must speak to issues or emotions that engage readers and viewers in speculation, fascination, and downright relish in the melodramatic excess of it all. Thus in spite of its frequent designation as a "scandal," the Clinton administration's Whitewater affair has yet to become one in the public view. It lacks drama, human interest, a clear sense of any moral codes being broken, and any excitement whatsoever. Neither the media nor the general public have a clear idea what the "story" of Whitewater is – there is no clear or compelling speculation and gossip, and there are few Whitewater jokes.

I have tried to place scandals in cultural context, seeing them as playing out moral dramas in extravagant terms. Scandal, and the delight we feel in it, have always been an integral part of news, and the many forms of communication that preceded "news" as we know it (Stephens 1988). The question now becomes: Is the enjoyment people derive from scandalous news something to be celebrated or decried? John Fiske has been a leading exponent of the school that sees popular culture as liberatory (Fiske 1989a, 1989b). Contrasting the news of "the people" with that of "the power-bloc," Fiske argues that "popular taste . . . is for information that contradicts that of the power-bloc: The interests of the people are served by arguing with the power-bloc, not by listening to it" (1992: 46–7). Thus tabloid news sources, such as *A Current Affair* or the *Weekly World News,* can be viewed as offering criticism of the power bloc, through the skeptical laughter that these shows produce as authoritative news is inverted and parodied. Popular news, then, can function as social and political critique, unmasking and mocking the powers that be.

Fiske's analysis of popular reception of tabloid news has much to recommend it; he clearly recognizes the oral, participatory dimension of that reception. In addition, his view of popular news as carnivalesque and excessive meshes nicely with a reading of popular news as melodrama. However, his argument ignores the fact that tabloid news is not always received with skeptical laughter and disbelief, although it may be. Stories about scandalous government cover-ups of UFO landings are taken seriously by many people (Bird 1992a) – hardly a progressive or politically critical stance to take. More important to this discussion of scandal is that Fiske misses the point that melodrama and carnival, like much of oral culture, tend usually toward the maintenance of the status quo, and so do media scandals. The functions of folklore that Bascom and other folklorists describe all work toward the validation of norms, and the restating of accepted values. In addition, the anthropological literature on gossip and scandal clearly indicates their role in maintaining conformity. This is not to say that these norms remain forever unchanging; oral narratives, like ongoing media scandals, do interrogate norms, allowing for questioning and some gradual changes. As we have seen, the interrogation of morality that accompanied the Gary Hart scandal produced a shift toward a more rigorous standard of personal conduct among politicians.

Nevertheless, one would be hard pressed to conclude that highly-popular news stories, whether scandals or not, have ever had any major subversive or liberatory outcome for "the people." If anything, they serve as distractions that help "the power bloc" get on with the business of maintaining power. Fiske himself recognizes that whether or not popular news has any real political impact is "a difficult question," arguing that "the pleasures of scepticism and parodic excess can be progressive," but "I do not wish to suggest that they are always or necessarily so" (1992: 54). In fact, the only concrete example he offers for the progressive value of popular news is the TV talk show, using an example from *Donahue*, in which a disaffected Drug Enforcement agent sparks an audience discussion of the dangers of drugs, and the possible role of the government in exacerbating the drug problem.

While Fiske sees this kind of discussion as a hopeful, progressive sign, the trend in popular news seems rather to be in the direction of ever more "stories" that actually have little to do with political critique or resistance. As Campbell points out in his study of *60 Minutes*, the appeal of that show is that it tells formulaic, neat, dramatic stories that engage the viewer's interest (Campbell 1991). At the same time, it and other shows like it inevitably reduce complex events to a tale of individual agonies and triumphs. A story about a homeless person becomes detached from the structural and institutional situation that put that person there, and becomes simply a tale of a personal setback. Radio and TV talk shows of the kind that Fiske admires for their liberatory potential revolve around personal experience, which is what makes them so gripping. They do indeed allow many voices to be heard, and they certainly encourage excessive and melodramatic exchanges – but how does that translate into effective political critique or involvement?

My concern, then, is that "story" news, instead of being one element in news, is moving toward becoming the only element. Daniel

Hallin (1992) makes a compelling if somewhat alarmist case that there is a growing "knowledge gap" between those who consume serious news and those who like only gossip, scandal, and personality stories. If the latter group forsakes serious news altogether, he argues, this will have significant consequences for democracy.

My own work with audiences of tabloids and news audiences does suggest that there are some people who avoid hard news altogether. But it also suggests that most do not. People read the *National Enquirer* and *Time*; they read local newspapers and watch *Unsolved Mysteries*. But clearly, the stories that stay with them are those that engage emotion as well as intellect, and which provide material for rewarding interpersonal communication. Scandals certainly do that. Are they pushing out serious news to the point at which public discourse is threatened? At present, I believe the answer to that question is a qualified no. The public conversation does not revolve solely around issues of scandal and personality; people still discuss political issues and complex economic questions. However, the media do have a crucial role in setting the agenda for public discourse, and with the proliferation in personality-driven news, and a decline in newspaper readership (Hallin 1992), the agenda is in danger of becoming increasingly trivial. In this chapter, I have tried to show how scandalous news is pleasurably useful, in that through these media morality tales, people come to terms with their own moral codes and values, as well as enjoying themselves immensely. All cultures need to do that. But if personal morality tales are all we are telling each other, then larger, more complex stories that ultimately affect us all will go untold. Then, perhaps, we really will see the triumph of a "power bloc" whose influence can escalate unchecked.

Notes

1 For those with a short memory for scandal, Donna Rice was the woman with whom presidential hopeful Gary Hart was believed to be having the extramarital affair that ended his candidacy; Marla Maples was the "other woman" credited with ending the marriage of mogul Donald Trump and his wife Ivana.
2 For a discussion of the range of methods that may be used in audience research, see Bird (1992b).
3 In selecting quotations from participants, I have attempted wherever possible to choose comments that seem representative of a point of view shared by many or all of the group. While the value of qualitative study lies in the

richness of its primary data, space limitations preclude the extensive use of numerous quotations that make the same general point.

4 The importance of narrative as a way of structuring human experience has been recognized and explored across many disciplines in recent years. For some discussion of this, see, for example, Fisher (1985); Mechling (1991); Mitchell (1981).

5 Often these jokes combine scandalous figures; for example, the joke that Tonya Harding and Michael Jackson have opened a race-track – she will do the handicapping, while he rides the 3-year-olds; or the bartender who invented the Tonya–Bobbitt cocktail – a club soda with a slice; and so on.

References

Andersen, R. (1992). Oliver North and the news. In P. Dahlgren and C. Sparks (eds), *Journalism and Popular Culture*. Newbury Park: Sage, 171–89.

Antoun, R.T. (1968). On the significance of names in an Arab village. *Ethnology*, 7: 158–70.

Bascom, W. (1954). Four functions of folklore. *Journal of American Folklore*, 67: 333–49.

Bird, S.E. (1992a). *For Enquiring Minds: A Cultural Study of Supermarket Tabloids*. Knoxville, TN: University of Tennessee Press.

Bird, S.E. (1992b). Travels in nowhere land: Ethnography and the "impossible" audience. *Critical Studies in Mass Communication*, 9: 250–60.

Bird, S.E. and R.W. Dardenne (1988). Myth, chronicle and story: Exploring the narrative qualities of news. In J.W. Carey (ed.), *Media, Myths, and Narratives*. Newbury Park: Sage, 67–87.

Campbell, R. (1991). *60 Minutes and the News: A Mythology for Middle America*. Urbana, IL: University of Illinois Press.

Carey, J.W. (ed.) (1988). *Media, Myths and Narratives: Television and the Press*. Beverly Hills: Sage.

de Certeau, M. (1984). *The Practice of Everyday Life*. Berkeley, CA: University of California Press.

Connell, I. (1992). Personalities in the popular media. In P. Dahlgren and C. Sparks (eds), *Journalism and Popular Culture*. Newbury Park: Sage, 64–83.

Davies, C. (1990). *Ethnic Humor from Around the World: A Comparative Analysis*. Bloomington: Indiana University Press.

Ellis, B. (1989). When is a legend: An essay in legend morphology. In P. Smith and G. Bennett (eds), *The Questing Beast: Perspectives on Contemporary Legend*. Sheffield, UK: Sheffield Academic Press, 31–54.

Fisher, W.R. (1985). The narrative paradigm: In the beginning. *Journal of Communication*, 35: 74–89.

Fiske, J. (1989a). *Understanding Popular Culture*. Boston: Unwin-Hyman.

Fiske, J. (1989b). *Reading the Popular*. Boston: Unwin-Hyman.

Fiske, J. (1992). Popularity and the politics of information. In P. Dahlgren and C. Sparks (eds), *Journalism and Popular Culture*. Newbury Park: Sage, 45–63.

Gans, H. (1979). *Deciding What's News: A Study of CBS Evening News, NBC Nightly News, Newsweek, and Time*. New York: Pantheon.

Gilmore, D.D. (1987), *Aggression and Community: Paradoxes of Andalusian Culture*. New Haven, CT: Yale University Press.

Goodwin, J.P. (1989). Unprintable reactions to all the news that's fit to print. *Southern Folklore*, 46(1): 15–40.

Gluckman, M. (1963). Gossip and scandal. *Current Anthropology*, 4(3): 307–16.

Glynn, K. (1990). Tabloid television's transgressive aesthetic: *A Current Affair* and the "shows that taste forgot." *Wide Angle*, 12(2): 22–44.

Gripsrud, J. (1992). The aesthetics and politics of melodrama. In P. Dahlgren and C. Sparks (eds), *Journalism and Popular Culture*. Newbury Park: Sage, 84–95.

Hallin, D. (1992). The passing of the "high modernism" in American journalism. *Journal of Communication*, 42(3): 14–24.

Haskins, J.B. (1984). Morbid curiosity and the mass media: A synergistic relationship. *Proceedings of the Conference on Morbid Curiosity and the Mass Media*, eds J. Crook, J. Haskins, and P. Ashdown. Knoxville, TN: 1–50.

Hogshire, J. (1992). Personal interview, March 13.

Johnson, R. (1983). *What is Cultural Studies Anyway?* Birmingham, UK: Centre for Contemporary Cultural Studies, General Series SP74.

Langer, J. (1992). Truly awful news on television. In P. Dahlgren and C. Sparks (eds), *Journalism and Popular Culture*. Newbury Park: Sage, 113–29.

Martin-Barbero, J. (1993). *Communication, Culture, and Hegemony: From the Media to Mediations*, trs, E. Fox and R.A. White. Newbury Park: Sage.

Mechling, J. (1991). *Homo narrans* across the disciplines. *Western Folklore*, 50: 41–52.

Mellencamp, P. (1992). *High Anxiety: Catastrophe, Scandal, Age, and Comedy*. Bloomington: Indiana University Press.

Mitchell, W.J.T. (ed.) (1981). *On Narrative*. Chicago: University of Chicago Press.

Oring, E. (1987). Jokes and the discourse of disaster. *Journal of American Folklore*, 100: 276–86.

Price, V. and E.J. Czilli (1996). Modeling patterns of news recognition and recall. *Journal of Communication*, 46(2): 55–78.

Stephens, M. (1988). *A History of News: From the Drum to the Satellite*. New York: Viking.

Zuckerman, M. (1984). Is curiosity about morbid events an expression of sensation seeking? *Proceedings of the Conference on Morbid Curiosity and the Mass Media*, eds J. Crook, J. Haskins, and P. Ashdown. Knoxville, TN: 90–124.

6 Character, Celebrity, and Sexual Innuendo in the Mass-Mediated Presidency

Bruce E. Gronbeck

The *Des Moines Sunday Register* ran two stories side by side in the front section on June 2, 1996. A three-column news feature unfolded under the headline "Dole says tide is turning, lashes out against Clinton's character." Assuring a Republican party leadership conference that he was "not in the race to discuss Bill Clinton's character," he nonetheless said that "but every time he talks like a conservative but governs like a liberal, he puts his character and credibility on the table."

That was set against a one-column story under the headline "Leach accents character issue in radio address." Representative Jim Leach, a Republican from Iowa, was in charge of the House's Whitewater investigating committee. He had had a good week in the wake of the convictions of three former Clinton associates. The scandal trail already was heavily trodden that month, as Paula Corbin Jones was asking the Supreme Court to allow her civil suit against a sitting president to proceed; Leach's remarks on personal indiscretion were abstract: "Public officials have a special obligation to tell the truth and conduct themselves and their affairs, be they public or private, in a manner above all reproach."

But, in the next paragraph, the *Des Moines Sunday Register* made sure its readers understood the upshot of Leach's remarks:

Leach did not directly address issues such as Clinton's involvement in the Whitewater land deal, his problems with a sexual-harassment lawsuit [the Jones action] or the controversy over the White House handling of its travel office – all issues Clinton opponents have used to challenge his character.

The Dole story also included the following paragraph:

Despite his protests, Dole and his campaign do want to make the president's character an issue, believing they can capitalize on lingering questions about his marriage, his draft record during the Vietnam War and his actions in office.

Three weeks later, the *Wall Street Journal* on its opinion pages ran an editorial, "Paula's day in court," next to a four-column story, "The complaint against the president," which reprinted excerpts from the sexual harassment complaint that Jones had filed two years previously. The following day, Albert R. Hunt's column "Politics and people" was entitled "For Clinton, trust issue is a time bomb," arguing that in 1992 "most Americans thought Bill Clinton was a draft-dodger and womanizer who inhaled." The rest of the article reminded readers of Whitewater, the White House possession of 700 FBI files on possible enemies, and Travelgate, all the while warning the president not to be overconfident about his then 17-point lead in the polls over Senator Dole in the campaign.

And yet, even while all of these stories about the president and his supposed moral shortcomings were circulating during the summer doldrums of Campaign '96, a *U.S. News & World Report* survey in June found that likely voters certainly questioned his personal morality but preferred his strengths, even his professional character, to Dole's. While 70 percent of the respondents described Dole as moral, only 41 percent thought Clinton was; yet more (44 percent) thought that Clinton shared their values than that Dole did (38 percent), and 59 percent called Clinton "right for the times," while only 31 percent thought Dole was. All of this may seem amazing, given that a *Newsweek* issue featuring "The politics of virtue" celebrated the "Virtuecrats" and reported a survey where a full 72 percent of the respondents in mid-1994 believed that "questions about Bill Clinton's character" would "hurt his ability to be an effective moral leader." But yet, as the bi-election year flowed into the election year, such concern about his moral leadership did not seem to stand in the way of his ability to produce a double-digit point gap between himself and Bob Dole in mid-campaign.

Given that many and probably most scholars of presidential campaigning see character as central, even determinative, of electoral outcomes, how can that be? Here is a candidate and then president whose personal morality, choice of friends, and habits of opportunism have been publicly challenged in ways designed to bring him down in what Garfinkel (1956) has labeled "degradation ceremonies." Yet he not only rebounds but seemingly prospers. Since Aristotle's observation that positive *ethos* – the perception of a speaker's good sense, good will, and good morals – is the absolute bottom line for success at public persuasion, how can candidates seriously tainted by charges of immorality and a pragmatic spirit survive?

Media scandals have brought down more than one politician. From the infamous Profumo case in Great Britain at the dawn of the 1960s (see Thompson, this volume), the Western world has reveled in a series of sexual episodes. For American politicians, most notably Wilbur Mills, then chair of the House Ways and Means Committee, and Fanne Foxe in 1974, and Wayne Hays in his liaison with Elizabeth Ray in 1975, the Hall of Shame has many rooms. The women involved in most of the episodes became celebrities in their own right; Foxe, Ray, Oliver North's Fawn Hall, and Gary Hart's Donna Rice, for example, all blossomed into public figures. Indeed, even the politicians accused of indiscretions engendered at least public interest and at most public celebrity; most recently, Senator Robert Packwood, accused of multiple sexual harassment, had opportunities to appear in both news and entertainment print and television formats. "Character" in its political constructions and "celebrity" in its social constructions seemingly merge.

For our purposes, "character" is to be understood in its original sense, as an explicit mark or stamp, in this case, of the ethical codes of a citizenry; even as late as Shakespeare's time (in *Twelfth Night*), a reference to character signaled the face or features of a person as "betokening," in the *Oxford English Dictionary*'s interesting formulation (1989), "moral qualities." When "character" understood in this way – as a mark, whether placed behaviorally or discursively on the visage of some person – mixes with his or her celebrity, that is, fame or even public worth, then most interesting and politically-charged articulations of someone's moral posture criss-cross the public prints.

And hence this chapter seeks to explore some of the complex relationships between political character and celebrity status on the contemporary United States scene, if only to dig at the paradoxes that surround the presidency of Bill Clinton. By the end of the chapter, I hope to have supported three interpretive propositions:

1 While character has always been central to the public construction of political leaders, it has taken on even more importance in
the era of the mass-mediated public sphere characteristic of large,
industrialized societies.
2 The American understanding of character has been extended –
and perhaps inextricably complicated and compromised – by its
merger in the public mind with notions of celebrity. During presidential campaigns, especially, the line between political and
entertainment reporting all but disappears; issues of character
(political morality) and celebrity (popularity, likability) are melded
in television and print coverage of campaigns.
3 Such an amalgamation of character and celebrity by the press has
made meta-politics and meta-ethics, rather than actual political
action and concrete morally relevant activity, the pivots upon which
electoral decisions turn. Hence the *scandalum* – etymologically,
the trap or snare set by an enemy to bring someone down – can
actually be, paradoxically, a catapult to public success.

Before turning to these propositions, however, we need to examine at least briefly an incident in which character and celebrity
status were worked out in the public sphere by a press focused on
sexual indiscretion. Certainly the paramount case of recent years is
the Gennifer Flowers–Bill Clinton episode of 1992. It rose in public
consciousness in spectacular fashion in January of that year and
was not completely disempowered until Clinton's convention film
in late summer. We, however, will focus on the public discourses
of February, 1992; the conversation was especially intense right
after the Clintons explained themselves in a *60 Minutes* interview
aired after Super Bowl XXVII, and hence this period allows us
access to the interpenetration of political character and social celebrity central to the arguments of this chapter.

The public construction of Flowers–Clinton, 1992

While the Gennifer Flowers story had floated in and through the
backwaters of Campaign '92, it became a raging river of sexual
excess as the caucus and primary season approached. *Penthouse*
had told tales of Clinton's extramarital affairs in late 1991; Cokie
Roberts, an American network news journalist, probed his reactions
to such stories in the candidates' debate of January 1992; and the

Star, a tabloid newspaper with high national circulation (3.4 million, more than twice that of the *Wall Street Journal*), even reported briefly Gennifer Flowers's accusations at that time. In the debate, Clinton seemed to dismiss the issue completely, and following it his popularity hit 39 percent in the New Hampshire polls. But then came the *Star*'s big story, "My 12-year affair with Bill Clinton plus the secret love tapes that prove it!", faxed to news organizations the week before the paper hit the stands (Blumenthal 1992).

At first, little happened. Papers such as the *New York Times* and the *Washington Post* ran small stories well back in their pages; CNN did not mention it. But Ted Koppel raised it on *Nightline* with guests Larry Sabato and Mandy Grunwald. While those guests pooh-poohed the story, its velocity accelerated. By the weekend, Clinton's approval rating had slipped in New Hampshire by fourteen points, to 25 percent according to the American Research poll (Blumenthal 1992). Bill and Hillary had to do something, so they went on *60 Minutes* in front of an estimated 40 million people (Klein 1992), with their interview edited to 11 minutes to fit into the CBS circus following the big game.

Interestingly, a *New York Times* op-ed piece by Anna Quindlen (1992) that appeared before the broadcast began to build a framework for construing the Flowers–Clinton episode in less than politically-damaging ways:

1 She attacked Flowers's credibility by innuendo: "How do you go from being a television reporter to being a nightclub singer? And whose idea was it to spell Gennifer with a G?"
2 She attacked the publisher: "Ms. Flowers told her story to *The Star*, which is that publication you can find right next to the gum and the little things that keep your glasses from hurting your nose at the supermarket checkout counter. You buy *The Star* by hiding it beneath your box of Total, pretending it fell onto the conveyor belt. *The Star* paid Ms. Flowers for her story."
3 She attacked the relevance of the story to electoral decision making and made its treatment more important than its facticity: First, she noted that any highly public person who has "the combination of megalomania and charisma needed to run for office" probably has "smoked pot at some time in their past" and "found ego gratification with actress/models or television reporter/nightclub singers, the kind of women who, when they go public, tend to have flattering 8-by-10 glossies readily available." Then she observed that: "In the the last 30 years, we have moved from

wondering whether it happens to wondering whether it matters. Now we care about how it is handled, about getting out of a jam with dignity."

That a journalist in the Sunday *New York Times* would offer such a pre-defense construal of the Flowers–Clinton relationship is fascinating. In denigrating the source of the information, the purveyor of it, and its relevance to present-day politics, Quindlen fashioned a perspective suggesting that (1) the affair might not have happened; (2) if it did, the public revelation of personal relationships for pay from a suspect source was more morally reprehensible than the adulterous act itself; and (3) if it did, it was part of the deep past of no relevance to contemporary electoral decision making.

That evening, the Clintons' interview was broadcast. On Friday night, John McLaughlin had said: "There is an answer that politicians ought to give [when charged with extramarital affairs], and that is to say, 'Look' – and particularly Clinton should give – 'I had a rough period in my life. I'm back with my wife. We're married. We're going to stay married. And that's it. I'm not going to talk about this anymore.'" That is essentially what the Clintons did. They offered background on their relationships with Gennifer Flowers, with Hillary saying even that she had met with "two of them [the women accused of having affairs with Bill] to reassure them they were friends of ours." Bill added, "there's a recession on. Times are tough, and, and I think you can expect more and more of these stories as long as they're down there handing out money."

The interviewer Steve Kroft then asked them to talk about their marriage and their problems. But as hard as he pushed, the Clintons would not talk about the fact (or not) of the extramarital affairs. When Kroft suggested the people needed to know more, Clinton replied:

> I have acknowledged wrongdoing. I have acknowledged causing pain in my marriage. I have said things to you tonight and to the American people from the beginning that no American politician ever has. I think that most Americans watching this tonight, they'll know what we're saying, they'll get it. . . . What the press has to decide is, are we going to engage in a game of "Gotcha"?

suggesting that neither affirmation nor denial would stop inquiries. Hillary concurred, saying that they needed "a zone of privacy." Bill went further, arguing that:

The only way to put this behind us, I think, is for all of us to agree that this guy has told us about all that we need to know. Anybody who's listening gets the drift of it. And then let's go on and get back to the real problems of this country. The problems are about what's going to happen to families in New Hampshire and the rest of this country in the future, and not what happened to mine in the past.

Hillary joined in with one of the most often-quoted segments of the interview:

We're going to leave the ultimate decision up to the American citizens . . . Look, I'm not sitting here – some little woman standin' by my man like Tammy Wynette. I'm sittin' here because I love him and I respect him and I honor what he's been through and what we've been through together. And you know, if that's not enough for people, then, heck, don't vote for him.

The Clintons' construction of the story was masterful insofar as it (1) was framed in socially (morally) acceptable ways and (2) drove the issues to a secondary or meta-level, specifically asking listeners and the press itself to focus on public treatment of the episode rather than the fact of infidelity. That Clinton was able to stay in the 1992 race and ultimately win the primary–caucus battles is a gauge of his success in controlling the dialogue among serious players in the public sphere.

The social–moral framework

Steve Kroft appeared frustrated on *60 Minutes* because Bill Clinton would neither confirm nor deny extramarital affairs. Rather, Clinton relied on two rhetorical strategies as foundations for his framing of the story: a *public–private distinction* and a *life pattern or timeline* that sealed off the past in order to concentrate on the present (the New Hampshire primary in particular) and the future (the direction of the American agenda).

Clinton had to find ways to balance his public and his private lives as well as his personal and professional reactions to the reporting of the story. And that he did: details of family-related life events were private even if the events themselves were public knowledge; maintaining a "zone of privacy," as Hillary called it, was a right even for publicly-accountable citizens; the complex feelings people associate with their personal lives – here, pity, sorrow, pain, love – need not be talked about publicly in order to be shared with others; while the fact of such feelings may be public knowledge, their force is resolutely private or at least ought to be.

The public–private distinction worked hand in hand with Clinton's efforts to control the time clock of life. Clinton buried the event in his past. In the *60 Minutes* interview, he regularly contrasted the past with the present: his association with "a number of young people who were working for the television stations around Little Rock" in the 1970s when he was attorney general (not even governor yet); a reference to this sort of story breaking long ago, in 1980; his constant use of the past tense to refer to "wrongdoing"; and an explicit argument that it now was time to move to the present and future of the "families" of New Hampshire and the rest of the country.

And thus the private–past was zoned off rhetorically from the public–present and public–future. Character was defined by Clinton as "leveling with the American people," and, by implication, as reconstituting rather than dissolving his marriage even while affirming its status (as did Hillary) as a relationship based on "love," "respect," and "honor." Such an erasure of the private–past set up for the Clintons an appeal to family values in a particular way. Though the active relationship of people might vary from time to time, stage to stage, so long as that relationship was grounded in mutual attraction (love), mutual regard for the other's talents (respect), and mutual recognition of the need to struggle to succeed (honor), then it demonstrated that such family values were operative and effective. And character – both personally and publicly or politically – was betokened by straight talk.

The Clintons' social–moral strategy, hence, was framed around the fundamental cultural anchors of space and time. If we accept Hall's (1957) argument that territorial and spatial orientations are the bases of cultural identity, then we can see in the Clintons' treatment of the private–past attempts to control such identity. We see them offering a spatial–temporal framework – private vs. public space, past life vs. present and future life – expansive and traditional enough to contain the Flowers–Clinton episode and to provide a culturally acceptable perspective on it.

That framework, as it turned out, was adopted and adapted by many commentators. *Newsweek* declared that "an anti-press, anti-phony puritanism backlash" was developing in New Hampshire. "It's almost as if voters would gladly forgive a politician his little peccadilloes [!] in return for some concrete solutions to the recession

health-care crisis." It sampled "voter reaction," with all 12 of
voters in its sample working out of the framework that the
Clintons had built, e.g.:

- Jane Gilson, secretary and Tsongas supporter: "We're voting for
  president, not pope. . . . We just don't care about Clinton's personal life."
- Suzanne Roux, restaurant manager and undecided: "We've all
  made mistakes. I would hope this country has changed since the
  Gary Hart issue. . . . It's the same old thing: dragging up dirt."
- Henry Beaudet, bowling alley owner and Clinton supporter: "His
  private life is his private life."
- Carl Dustin, agency administrator and undecided: "Sometimes I
  think if you have a candidate who's never strayed from the
  straight and narrow, you have someone who's never taken a
  risk. . . . We've all done things we're not proud of."

The next week, *Newsweek* reported that Hillary, standing in for Bill
at a function, said that "Bill Clinton is with the other woman in his
life," referring to a father–daughter event in Little Rock. Family
values were strewn all over the place, even in an interview with
Deborah Mathis, another woman suggested as a bedmate of Bill;
both she and Hillary treated the charge with pointed humor less
than two weeks after the *60 Minutes* interview.[1]

The *New York Times* immediately did a full report of the Clintons'
positions on the affair and on their relationship. As the story came
to a close, it reported that Larry Nichols, a former Arkansas state
worker who in a lawsuit against Clinton named women he said
Clinton had slept with, was dropping that suit. The following is
part of that section:

> In a signed statement, Mr. Nichols said that it was "time to call the fight
> with Bill Clinton over." Mr. Nichols said he had set out to "destroy" Mr.
> Clinton but that the results had got out of hand. He apologized to women
> he named in the suit, including Ms. Flowers, but did not retract his accusa-
> tion that Mr. Clinton had been involved with them.

The next day, Gwen Ifill included in a *New York Times* story a
prayer from a breakfast for Clinton supporters: "May we concentrate
on winning races, not ruining lives." Ifill also noted that Democratic National Committee chair Ron Brown said "We should pull
the plug on trash journalism and titillation television." And apparently America bought the Clintons' rationale, the story finishing

with a report of an overnight poll by ABC News that showed 73 percent of respondents agreeing "with Gov. Bill Clinton that the question of whether he had had an extramarital affair was between him and his wife."

That reporters from the mainstream press and representative citizens both individually in street interviews and collectively in polls tended to view the social–moral aspects of the episode through the Clintons' eyes perhaps is not too surprising. Maybe columnist Ellen Goodman was right when she noted that "The old religious right worried about sin. Younger moderns are concerned about 'relationships' and the 'wife's pain.'" And certainly *Newsweek* understood the public reaction when it suggested that Clinton "may have humanized himself and won points for upholding the institution of marriage." That same issue ran an interview with Hillary that focused on such matters as where her sense of social responsibility came from, the features of Bill that affected her perception of him as "husband and father," her views on childraising, and her defense of their continuing work on a marriage. Softball questions opened space for political–social melodrama, with the Clintons as heroes. A potentially harmful episode became an opportunity to actually improve a candidate's character rating.

The journalistic–moral framework

Such speculation is interesting and in a sense borne out by the end result – Clinton's election that November. Presumably a plurality of the voters did not find his marital difficulties an encumberance. But yet, the social–moral framework gives us only half the story. The other half surrounds the Clintons' references to the fourth estate's delight in playing "Gotcha." The Flowers–Clinton story was subordinated to the state-of-political-journalism story. The ethics and politics of the Flowers–Clinton events were transformed into meta-ethics and meta-politics: stories-about rather than stories-of, meta-narratives rather than narratives.

The nub of the issue was given concrete expression by a midwest newspaper editor quoted in *Time*: "'People talk about the media as if the *Star*, ABC, the *Eagle* and the *New York Times* were all the same,' says David Merritt Jr., editor of the Wichita *Eagle*. 'When we blur the lines by picking up from the *Star* we invite that very devastating comparison.'" Yet in fact that comparison was invited;

Los Angeles Times national editor Norman Miller might indeed have "felt sick" when he was given the faxed copy of the *Star* story – but he published it. And it became centered in many of the February reports of the Flowers–Clinton episode. In the phrase turned by former Democratic Party chair John White, "It just sucked up all the oxygen in the room." New Hampshire station WMUR's co-anchor said "let's try to get to the issues," but of course campaign journalism became the big issue.

U.S. News & World Report correctly surmised that "Attacking the *Star* was central to Clinton's damage control, especially the effort to embarrass mainstream publications into ignoring the story," yet it soon was obvious that the mainstream publications were going to worry about the ethics of their practices all by themselves. Perhaps the strongest indictment of the press came from Sidney Blumenthal writing in the *New Republic*:

> [T]he spread of the K-Mart economy has been accompanied by a parallel explosion of a tabloid culture, not only at the checkout lines but on television. Politics itself has been consumed in the maw of Oprahfication. Pseudo-news shows such as "Hard Copy," "Inside Edition," and "A Current Affair" have set parameters for public discussion that the broader political world has only just begun to assimilate, and still vainly attempts to resist.

And thus, Blumenthal saw the Flowers–Clinton affair as more than a "media epiphenomenon," because of the weakness of the rest of the Democratic hopefuls, yet a media epiphenomenon nonetheless, 1992's "version of *The Scarlet Letter*." That journalism had run amok was a theme echoed by Joe Klein in *New York* (1992): "The real challenge of the Bimbo Primary was to tame the gluttonous, chaotic, undiscerning, and uncontrollable media machine that was, in its way, a perfect reflection of the cynicism and voyeurism at the heart of the national anomie. . . . The Great American Media-Driven Scandal has become the signal ritual of our public life." "Pornographs," Thomas Oliphant of the Boston *Globe* suggested, "hijack democracy." The fact that both New York's *Newsday* and its *Daily News* featured identical banner headlines – "SEX, LIES, AND AUDIOTAPE" – on January 24, 1992, was taken by Edwin Diamond in *New York* as a sign of the depths to which newspaper journalism had sunk.

Newsweek expressed the same sentiment in noting that "Once again last week, anyone turning on the TV felt like a voyeur," later observing that:

Instead of waiting for credible evidence of whether the audiotapes trumpeted by the *Star* were in fact incriminating, the mainstream press – first gingerly, then eagerly – leaped into the fray. ... [N]early every self-respecting news organization was having its chain yanked by a publication whose cover headline the previous week was ROSEANNE LOSES 40 POUNDS ON NEW DIET – AND SO CAN YOU.

The editorial pages joined in the discussion. *Time*'s editorial, "Who cares, anyhow?" (Morrow 1992), offered four lines of analysis:

1 Bad issue: "Did Bill Clinton have an affair with Gennifer Flowers? The question must get in line behind real news: drugs and drug murders, AIDS deaths, illiteracy, a population getting dumber, 74,000 jobs lost at General Motors, Pan Am and Eastern folding, the highest homicide rate in the Western world."
2 Bad politics: "The nation cannot afford to waste good candidates. There are not many to spare."
3 Bad journalism: "The Clinton mess last week suggested something about a certain brainless overstimulation of American media life. . . . Bill Clinton, wholesome, ruddy Arkansas boy, found himself handling poisonous snakes. Ugly stories have a slithering life of their own."
4 Bad political judgment: "Too much sexual buzz interferes with people's instruments and makes it harder to judge a candidate on important questions – his or her stability, judgment, decency, intelligence, ethics, strength of will, experience, truthfulness."

Morrow thus drew a bead on the voyeuristic press, the gullible public, and a political system threatening to drive away good candidates. All of these charges were laid at the feet of a press responsible for "the pseudo-moral attention lavished on this spectacle."

Two weeks later, *National Review* editor John O'Sullivan (1992) rode his hobbyhorse to even higher plateaus, assuring his readers that he had "no hesitation" in turning down a story about the sex life of a potential presidential candidate. He did so because "Any sensible taxpayer would much prefer to be governed by an adulterer of sound anti-inflationary views than by a socialist monk"; "the stress on private morals, uniting tabloids and fundamentalists, may even be misleading as a guide to public policy on moral grounds." He turned away from "the establishment media" and their "anxious self-criticism" because it was a sign they had no principles to fall back on; "they simply pick up and discard whichever principles happen to be useful at the time," as could be seen in their protection of Anita Hill but attack on Gennifer Flowers. "Don't say it with Flowers" was the headline for this editorial.

The story of Flowers–Clinton had gone meta:

1 The ethics were meta-ethics; that is, talk about what sort of ethics were applicable to sexual innuendo in politics and about the ethical standards that ought to be observed by journalists covering campaigns.
2 The political questions were meta-political insofar as relationships between the press and politics became featured instead of the sexual and political acts of Flowers and Clinton.
3 The story that took center stage was a meta-narrative, the story of what stories ought to be told in political reporting of the campaign in New Hampshire, not of the campaign itself.

The press's self-reflexivity deflected attention away from Gennifer Flowers's claim, the Clintons' personal and political lives, and the primary and caucus process in American politics. The events that comprised the Flowers–Clinton encounters were subjugated to meta-analyses of ethics, politics, and journalistic storytelling. The Flowers–Clinton connection was put into the past tense within two or three weeks of the interviews in the meta-discourses of 1992.

It thus was comparatively easy for the Clinton campaign to finally bury the episode, which it did in the Clinton convention film in late summer. That film, *A Place Called Hope*, the story of Bill Clinton's life, included a segment on the accusations and the *60 Minutes* interview. Bill and Hillary indicated in the film that their daughter Chelsea asked to watch the interview with them. Afterward, he said (gulping), "What do you think?," to which Chelsea replied, "I think I'm glad you're my parents." "After that," said Bill, "I knew that whatever happened would be all right." And from there, the film rolled into a segment of a campaign speech, with Bill saying:

> When the history of this campaign is written they may say, well, Bill Clinton took a lot of hits in this campaign. Well, I want you to know something. The hits that I've taken are nothing compared to the hits that the people of this state and this country are taking every day of their lives under this administration.

The historicization of the Flowers–Clinton episode within a construction of his life, the blessing offered to the Clintons' story by their very own daughter, and the amalgamation he offered between his past–private pain and the present–public pain of his listeners were all part of a remarkable transformation of scandalous extra-marital sex into what Kenneth Burke (1950) called a "representative anecdote" – a story capturing the mythos of a time, of politics in late twentieth-century America. The Flowers–Clinton story had a happy ending for the Clintons and, presumably, the American public, now assured that he could feel their pain because of his own. Private vice was transformed into private virtue and, thence, into public virtue.

Character, celebrity, and the mass-mediated presidency

In wrestling with the idea of postmodernity, Ien Ang (1996: 2) wrote that postmodernity "doesn't mean that chaos is the order of the day, but that any sense of order, certainty and security – i.e. of structure and progress – has now become provisional, partial and circumstantial." That sense of the provisional, partial, and circumstantial assuredly marks what we might call political consciousness in our time. Less than half of those voting in presidential elections belong to political parties. Jesse Jackson's metaphor of politics as individualized, demographically derived squares stitched together rhetorically by politicians to make a majoritarian quilt is used so much as to be all but dead; coalition politics is, simply, mandated in our time. Collective distrust of politicians and the press that is covering them is at an all-time high. A cloud of ennui has been hanging over American politics for most of at least a decade.

The press is no better appreciated. Neil Postman (1985) has accused it of serving up only "peek-a-boo" politics – sound bites or video clips that can provide us with but a spot of feelings or a dot of ideas. Perhaps Lance Bennett (1988: xv) is correct when he suggests that we have substituted minimalist stories and overwrought dramatizations for actual information: "Mysteries, melodramas, and rationalizations are all poor substitutes for explanations," he notes, "since none provides a solid basis for critical thinking or effective action."

With politics and the press on the run, with the books of virtue (e.g. William Bennett's *The Book of Virtues* [1993], Peggy Noonan's *Life, Liberty and the Pursuit of Happiness* [1994], Stephen Carter's *The Culture of Disbelief* [1993]) on the ascendency, we face most difficult questions concerning character, virtue, and the presidency. Let me approach them via the three propositions that I suggested near the beginning of this chapter.

The centrality of character to politics

First off, no matter how difficult it is to untangle Bill Clinton's political reputation, one fact seems incontrovertible: Matters of character (*ethos*) are central to the public construction of politics and political leadership, especially now, in the era of a mass-mediated public sphere so characteristic of late-capitalist, large, industrialized societies. In an epoch of Western life dominated by not only postmodernist sermonettes but also chaos and complexity theory (e.g. Lewin 1992), in an era where the great majority of people fail to grasp economic interconnections between the global and the local, to understand the feedback loops built into the welfare system and the lives of the underclass, and to comprehend the social and economic dimensions of militarism – in such a period of world history, politics almost of necessity becomes character-centered. Because there are so few decision rules upon which a people can base their political actions, leadership in Lewin's terms must always be emergent rather than systemically predictable, and the authority of emergent leaders has always been grounded to a considerable degree on their character.

The citizenry has precious few ways of basing electoral decisions on policy recommendations. If issues are too opaque and entangled to be understood, candidates' stands on them are no guides to voting. How can I know the effect of monetary policy on quality of life? Do I as a voter have the knowledge of welfarism to judge which plan really will reduce cost and yet protect the needy? In such situations, voters can but hope that they have elected as leaders people with the vision, good sense, practical skills, and commitment to social responsibility to make the best possible legislative and executive decisions, situation by situation. They look to character as a guide to electoral decision making.[2]

The amalgamation of character and celebrity

In a world running on the provisional, the partial, and the circumstantial, however, we are forced, I think, to enlarge our understanding of "character." We must return to the ideas lying beneath its originary meanings – to the marks of community commitments that are visible in someone's behavior and discourse. We must rid ourselves of a narrow, merely moralistic understanding of character and construct in its place a concept big enough for even the Clintons to move in.

Aristotle's triad of bases upon which audiences grant a speaker positive *ethos* – good sense, good will, and good morals – is an excellent place to begin. "Good morals," Aristotle knew, are not sufficient grounds upon which to adjudge someone communally homologous to members of his or her audience. Speakers also have to demonstrate good sense (the ability to analyze problems and to frame workable solutions, i.e. leadership) and good will (a visible commitment to an audience's best interests, i.e. friendliness or other-directedness).

Good will, especially, brings us at least potentially into the realm of celebrity. To be celebrated – famous, likable, worthy of public interest – is in part a matter of accomplishment in some area of endeavor, but also a matter of attractiveness. Further, celebrity status is an interactive variable; that is, celebrity is conferred upon a personage by a public, for to be known as likable and worthy of attention is to be molded into a kind of honored or appreciated object by another. And, of course, the kind of object into which a person is made depends, once again, upon tokens – visible behavior and discourses that serve as markers. All of this in our time, I think, leads to a collapsing into each other of judgments about character and celebrity. The celebrity is a kind of fetish – an evil object in the case of a Charles Manson, a precious object in the case of the 1996 Olympic medal winners – that manifests the various grounds for an audience's positive and negative judgments. Those behaviors and discourses, regardless of where and when they are seen, become the bases for judgments about character.

We live in an era where it is impossible to separate questions of good morals from questions about good sense and good will. As I have argued at some length elsewhere (Gronbeck 1996), the American president, especially, is constantly in the living rooms of the electorate. In the period 1992–6, we watched President Clinton not only signing bills and greeting dignitaries in the Rose Garden but also taking his daughter to basketball games, traveling with his wife, jogging around the District, stopping at McDonalds, hunting, passing out clean water in Des Moines during the floods of 1993, picking through the ruins of the federal building in Oklahoma City, and burying his mother. Such actions, of course, could technically be sorted into two piles – presidential actions and personal actions – but it was President Clinton, the man in that office, nonetheless carrying all of them out; all of those sightings of the president were made relevant by the press to assessment of his leadership. The marks of Clinton's character were visible in all of these contexts because all of those actions were defined as political by the press. Few in the electorate separated those actions into different categories.

And thus, in the era of electronic journalism and visualized news, one wherein journalists and the subjects of their stories are larger-than-life talking heads in our living rooms, the tokens of character and celebrity tend to merge. We here enter the problematic world of what Boyne (1995: 61) calls "contemporary representations of subjectivity" – in our case, the representations of another's (a president's) *ethos* in multiple public and private, past and present manifestations. A president's behaviors and words, especially in the television age, are paraded before us constantly and, for better or worse, almost inevitably made relevant to political contexts.

Meta-politics and meta-ethics in the press

And here, at last, we get to the nub: In the processes whereby a public collectively assesses the character of a leader such as President Clinton, the press plays two crucial roles in our time – as source and adjudicator of relevant information.

Should the print and electronic press have passed on rumors about Clinton's sexual promiscuity? The press is the source (or not) of our knowledge about such rumors. Do the tabloids differ significantly from mainstream press organs as sources of political information? For that matter, are there differences in credibility between domestic and foreign outlets, Top 10 and other newspapers, *20/20* and MTV's "Rock the Vote" slots, evening news and morning magazine shows, Dan Rather and Geraldo Rivera? Sources of public information simply must be tested by an electorate over time before it can confidently accept this or that print or electronic source of political information as trustworthy. But, unfortunately, it seldom administers such tests, and so it picks up political information where it can, indiscriminately (Kern 1989).

Not only quality of information but also the matter of adjudication – of contextualization or perspective taking – must be examined. Into what contexts was the question about Bill Clinton's extramarital relationships put?

1 They were put into *Penthouse* so as to frame a politician's sexual activeness in both voyeuristic and moral–judgmental contexts.
2 Cokie Roberts used the question to test Bill Clinton's coolness under fire – an important test for a presidential candidate.
3 The *Star* reportedly upped its sales significantly the week it published Flowers's story and such stories helped inflate its stock prices in 1991–2 (CNN Moneyline); the story played well in a financial context.
4 ABC employed the story on *Nightline* to hold its late-evening share and to broaden the political conversation in 1992 to include relationships between personal activities and political electioneering.
5 *60 Minutes* used the Clintons' experience to bolster its reputation as the most blunt and successful newsmagazine for a quarter of a century.
6 *Time, Newsweek, U.S. News & World Report*, the *New York Times*, all of the other newspapers with front-page stories on the brouhaha, and dozens of other journalistic outlets replayed the story in part to comment upon the New Hampshire primary, in (maybe even larger) part to comment on the roles and responsibilities of the press in the political arena.

The main point here is, of course, that a story involving a president, a reporter turned back-up singer, an at-times rocky marriage, and the heat of the presidential primary and caucus period can slam through multiple contexts in an amazingly short period of time, thereby giving the electorate multiple, simultaneous perspectives on such a story and hence more likely confusing it than giving it direction.

For that reason, the meta-contexts – meta-ethics, meta-politics, and a meta-narrative – often take center stage. Not only were warriors from the so-called mainstream press actually concerned about their own ethics in reprinting stories from the *Star* (and we have no reason to doubt the sincerity of their concern), but of course the best among them knew that the country, which had been fed so many perspectives from which to view the story in a matter of a few days, needed help. Talk *about* ethics, talk *about* politics, talk *about* storytelling in American society, we should expect, will take center political stage when the main story is as confused as the Flowers–Clinton story seemed.

The Clintons thus ultimately were released from the trap set by a greedy tabloid newspaper, by a woman willing to tell a/the story about her sexual life to others, and by a press finally willing to circulate that story – not only because they apparently convinced much of the American public momentarily to separate character from celebrity (the past from the present, the private from the public) but also because the press went meta, making its own story more important politically than the Flowers–Clinton one. In going meta, the press effectively took the titillation and the political consequences out of the scene. The Clintons became even more more valued fetishes for having escaped the steely jaws of the *scandalum*.

Concluding thoughts

Kevin Robins (1994: 309, 310) has written that:

> we confront moral issues through the screen, and the screen confronts us with increasing numbers of moral dilemmas. At the same time, however, it screens us from those dilemmas; it is through the screen that we dis-avow or deny our human implication in moral realities. . . . If we are to come to terms with this moral condition, we must consider the nature of our engagement with screen culture.

This examination of character, celebrity, and sexual innuendo in the mass-mediated presidency assuredly bears out Robins's claims. The screen brought us the Clintons at first confronting important moral dilemmas about matters of sexual activities in private and public contexts, and then six months later delivered to us at the Democratic National Convention a disavowal of those dilemmas. The disavowal was credible in large part because the screen already had historicized the behavior under scrutiny and depoliticized its implications. The screen focuses in tightly on individuals, letting us see them sweat, but then, cutting from picture to picture, context to context, calls attention to its own roles in constructing social–political – i.e. moral – scenes for our envisioning. The screen draws us in, then distances us; television is simultaneously intimating and yet depersonalizing.

And the same can be said about most of the political press, print or electronic. In presenting (or not) various categories of information, and in discursively constructing the contexts in which we examine that information (or our lack of it), the press endlessly engages us with its up-close-and-personal photos and language, only to offer enlarging and disengaging commentary upon those pictures and thoughts. In the constant flow of new and relevant information, which immediately calls for more and refocused contextualization, a citizenry comes to believe, I think, that ethical principle is less important than political competency.

We likely will never know what went on between Gennifer Flowers and Bill Clinton. For that matter, we have not answered satisfactorily the question of whether those events are at all relevant to judgments about the quality of his leadership – of whether sexual innuendo can bait a *scandalum* strong enough to bring down a presidential candidate in these times. Political ethics needs some additional development. But, worse, as a society we may have bought into some journalists' position that a key mark of political character is the ability to escape moral traps of the sort set for Bill Clinton. The escape artist is granted skill points, he or she becomes known as competent, and, over time, we construct a sense of his or her character out of bits and pieces of competent action and talk. That is dangerous.

Barry Brummett (1991: 197) has argued that "No experience is 'safe' from *the influence of influence*," by which he means that an episode in a person's life can be made rhetorical, i.e. turned into an index of cultural life, a generalization to be seized, a lesson to be learned. If that is true, then certainly there is no practicable difference between celebrity and character, for the marks of attractiveness or renown differ little from the marks of morality. If in fact efficiency and likability translate into positive assessments of *ethos*, then we face a media scandal far larger than any treated in this book.

Notes

1 For similar stories, see *Time*, 3 February and 10 February, 1992, and *U.S. News & World Report*, 3 February, 1992.
2 There is another guidance system to which voters seemed to have looked in recent years: hot-button moral issues. For example, in the 1994 Iowa gubernatorial election, crime and the death penalty, according to a *Des Moines Register* survey, was the single issue separating the two candidates (GOP incumbent Terry Brandstad and Democratic Attorney General and challenger Bonnie Campbell). That voters in a state with one of the lower per capita crime rates in the nation would turn to this issue – as well as abortion – is a signal that primarily moral issues are thought by the electorate to be easier to understand and use as a basis for electoral decision making than primarily economic, educational, or social service issues. Moral issues seem reducible to binary decision making – yes/no, him/her, Republican/Democrat – while other sorts do not. Thus, only the moral issues seem to have the power to rival character issues in our time.

References

Ang, I. (1996). *Living Room Wars: Rethinking Media Audiences for a Postmodern World*. New York: Routledge.
Bennett, L. (1988). *News: The Politics of Illusion*. 2nd edn. New York: Longman.
Bennett, W.J. (1993). *The Book of Virtues: A Treasury of Great Moral Stories*. New York: Simon & Schuster.
Blumenthal, S. (1992). Bill and Ted. *New Republic*, February 17: 13, 16.
Boyne, R. (1995). Fractured subjectivity. In C. Jenks (ed.), *Visual Culture*. New York: Routledge.
Brummett, B. (1991). *Rhetorical Dimensions of Popular Culture*. Tuscaloosa: University of Alabama Press.
Burke, K. (1950). *A Grammar of Motives*. New York: George Braziller.
Carter, S.L. (1993). *The Culture of Disbelief: How American Law and Politics Trivialize Religious Devotion*. New York: Basic Books.
Character questions (1992). *Newsweek*, February 10: 26–7.
Garfinkel, H. (1956). Conditions of successful degradation ceremonies. *American Journal of Sociology*, 61: 420–4.
Gronbeck, B.E. (1996). The presidency in the age of secondary orality. In M.J. Medhurst (ed.), *Beyond the Rhetorical Presidency*. College Station: Texas A&M Press.
Hall, E. (1957). *The Silent Language*. Garden City, NJ: Doubleday.
Hunt, A.R. (1996). For Clinton, trust issue is a time bomb. *Wall Street Journal*, June 27: A: 19.
Kern, M. (1989). *30-Second Politics: Political Advertising in the Eighties*. New York: Praeger.
Klein, J. (1992). The bimbo primary. *New York*, February 10: 22–6.
Lewin, R. (1992). *Complexity: Life at the Edge of Chaos*. New York: Macmillan.
Morrow, L. (1992). Who cares, anyhow? *Time*, February 13: 15.
Noonan, P. (1994). *Life, Liberty and the Pursuit of Happiness*. New York: Random House.
O'Sullivan, J. (1992). Don't say it with Flowers. *National Review*, February 17: 6.
Oxford English Dictionary (1989). 2nd edn. Oxford: Clarendon Press.
Paula's day in court. (1996). *Wall Street Journal*, June 26: A: 19.
Postman, N. (1985). *Amusing Ourselves to Death: Public Discourse in the Age of Show Business*. New York: Viking.
Quindlen, A. (1992). Public and private: The adultery watch. *New York Times*, January 26: 4, 19.
Robins, K. (1994). The haunted screen. In G. Bender and T. Druckery (eds), *Culture on the Brink: Ideologies of Technology*. Seattle: Bay Press.

7 (Don't) Leave Me Alone:

Tabloid Narrative and the Michael Jackson Child-Abuse Scandal

Stephen Hinerman

> Michael is not of this world.
>
> *Brooke Shields, 1993.*

In the video of Michael Jackson's song "Leave Me Alone," the world, in the form of the body of the singer, is turned into a giant amusement park/sideshow, populated by animals, cameras, phones, and, most of all, the presence of tabloids. By employing what Andrew Goodwin has termed his image of "fantastic otherworldliness" (1992: 112), Jackson then becomes a modern space traveller who is seen gliding through this display. As he moves past numerous computer-enhanced images, the viewer sees references to children, to the fantastic, and, most interesting of all – within the images of tabloid newspapers – to many of Jackson's own reported "scandals," from buying the Elephant Man's bones to a fascination with Liz Taylor and plastic surgery.

Michael Jackson and scandal – the two appear to be locked in an eternal equation, one that Jackson himself seems to acknowledge. As the video tells the story, the hounded Jackson, afloat and singing in his spaceship, is able not only to laugh at his tabloid public image as it passes by his window, but to transcend the whole controversy. Jackson proceeds through his public body as (apparently) effortlessly as he can sing, proving that, however much he is attacked, he can always triumph through the power of pop song and superstardom.

The actual "source" song for the video is almost forgotten in the blur of color and movement the video images provide, and viewers could be forgiven if, watching the video, they came away only remembering the song for its driving drumbeat and the swooping Jackson voice.[1] A closer hearing of the song apart from its video representation reveals that – lyrically, at least – the song *seems* to be (and its references are, one suspects, purposely vague) about a personal betrayal, the story of someone who has been loaned or has taken money and been granted other favors, only to then ask for "more" once too often. This "subject" is never represented in the video, because it probably would be the last story Jackson wished to tell. For someone with a career (and a life) grounded in carefully calculated business moves, Jackson has always been careful to hide such machinations from the public eye.[2] But there is another reason that the images chosen for the video make perfect sense: it had become impossible by the time of the video to view Michael Jackson outside of his relationship to the tabloids.[3]

In 1993, that impossibility threatened to overwhelm everything else about Jackson's career, his life, his music, and his commercial endeavors. In the early fall of that year, the young son of a southern California doctor accused Jackson of sexual abuse. In the ensuing five months, the Jackson child-abuse case became the main story of the tabloid industry, and the resulting scandal became topic A on the list of stories Americans were talking about. It soon became clear that Michael Jackson could no longer navigate above these accusations the way he did in his video universe, floating above the rumors incorporated into "Leave Me Alone." And whereas at the end of that video, a Gulliver-like Jackson tears himself free from the Lilliputian tabloid universe, this scandal threatened to reduce the self-proclaimed "King of Pop" to a social outcast.

An out-of-court settlement finally took the story out of the mainstream of public consciousness. But looking back at the tabloid coverage of Jackson and the accusations, a number of questions remain. Why did the scandal capture the public imagination so completely? What is it about Jackson that made the allegations so plausible and yet so shocking? And what does the scandal itself tell us about the nature of stardom, the tabloid press, and news in the postmodern media environment?

This chapter addresses these questions. First, I will discuss the theoretical literature which analyzes how stardom functions in the tabloid universe. Next, I will show how the specific Jackson star image had been articulated in the press up to 1993, looking at it through three stages of development. Finally, I will examine coverage of the Jackson sex scandal in tabloid television and newspaper accounts from the fall of 1993, illustrating how the constellation of images in place previous to the scandal was disrupted by the scandal reports, and how the resulting tabloid coverage gives us insight into the nature of modern scandal and its relationship to stardom in general.

Stardom and the tabloids

It is virtually impossible to discuss the nature of media stardom today without taking into account both scandal and the tabloid press. Tabloid television shows and newspapers are pervasive, often featuring narratives of stars as their primary focus. These media outlets display for their audience the private lives of stars, their public adventures, and their shocking secrets. As a primary star of the 1980s and 1990s, who appears to have more than his share of secrets and enigmas, Michael Jackson has always been a tabloid favorite.

Yet what it is it about the nature of stardom and the role and function of tabloids that shapes the narratives of scandals like that of Jackson and his accuser? To answer this question, it is necessary to understand how stardom operates today in the context of its audience, and how the tabloid press uses this "image system" on behalf of its readers.[4]

Since the development of the film star, everyone from gossip columnists to academic scholars has attempted to understand the relationship between stars and audiences.[5] Reasons for the mere establishment of such a relationship, at least on a superficial level, seem obvious. Modern stardom is partly about the circulation of popular, recognizable image systems. Insofar as many of these circulating systems are film or video, one way that stars are made in the twentieth century is through consistent patterns of visualization constructed in various (often analogous) narrative settings, which are then repeated until recognized by audiences as being associated with a particular star. In addition, certain verbal descriptors attach to the stars of pop culture. Written accounts of those stars will often employ these predictable descriptors.

Out of this process, stars accrue particular sets of meanings for audiences. Audiences look at the star's skill level or talent, performances, look, and personality, and from these factors stars take on symbolic meaning for their publics. Given the specific culture of the star and the audience, these meanings can vary and mutate, but in all cases, the image systems of stars always say something about cultural values and attitudes. Audiences develop relationships with stars who simultaneously reflect and help construct their cultural practices. At this fundamental level, Richard Dyer notes that stars repeat, reproduce, reconcile, and even displace and compensate audience values within particular cultural formations (1979: 30).

Examples of this process are numerous. If one looks, for instance, at the image of John Wayne, the American actor, it is clear that from the film *Stagecoach* on his visual image as a tall, solitary cowboy is repeated over numerous movie texts. This image soon becomes one with the actor, and verbal descriptors like "brave," "courageous," and "American" soon attach to Wayne. When these meanings are taken into the everyday politics of a country, Wayne's impact on American values and the way they are seen in his own country and in much of the rest of the world is undeniable. Indeed, Wayne is soon seen to "stand for" something unique to the American psyche, a moral code that moves quickly from reflection to action on behalf of mainstream values. That John Wayne managed to avoid any hint of scandal during his life meant that these values remained unchallenged until certain outside political events of the 1960s made Wayne a figure of symbolic contestation.

It is in the narrative of scandal that this relationship between stardom and cultural values is most apparent. If we take as our starting place that the media scandal is a narrative of a disruption, where a particular set of acts is seen to violate the moral boundaries of a culture, then stars, with their uniquely telling cultural signifiers, are likely candidates for morality tales. Such tales tell us about a culture's moral constraints and its moral values.

Authenticity and morality

To give an example of how this process unfolds, various tabloids reported at one time that Tim Allen, the star of an American hit television series, *Home Improvement*, had been imprisoned as a young man on drug charges. The reasons that this event may be termed a scandal seem obvious. First, imprisonment on drug charges for any person is seen by most as constituting "immoral behavior" in America. Second, Allen has certain specific meanings for his audience related to his role on the program. His image as the "every-man family person" clearly contradicts his drug use and imprison-ment. No doubt, a scandal narrative was ripe for tabloid television and newspapers. But what saved Allen from a protracted and even more damaging scandal was that the arrest took place before his star had risen, allowing audiences to attribute his indiscretion to "youthful living." The scandal, therefore, was soon gone from the airwaves, and faded quickly in the public mind.

Why do audiences in cases such as this assume that the roles played on television or film – and the values of that character – are in any way related to those of "real life?" Why do audience mem-bers perceive stars of fictional programs as indicators of the real world's moral or immoral behavior? The reason is simple: *for audi-ences, modern stardom entails a belief in the ideology of authenticity.*

With roots in the Enlightenment view of "man" (often gender-specified), the notion of authenticity derives from the idea that a person is an integrated individual with inner and outer selves, public and private "personalities," which may or may not overlap.[6] Dyer suggests that all modern stardom "reproduces the overriding ideology of the person in contemporary society" by its use of the concept of authenticity (1986: 14). According to Dyer, stars are clearly seen by audiences as "individuals," persons with identity and con-sciousness, with public roles and private lives. This not only allows for identification to take place in the audiences' relationship to the star; it also allows the star to carry over the effects of previous work and notoriety into new projects, as audiences desire to view the relatively stable person behind the new public persona.

Indeed, the notion of authenticity appears inseparable from that of stardom. Audiences see stars as persons who are at once their roles in public and at the same time (to varying degrees) separate from those roles in private. For instance, in the midst of the *Dirty Harry* films, Clint Eastwood was seen by his fans not as a gun-toting vigilante, but as an actor in a role. Yet Eastwood's assumed "private authentic self" – a tough and uncompromising male figure – brought a certain depth to the character, while the part further defined for audiences who Eastwood "might really be." As Dyer notes (1986), some stars are valued due to the high correspondence between their public and private roles; some are valued in the way their star turns are so "unlike" their "real selves." But all stars operate in this nexus of authenticity.

The public/private conception of authenticity introduces the notion of morality, which is key in scandal narratives, into stardom.

Stars are seen by audiences to act out of private sets of values, which may or may not impinge upon their public image. It is this moral center that all stars (indeed, all post-Enlightenment individuals) are supposed to have. The moral center should dictate public choices and, therefore, public images. Thus, a scandal can occur when a star's existing public image system, one which has been circulated and repeated, and which bears a connection to a particular cultural formation, is disrupted by some "immoral" private action at odds with both cultural norms and the star's image. Suddenly, the "authentic" star, with a cultivated public and private image, is thrown into crisis. For example, in the case of Hugh Grant, the public image drawn from roles played in movies (of the reserved, shy Englishman) was put into crisis by private behavior at odds with the image (paying for sex on the streets of Los Angeles). That this private act also violated normative behavior created a sense of scandal among the public. This certainly could account for the numerous women who were heard to ask, "Why would a man that handsome – and a star – have to pay for it?" Or, to look at another example, one may see a similar process at work in the case of the Olympic skater Nancy Kerrigan, whose public image throughout the early stages of the Tonya Harding skating scandal was that of the quiet, pretty victim. We can observe how this image was disrupted when members of the media overheard her make slurs on Disney characters ("That stupid Mickey Mouse"), revealing a private self at odds both with a public image and with cultural practices of respect. In the case of both Grant and Kerrigan, the public became confused as to who the authentic, real star was. Was it the private person who seemed to be so disrespectful or the public person who seemed so good and innocent? In many ways, narrativization of the crisis – the media scandal – was an attempt to address this confusion so that audiences could resolve the seeming contradiction. In this sense then, scandals can begin a process of restoring a star's authenticity, at least within certain cultural boundaries.

Returning to the career of Michael Jackson, and in light of this discussion over authenticity, we see that a series of image systems has been developed to write about him. These categories help writers and audiences to link up the "past" Michael Jackson with the current one, and they assume that there is an individual linking various projects, an identity ("Michael Jackson") which has a private constancy from which creative work springs. These images allow fans to stay loyal to Jackson while helping them more easily negotiate new information about his life and work. However, when information arises about a private Jackson that is at odds with the public image and normative moral codes, a crisis occurs.

The role of tabloids

When scandal emerges in the public life of a star, tabloids quickly enter the process. They have often been instrumental in cementing a star's image system, and are crucial institutions for explaining the seeming contradiction which the scandal reveals in the authentic star.

The presence of the tabloid has been well documented.[7] In relation to scandal and stardom, tabloids have specific roles and functions which shape the resulting narrative. These arise from how tabloid journalism becomes, for readers, an authoritative source on events in the star's life. It does this by promising the reader access to the private world of the star, thereby playing upon the public/private dichotomy of authenticity. The reader is offered a look at the "real, authentic" star away from the public work he or she does. Then, when a scandalous private act exposes a gap between the public and private images of a star, the tabloid, by showing the reader something a star does privately that impinges upon the public image, and by granting some answer as to what the truth of this scandal was, becomes a kind of guarantor of public morality. The tabloid passes judgment on the star by standing in for the reader. Tabloid tales thus "set out to teach moral lessons by exposing worthy and unworthy actions" (Connell 1992: 77).

It is important to note that for tabloids to fulfill their function in covering star scandals (and sometimes in restoring star images), there must be a "truth" to be discovered. When tabloids use their authority to uncover private secrets, those secrets must be there in the first place. In this sense, as we will soon see, the Jackson child-abuse scandal presented a troubling situation for tabloid reporting, for it has been next to impossible to fix the sexual "truth" of the Jackson private life, and therefore to find out who the "real" Michael Jackson is.

I will now seek to identify and explain the image system of Michael Jackson as he operated in and through the popular press. This will allow us to see the star as he appeared to be on the eve of the child-abuse scandal, and will help illustrate how the narrativization of that scandal in fact drew upon descriptors of Jackson previously in place.

Michael Jackson as a star

If one examines the coverage of Michael Jackson in the mainstream press from 1970 to 1993, it becomes clear that his image system goes through three fairly distinct stages. These are not absolutely demarcated, of course, but they are general ways in which Jackson has been talked about during those years. Stage 1, beginning in 1970, presents Jackson as a particularly talented member of his family. Stage 2, which begins in 1983 and goes through 1985, presents Jackson as a solo artist and "Peter Pan" figure. Commentators speak about him as if he were some strange combination of child and man, white and black, woman and man, sexual and asexual creature. Finally, by 1987, stage 3 begins. Now, Jackson becomes even more "eccentric" and begins to appear associated with strange incidents and whims, behavior that causes him to be labeled as a tabloid favorite. As the eccentricity becomes more pronounced, Jackson now becomes described as "weird."[8] In the course of these stages, Jackson's sexuality, age, race, and gender are of increasing interest and debate. By the time of the child-abuse scandal in 1993, Jackson's image is firmly set in the public mind, and it is that image system which the scandal disrupts and displaces.

Examining these three stages, we see that in 1970 the mainstream press showed little interest in the Jackson family or Michael in particular. But *Ebony* did offer an initial portrait of the family that singles out Michael and establishes themes that reappear later in discussions of his image. Not surprisingly, the major aspect of Jackson it noted was his showmanship. It states that Michael Jackson is a "singer and dancer with bold and innovative showmanship astounding in one so young[.] Michael is viewed by many as being a potential equivalent to Sammy Davis Jr. and James Brown" (Robinson 1970: 152). Here, the article has done what must be done with all new stars: it places them in the context of stardom existing at the time, contextualizing the Jackson talent in light of a tradition that helps readers interpret the new style. So, Jackson is compared to earlier performers but shown to be somehow "new" and "innovative."

Interestingly enough, Jackson's personality is ignored in the *Ebony* piece. But the family as a whole is commented upon, in much the same language as will later be used to describe Michael. Because the Jackson Five are still children, they must take "limited and well-chaperoned trips to nearby parks and the like, but little else. This,

coupled with the demands of school, rehearsal, recording sessions
. . . and appearances means that the Jackson Five, for all their celebrity, enjoy a lot less fun than the average teenager" (Robinson 1970:
153). Here, an important theme appears: because Jackson began his
career as a child, his development as a person was not "normal,"
giving rise to his status as "unique," "not average," and "special."
That these categories also are those inevitably linked to stardom
only makes his later ascension easier to explain.

In 1980, Michael Jackson recorded his *Off the Wall* album, but it
was in 1983, with the release of *Thriller,* that he finally agreed to be
profiled and interviewed apart from his family. And it was here
that his image began to take on further attributes. In the period
between 1983 and 1985, Jackson was increasingly written about as
an androgynous figure who on the one hand was childlike (shy,
gentle, and innocent), but on the other was a man who operated in
the adult world of record production and sales. A whole series of
uncertain dichotomies was posited as to who Jackson might "really
be": a man or a child; a sexual or asexual being; a hetero- or homosexual; a man who was white in some ways but black in others.[9]
In addition, a series of image systems was seemingly placed outside any debate – that Jackson is a superstar who is affectionate
with children, and a harmless innocent who is adored by millions.

Jackson's shy and childlike nature was clearly seen as an out-
growth of a life in show business. In an interview in *Rolling Stone*
in 1983, Gerri Hershey wrote that Jackson appears to be "excruci-
atingly shy . . . [one who] guards his private life with an almost
obsessive caution 'just like an hemophiliac who can't afford to be
scratched in any way'. [The analogy is his]" (1983: 11). Director Steven
Spielberg compared Jackson to the fictional film character ET, noting that Jackson is "an emotional child star" (Hershey 1983: 13).

The idea that a 24-year-old, multi-talented, multi-platinum performer could still be seen as a "child star" was common in articles
written in the mid-1980s. *Newsweek* labeled him "the Peter Pan of
pop" (one suspects Jackson himself of responsibility for the label)
and spoke about his childlike love of a pet llama named Louis and
a boa constrictor named Muscles. Clearly, this Peter Pan was a
puzzle even Disney couldn't figure out, a grown man with the soul
of an animal-loving child:

Despite his showy style, Michael Jackson remains something of an enigma.
Onstage in one of his sequined jump suits, he's a flamboyant picture of
grace, a sleek jaguar ready to pounce. In photographs he's a creature of

sweet sensuality, beguiling, angelic, androgynous. In person, though, he's quiet and reserved, a gangling young man of cagey reticence, with a childlike aura of wonder. (Miller 1983: 52)

Such contradictions are reinforced when producer Quincy Jones calls him a "truth machine. He's got the balance between the wisdom of a 60 year old and the enthusiasm of a child" (Miller 1983: 53). In a logical extension of the problems of 1970, *Newsweek* concluded, "Here is a black giant who sacrificed his childhood to become a pop idol, a demigod detached from his fellow men, now sealed in a transparent bubble – a lonely prophet of salvation through the miracle of his own childlike, playful, life-giving music" (Miller 1983: 54). Already then, Jackson's image was piling on contradictions, from child to man, one in control but playful, possessor of pure wisdom and pure innocence. That all of this could be attributed to an unusual upbringing may or may not be as important as the Peter-Pan-like curio into which he was developing.

Rumors of strange behavior began to add to the image fascination. In 1984, *People Magazine* reported on the visit of Jackson to the Reagan White House, where, expecting to see just a few children, Jackson was surprised by some seventy-five adults, causing the singer to retreat into the men's room off the presidential library (Why Michael hid out . . . 1984: 75). And the one-sequined glove, worn during the visit, became an object of fascination for the world. *People*, in an issue later that year, featured the glove in a full-page photograph where it looked like nothing less than a Hollywood version of the Turin Shroud (Arrington 1984: 98). Indeed, Michael Jackson was becoming a royal figure, but still a creature who could only be described in contradistinctive adjectives. *McCalls* weighed in with precisely this judgment, calling Jackson, in a summation of the contradictions of his image during this period:

part man, part child; part lover; part son; black with almost Caucasian features; urban, streetwise, trendy-slick *and* ethereal, pixielike, otherworldly; a fantastically polished professional who's as shy as the darting fawn he in fact resembles; a man, yes, but – with his dreamy, high voice, his facial hairlessness and sheer prettiness – so boldly possessed of the female as to seem androgynous. (Weller 1984: 40)

As *McCalls* notes, Jackson's sexuality was also a matter of speculation. *Parade Magazine* wondered if Jackson was taking hormones to keep his voice girlish (reported in Miller 1983: 69). *Newsweek* also addressed questions of Jackson's virility, reporting that one journalist met Jackson at his home and found his hand to be "like a cloud." Indeed, speculation reached such a peak that in 1984 *Discover* magazine asked psychologist Carin Rubenstein to address the question of what it means when young people become worshippers of "an androgynous admirer of Peter Pan." The conclusion was that, "In a society obsessed with sex, there could be worse role models for young people" (Rubenstein 1984: 70). By 1984, then, much of the Jackson image repertoire that was later involved in the child-abuse scandal was already in place. These images were elaborated in the next round of Jackson publicity, in 1987, when his behavior was seen to become even stranger and speculation abounded as to just how "weird" Jackson really was.[10]

The flurry of publicity that surrounded Jackson in 1987 seemed predicated upon the release of his third solo album, *Bad*. But when the 1987 stories began, it was as if the contradictions laid out in the early 1980s had grown progressively more strange. In 1987, *Rolling Stone* noted the increased fascination with the star:

> For the past three years, Michael Jackson has been conspicuous mainly by his absence, and fans have made do with odd tidbits of info gleaned from tabloids. Less has been known about his artistic endeavors than about his attempts to purchase the remains of the Elephant Man, to marry Elizabeth Taylor, to levitate himself and to prolong his life through hyperbaric treatment. (Good news . . . 1987: 11)

A Davitt Sigerson record review in *Rolling Stone* (1987: 87) later that year began not by discussing the new album, but by reciting his recent scandal history:

> Michael Jackson is a man. Agreed, he is a young man, emotional age about thirteen, with a young man's interest in cars, girls, scary movies and gossip. But adolescent stardom, Jehovah's Witness wackiness and unadulterated genius have kept this faux-porcelain elephant man more childlike than any oxygen-tank sleeping device ever could.

A *People* article that same year addressed this concern directly, asking the question: "Is Michael weird or what?" While conceding that Jackson "beggars description," the article then proceeds to describe him anyway, as both creative and normal – Quincy Jones is quoted as saying Michael is "one of the most normal people I've ever met" – and eccentric and strange (Durkee 1987: 87). In terms of the latter, visual evidence is offered, from a record of his plastic surgeries with accompanying photos of the changing face, to his oxygen chamber photograph, to snapshots of his being accompanied by young boys more and more frequently.[11]

For our purposes, what makes Jackson a particularly interesting figure during this time is the confusion over who the "real" Michael Jackson was. It is as if the modernist conception of the human, a person with a stable and consistent private center, is now foreign to much of Jackson's image system. Certainly, he is seen as innocent and giving in his love of children, and childlike himself, but even these descriptions are hedged in press accounts. Allusions remain to a calculation and skill in Jackson that only a full adult could possess. In a very real sense, the Michael Jackson pictured from 1987 to the first half of 1993 was still a star in the making, fascinating precisely because he seemed so far from other stars in the way his multiple private and public selves consistently assumed and displaced identities. That this very confusion over identities gathered around those mirrored by the larger society where his stardom had such great meaning (i.e. around gender, race, sexuality) meant that Jackson not only was a great performer, but represented classic fissures of modern culture and society.

Therefore, when the child-abuse scandal hit, the image of Jackson as a mass of contradictions clustering around age, race, sexuality, and gender had clearly solidified, as had specific questions about his behavior. So while pictures of Jackson in the company of young boys were seen as evidence of his childlike quality in 1987, six years later those same pictures were to be offered as evidence for quite another set of image markers.

Tabloid coverage of the scandal

The allegations that Michael Jackson had sex with young boys seemed tailor-made for tabloid scandal coverage. It was a clear case of the secret, private actions of a star which lay at odds with public morality. And if the tabloids, with their function as fearless organs of "truth" on behalf of their audiences, could only discover the reality behind these allegations, then moral judgments could readily be offered by them as to the star's behavior.

Yet Jackson's image was not like many stars'. Authenticity assumes a certain consistency of personality. While many stars are seen to have "wild" or "crazy" private sides, they are usually perceived as consistent in that craziness by much of the public. Madonna, for instance, could have a baby out of wedlock, but few of the public were likely surprised by that feat. Her image system allowed such behavior to be consistent with her previous actions. She may be wild, but you can count on her being wild.

Jackson was anything but a clear figure. What was the "truth" about Michael Jackson? Was he gay, straight, sexual, asexual, a child or a man? For all of the talk of who the "real" Michael Jackson might be, it was the child-abuse scandal that was seen as able to finally provide a clear set of answers. It was clear that Jackson could be a child molester. He was, after all, weird, unusual, and of indeterminate sexuality, and his fondness for the company of young boys was well documented. It was equally possible that he was simply a strange, childlike man who enjoyed the company of those pre-adolescents. If the allegations were true, then Jackson seemed to be (in private, at least) a very sexual, not innocent man who preferred the company of young boys to women or girls. However, if the allegations were the result of an opportunistic Hollywood social power play or a money-making scam, then the possibility remained that Jackson was a true innocent – a child in an honest-to-goodness never-never land of platonic playfulness.

The intrigue of the scandal was that the Jackson image, in all its complexity, rendered either answer equally plausible. It was up to the tabloids to uncover which truth was the more likely one, thereby restoring Jackson's image to acceptable cultural moral practices, at least in the sense that a majority of Americans might use the term, or banishing him into the netherlands of an especially "sinful" world. This search is clearly the driving force behind the narrative of the Michael Jackson child-abuse scandal.

The "truth" of scandal

Establishing the "real truth" of the scandal is clearly what both TV and print tabloids attempt to do when such a story breaks. First, they report the "news," informing the audience of allegations that have been made. Next, they draw upon the previously circulating star image system as a way of suggesting the truth of what might have really happened in private, "behind closed doors." The tabloids look for authoritative answers. If they find few, they may pose a series of "what-if" questions. They can then search out spokespeople, insiders, and confidants, continuing to reveal secrets about the "real" star.

The problem is that what happened behind those doors in the Michael Jackson case remains, even today, a matter of speculation. Without the ability to establish truth with specific evidence, the tabloids could act as neither authoritative voices nor guarantors of morality. Therefore, their coverage of the scandal became a series of fluctuations, of speculations and competing claims given equal coverage. Finally, in an air of confusion, the scandal simply died, unresolved.

Let me offer a few brief examples of how this process actually unfolded. Early in the scandal, less than two weeks after the abuse investigation began by the Los Angeles Police Department, the tabloid TV show *A Current Affair* broadcast an episode appropriately entitled: "Michael Jackson: The curtain closes"[12] (*Current Affair*, 1993a). This show began with a review of the Jackson image system, as host Maureen O'Doyle stated, "Michael Jackson was everything we wanted him to be – the ultimate entertainer . . . at once a grown-up whose music pulsated with sensuality; yet the eternal kid, whose greatest joy was having the other kids visit the home he calls Neverland Ranch." The narrator, over "exclusive" grainy footage of Jackson and a young boy at play in a closed-down amusement park, then amplified upon this image system, noting that Jackson is seen in the tape "being Michael – rich, eccentric and a child at heart." In the following few minutes, Jackson was also described as "definitely our Peter Pan," "remind[ing] us of the child we all have inside," and as an "icon of eternal youth."

In this sense, the program is simply drawing upon previously articulated sets of Jackson characteristics. Yet the allegations threatened to disrupt this series of oppositions. As the show notes, there may be more to the image than we know (the "image we take at face value," according to the program, may not be all there is). The narration then comments that, in the video of Jackson playing with the young boy, the visuals "sum up the image" of Michael Jackson:

> [He is] a millionaire idol with the quirky but willful energy to rent an entire amusement park for the night just so he and another kid could play. It may be indulgent, it may be eccentric, it may be weird, but it's a rare glimpse of pure Michael Jackson – the childlike joy that is catching and yet for those who would make Michael Jackson a target, it's a convenient circumstance.

These observations are fascinating on at least two levels. First, notice the degree to which the "real" Jackson is still presented as a child ("just so he and *another* kid"), yet entertains the possibility that the private Jackson is an adult who knows more than he lets on. Yet, without firm evidence to move the image from one side of the opposition to the other, the tabloid story hedges its bets. The tapes of Jackson and the young boy playing are said to give ammunition to "those who would make Michael Jackson a target." The show clearly distances itself from these people, yet, by showing the tape and discussing Jackson's "eccentric" behavior, it at least leaves open the possibility of his guilt. It is clear *A Current Affair* wants to have it both ways, presenting a wonderful, childlike Michael as his fans see him yet hinting that Michael might be an adult criminal.

Tabloid newspapers at the time show a similar ambivalence. The *Globe* of September 7 used an earlier interview of Jackson to paint him as admitting to "prefer[ring] the company of children to adults." He is secretive, a man "who guards his privacy like a king guards his gold" (Tragic . . . 1993: 8). Therefore, his prior image as a child whose true, private personality is unknown is employed to suggest that the charges might be valid. Indeed, in this sense, Jackson's image certainly appears to make the charges plausible.

In order to get at the "truth" of the charges, the paper then recounted the results of an investigation by a "top psychologist," Marvin Fredman, who relates that Jackson's unusual love for the company of children revealed "he's still a little boy trapped in a man's body. Because he couldn't bond with his tyrannical father, his emotional development was stunted" (Why I prefer . . . 1993: 9). Still, even with this insight, the paper utimately refused to "fix the truth" of what really happened, and made no definitive judgment as to guilt or innocence.

This ambivalent coverage continues, and is perhaps best summed up in a graphic which appears first in the *Globe* on September 14 (Michael's fatal . . . 1993: 2). In a small box, two pictures of Jackson are featured side by side. In one, Jackson appears to be looking up while his hands are folded as if in prayer in front of his face. In the second, a darker, more sinister Jackson glares out behind heavy make-up. The caption is carried on the top and bottom of the picture in the words: "Peter Pan/or pervert?" This graphic will appear in much of the *Globe* coverage which follows in the coming months, and it is this question which cannot be answered in the remaining five months of tabloid coverage of the scandal.

By December, reports increasingly turn to "insider accounts" to uncover a possible "truth" to the allegations. A *National Enquirer* report of December 14 carries allegations by Jackson's former chef, Johnny Ciao, who states he saw Michael emerge from his "secret playroom" where he had been with young boys "in only his under-wear" (Michael Jackson's weekends ... 1993: 26). Yet the real activity that took place in that playroom remains a matter of spe-culation. Tabloid television shows offered much the same material, as a plethora of former Jackson employees came forward with their stories. *Hard Copy*, on December 14 (1993a), revealed the allega-tions of former Jackson maid Blanca Francia, who is presented as "the one person he trusted inside his home ... inside his bedroom" (therefore promising, at last, the true account). Francia states she saw Jackson "naked" with other young boys, and the show states that "her painful secret" is all the more valid because she is more than an "eyewitness," she is the "mother of a son." The next day, Francia returned to *Hard Copy* (1993b) to reveal Jackson's private nickname for his playful games with young boys ("rubba"), and the day after that, she revealed Jackson's "secret hideaway," where she "witnessed very private behavior" of Jackson and young boys. But since Francia never actually witnessed abusive acts with the young boys in question, her account too is unable to establish a definitive truth about the scandal or about who the "real" Michael Jackson is.

The search for the "truth" to the scandal continued unabated, even after Jackson himself delivered a televised denial from his Neverland Ranch on December 22. A December 23 broadcast of *A Current Affair* (1993b) offered voice analyst Steven Lamb, who analyzed a soundtrack of Jackson's Neverland denial. According to Lamb, Jackson is "not totally innocent" of the charges. The ques-tion as to whether or not he is "totally guilty" is left unanswered.

Throughout the scandal narrative, then, the tabloids attempt to uncover the secrets that take place behind the closed doors and curtains of Michael Jackson's life. But the absence of agreement as to the "authentic" Michael Jackson – which turned out to be more a series of ambiguous contradictions than a coherent personality – make such a truth difficult to come by. One side of Jackson could have been guilty and another could just as easily have been innocent.

Therefore, the normal authoritative function of the tabloid press was reduced in this scandal to presenting a series of competing claims, driven only by new witnesses and promises of further glimpses into the family secrets which awaited a public trial for final certainty. But no trial was forthcoming, for the charges were settled out of court by Jackson and the boy's family. It is interest-ing to note that even the statement by Jackson's manager, Sandy Gallin (reported by the *Star* on February 8, 1994) relies upon the established image system of Jackson to attempt to absolve him of guilt: "Michael's innocent, open, childlike relationships with children may appear to be bizarre to adults in our society who cannot conceive of any relationship without some sexual connotations. This is not any kind of reflection on Michael's character. Rather, it's a symptom of the sexual phobias of our society" (How Michael Jackson plotted . . . 1994: 5).

So, five months after the scandal began, Michael Jackson was still, according to his management "innocent," "open," and "childlike." Some members of the public clearly agree with the assessment, some do not. But one still has the sense that the "real" Michael Jackson remains shrouded in mystery, just as enigmatic as always. Only one fact is beyond controversy: he remains always a star who cannot be left alone.

Conclusion

The Michael Jackson child-abuse scandal is, for all intents and purposes, over.[13] Yet it still gives us a fascinating look at the media scandal generally, and how it operates in the world of stardom. Michael Jackson had become a series of image descriptors, many of which were contradictory in nature. These contradictions may have made him, along with his voice, dancing, and other talents, a "larger-than-life" star. Yet these contradictions were also tailor-made for the kind of scandal in which Jackson found himself. One could always pick and choose which Michael Jackson was the authentic one, and the scandal gave audiences the chance to take sides. Jackson was the perfect polysemic figure, in that anyone's interpretation could never be completely wrong.

The tabloids attempted to close the argument by acting on behalf of its audience to uncover the truth. But what happened or did not happen in the secret rooms of Neverland Ranch never saw a public "final truth" reached in a courtroom. The Michael Jackson sex scandal became a narrative without an ending. The story had begun with a mass of contradictions already in place, and its middle contained a mass of "maybe/maybe not" allegations. While this certainly frustrated the tabloid press, which had hounded Jackson for months looking for answers, it did have one positive benefit for the industry. It gave the tabloids a high-profile, ongoing subject. Even if they were ultimately unable to find a truth, the Jackson story gave them a profitable, lengthy narrative to focus on. The "Did he or didn't he?" question did not have to be answered so much as asked – and asked, and asked, and asked. The Michael Jackson scandal as it appeared in the tabloids was about the telling of a story that was never quite finished, about making promises that were never quite kept, and about giving its audiences something enduring to talk about. Whether or not the real Michael Jackson was ever uncovered, this scandal narrative sold lots of papers and brought in plenty of rating points.

In the end, the authentic Michael Jackson remains ambiguous. He is painted as a mirror, one who simply reflects the world rather than creates it. Perhaps this is where postmodern stardom is ultimately most comfortable, where the "authentic" star is whatever the audience is – devoid of motive, drive, or desire independent of that contained within the fans. In this sense, keeping one's image system a mass of contradictions which appear unresolvable is more than just a way to avoid getting caught in a career-ending scandal; it is the ultimate in postmodern marketing. There are always "halls of mirrors" for the mass-mediated, postmodern star to be reflected in; if one mirror shatters, the star can always point to the "real me, over there," in another reflection, one that could itself shatter at any moment. We sometimes speak of criminals staying "one step ahead of the law." What Michael Jackson has shown is that for public figures, it is best to always stay one step ahead of having a singular authentic identity. In this sense, Jackson is perhaps only the most spectacular example of postmodern stardom, a classification that now includes others whose contradictory and ever-changing image systems seem to allow them to escape the handcuffs of moral judgment, a line-up including, some would argue, figures as far afield as Bill Clinton and O.J. Simpson.

Of course, this was never the intention of Michael Jackson's image making, and while he has survived the child-abuse scandal, unbroken if not unbent, the threat it posed to his career and to his freedom was very real. In his early video, Jackson's cries of "leave me alone" clearly are muted; the last thing a star, particularly one like Jackson, desires is to be left alone by the publicity machine or by the public. But one should not forget that the cries he uttered on December 22, 1993 – his apologia broadcast from Neverland Ranch in the midst of scandal – were real. They sounded so desperate because Michael Jackson knew, better than anyone else, what was at stake in the outcome.[14] For as the scandal played out, it quickly became, for Jackson, a tale about the struggle over the one thing he knows he needs to remain a star: control over his own image. That this most important element of his life, his career, and his marketing began to slip from his control to that of the media and the public must have been the scariest thought of all.

Notes

1 I wish the reader to keep in mind a caveat here. Jackson is, above all, an extraordinary singer, and it is as a singer and melodist that he reaches people in the first instance. And if it were not for that first instance, I feel the tabloid coverage would be unnecessary. It is because he has the voice and stage actions, i.e. talent, that Jackson is tabloid fodder, not the other way around. When Kobina Mercer says, "It is the voice which lies at the heart of [Jackson's] appeal," he is cutting to the heart of the matter (1993: 93).

2 This becomes readily apparent when one reviews the remarkable correlation between articles on Jackson and Jackson's own efforts to promote a new product, be it album or tour. Jackson often literally vanishes from public view in the years between these projects. Then, when the merchandizing is underway, he emerges in a wide range of popular press reports, all of which seem to comment on his recent "reclusive" absence. The interesting aspect of this is that the logical explanation for his absence (that Jackson is consciously controlling his image proliferation in order to maximize sales when a product is new and available) is somehow effaced, replaced by the "mysterious" tendency of Jackson to appear and disappear. This not only illustrates just how much the business side of pop culture is hidden from public view; it also says something about the image of Jackson as innocent or childlike, which would seemingly preclude him from being in conscious control of his own marketing.

3 While a precise definition of what constitutes a tabloid is difficult to come by (generally, it is one of those things one knows when one sees it), I will argue that the item is known by the characteristics suggested by Bird. For her, tabloid publications and shows are heavy on "human-interest" stories and gossip, usually with a "sensational twist," told "graphically," visually intensive, with stereotyped prose or narration. See Bird (1992: 8) for more discussion of what defines a tabloid.

4 For a full discussion of "image systems," see Lull (1995: 9–21). I use "image system" in much the same way here. I am particularly concerned with how such systems are employed to "encourage audience acceptance and circulation of . . . dominant themes" (Lull 1995: 9).

5 See Bowser (1994: 103–20).

6 See Hamilton, who notes that the idea of the individual from the Enlightenment embodies "the concept that the individual is the starting point for all knowledge and action . . . Society is thus the sum or product of the thought and action of a large numbers of individuals" (1992: 22).

7 See Bird (1992).

8 It should be noted that, in stardom today, there is "weird" and there is "weird!" It certainly is an asset at times to be seen as eccentric. Yet to violate commonly-agreed-upon moral standards (such as a ban on child

molestation) moves the star beyond eccentricity and weirdness into the reprehensible.

9 These characteristics not only stood in opposition to one another; they often defined themselves in dynamic relationship to other characteristics, while the very classification categories changed as often as Jackson's own skin color.

10 Characteristically, Jackson "disappeared" from public view from 1984 to 1987. The best explanation – as I noted above – is that he had no new product to merchandise.

11 While it is outside our emphasis here, the image of Jackson as a shrewd businessman also begins to appear at this time, as does his image as a philanthropist (Gold 1988). The fact that a number of pieces with the same theme appear in the same year may not be coincidental – Jackson, after all, does employ press agents. Indeed, one of these accounts, that Jackson slept in a special chamber to preserve his youth, was, it is claimed, given to the tabloids by Jackson himself. According to an editor of the *National Enquirer*, Jackson furnished Polaroids to the tabloid picturing him lying inside the machine. When he was informed that these were not of publishable quality, Jackson went back into the chamber and had the series reshot so the tabloid could feature them (*Frontline* 1994). This makes it ironic, to say the least, when the video of "Leave Me Alone" presents a tabloid picturing Jackson in the machine as some kind of threat to Jackson. Such irony is now, no doubt, just another kind of postmodern pop currency.

12 Images of curtains, pulled back by the authoritative narrators to reveal secrets, are common in the coverage of tabloid scandals.

13 As I write in early 1997, Jackson has married his dermatologist's assistant. It is his second marriage, following his divorce from the daughter of Elvis Presley, Lisa Marie Presley. The couple has just made Jackson a father, and the child has been named Prince. While the cynical among Jackson watchers may wonder if this event merely forecasts an upcoming record release or tour, it is interesting to note that the pregnancy and birth cannot be viewed by the press (and public) apart from the earlier scandal, which has exhibited real staying power in the discourse about Michael Jackson.

14 The question as to the scandal's effect upon Michael Jackson's record sales remains a point of debate. In an interview aired in late November, 1996, on the American music channel VH-1, Jackson denied published reports that his record sales were down and urged fans to "believe me" and not the media and tabloids. The levels of irony in this defense are multiple, but it is interesting to see that here, at least, Jackson seems to indicate that there is a "me" stable enough for fans to believe in.

References

Arrington, C. (1984). Hands up for all those who think Michael Jackson's glove is a many splendored thing. *People Weekly*, March 19: 98–9.

Bird, S.E. (1992). *For Enquiring Minds: A Cultural Study of Supermarket Tabloids*. Knoxville, TN: University of Tennessee Press.

Bowser, E. (1994). *The Transformation of the American Cinema: 1907–1915*. Berkeley, CA: University of California Press.

Connell, I. (1992). Personalities in the popular media. In P. Dahlgren and C. Sparks (eds), *Journalism and Popular Culture*. London: Sage, 64–83.

Corliss, R. (1993). Peter Pan speaks. *Newsweek*, February 22: 66–7.

A Current Affair. (1993a). Broadcast date, September 3.

A Current Affair. (1993b). Broadcast date, December 23.

Durkee, C. (1987). Unlike anyone, even himself. *People Weekly*, September 14: 88–99.

Dyer, R. (1979). *Stars*. London: BFI Publishing.

Dyer, R. (1986). *Heavenly Bodies: Film Stars and Society*. New York: St Martins Press.

Frontline. (1994). Broadcast date, February 15.

Gold, T. (1988). On tour, he's still "Michael!" But his charity work has won him a new title: Dr. Jackson. *People Weekly*, March 28: 36–7.

Good news, bad news. (1987). *Rolling Stone*, August 13: 11.

Goodwin, A. (1992). *Dancing in the Distraction Factory: Music Television and Popular Culture*. Minneapolis: University of Minnesota Press.

Hamilton, P. (1992). The enlightenment and the birth of social science. In S. Hall and B. Gieben (eds), *Formations of Modernity*. London: Open University Press, 18–59.

Hard Copy. (1993a). Broadcast date, December 14.

Hard Copy. (1993b). Broadcast date, December 15.

Hershey, G. (1983). Michael Jackson: Life in the magical kingdom. *Rolling Stone*, February 7: 10–11, 17.

How Michael Jackson plotted for 2 months to pay off teen accuser. (1994). *Star*, February 8: 5.

Lull, J. (1995). *Media, Communication, Culture: A Global Approach*. Cambridge: Polity Press; New York: Columbia University Press.

Mercer, K. (1993). Monster metaphors: Notes on Michael Jackson's Thriller. In S. Frith, A. Goodwin, and L. Grossberg (eds), *Sound and Vision: The Music Video Reader*. New York: Routledge, 93–108.

Michael Jackson's weekend with boys in secret playroom. (1993). *National Enquirer*, December 14: 26.

Michael's fatal attraction for little boys. (1993). *Globe*, September 14: 2–4.

Miller, J. (1983). The Peter Pan of pop. *Newsweek*, January 10: 52–4.

Robinson, L. (1970). The Jackson five. *Ebony*, September: 150–4.

Rubenstein, C. (1984). The Michael Jackson syndrome. *Discover*, September: 68–70.

Sigerson, D. (1987). Michael grows up. *Rolling Stone*, October 22: 87–8.

Tragic youngster trapped in Jackson sex scandal. (1993). *Globe*, September 7: 8.

Weller, S. (1984). The magic of Michael Jackson. *McCalls*, May: 38–40, 43–4.

Why I prefer kids to grown-ups. (1993). *Globe*, September 7: 9.

Why Michael hid out in a White House men's room, and other tales of the day power played host to fame. (1984). *People Weekly*, May 28: 74.

Producing Trash, Class, and the Money Shot:

A Behind-the-Scenes Account of Daytime TV Talk Shows

Laura Grindstaff

Behind the scenes

I took my seat in the control booth just as the director started the countdown. The room was cool and dark, illuminated primarily by the double row of television monitors on the far wall above the editing console. The sound board looked like a miniature city block sprinkled with neon lights. It was my job to answer the phones in the booth so those working there were not disturbed during taping. For me it was the most interesting of all the intern duties because I got to witness two performances at once: that of the host and guests on stage and that of the production staff around me. "Cold open – no music, no applause!" the director shouted. "Three! Two! One! *Roll tape!*" The camera was tight on the first guest, Karen, a victim of childhood molestation, who spoke of the abuse she suffered as a child every holiday when her uncle came to visit. Her voice was high and clear, with a faint Southern accent. Diana, the host, prodded for more details, and Karen obliged, tears welling up in her big brown eyes. I could feel the tension rise in the control booth; we were simultaneously horrified by her suffering, incredulous that she would discuss it on national television, and elated that she was doing so with such visible emotion – especially with the November ratings sweeps just around the corner. When the woman broke into sobs describing the time her uncle "shared" her with a friend, the look of triumph on the producer's face told me this show was indeed a "sweeper." The segment ended with the introductory credit sequence accompanied by the trademark *Diana* music, and then the director cut to a commercial. As soon as the stage manager gave the "clear" signal, the silence in the booth gave way to the buzz of conversation.

I spent more than a year as a student intern and fieldworker at two nationally televised daytime talk shows I will call *Diana* and *Randy*. Daytime talk is undoubtedly one of the most popular yet derided forms of mass culture. Geared primarily toward women and focused on a wide range of topics from sexual abuse and marital infidelity to family feuds and prostitution, talk shows take the backstage of people's lives and put it up front, on stage; they make public issues of personal experience, and they do so by privileging emotion, confession, and conflict among "ordinary" people over rational debate among experts or the pleasant chatter of celebrities.[1] Daytime talk thus challenges conventional boundaries separating public from private, reason from emotion, news from entertainment, fact from fiction, and expert knowledge from common opinion – binarisms which also tend to distinguish "high" from "low" culture. Indeed, talk shows are one of the most debased of all television forms, characterized in the popular press and elsewhere as trashy, sleazy, and even pornographic. Most people I know hold the genre in contempt, and are at a loss to explain its attraction for participants. At the same time, they are fascinated by talk shows, and by my work behind the scenes – it is as if I had infiltrated a cult or underground drug ring.

I went behind the scenes in order to gain first-hand knowledge of the production process, including how topics and guests are chosen, how a show is put together and carried off, and the nature of the relationship between producers and guests. Besides taking fieldnotes and conducting formal interviews with producers and guests, I attended live tapings of talk shows in New York, Chicago, and Los Angeles, and in preparation for the fieldwork watched more than 1000 hours of videotaped talk-show programming.[2] The incorporation of ordinary people into the regular machinery of the television industry poses some unique challenges from a production standpoint, for the very physical and emotional theatrics that make the genre popular and compelling are the most difficult to produce on a daily basis. Talk shows are just that: talk and show. They are performative conversations about real-life events that must strike a delicate balance between information and entertainment, scriptedness and spontaneity, freedom and control. Negotiating this tension is not simply a matter of individual effort, but is built into the structure of the production process. So how do producers orchestrate public performances based on private revelations? How does an industry devoted to the manufacture of experts and celebrities transform the stories of "just folks" into mass entertainment? At some level, of course, these folks themselves are the "stars" and "experts" of the show; however, what constitutes one's expertise or celebrity status is clearly different for so-called ordinary people, who are expected to yield dramatic performances that therapists, professors, and Hollywood stars generally are not. They are ordinary people who must do and say *extra*ordinary things.

This chapter is based on my experiences backstage at *Diana* and *Randy*, and aims to link a discussion of daytime talk to the notion of media scandal. If "scandal" is defined broadly as the public disclosure and narrativization of private transgressions, then talk shows are nothing if not scandalous. But while the term "media scandal" usually refers to specific events such as the O.J. Simpson murder trial, the Hill/Thomas sexual harassment hearings, or the controversy that ensued when Lorena Bobbitt severed her husband's penis (all of which were featured on daytime talk shows), I want to position daytime talk as "scandalous" in a more generic and institutional sense. The public disclosure of personal intimacies and the incorporation of ordinary people into an entertainment context are not in and of themselves bad things. In fact, daytime talk often gives voice to those normally denied representation on television, especially women, the working class, and sexual and racial minorities, and in doing so frequently addresses issues too "private" or "offensive" for the more "respectable" media. What is problematic about the genre for many scholars and critics is the *way* ordinary people are brought into this context: not only the topics they are asked to discuss, but the performances they give, and the orchestration of these performances behind the scenes. Of central concern here is the authenticity of the guests and their stories, and, related to this, the perceived manipulation of guests by producers – the questionable tactics producers employ in order to elicit from guests the desired physical and emotional displays. These tactics themselves became something of a media scandal after the March, 1995, incident known as the *Jenny Jones* murder, an incident that thrust talk shows into the national spotlight as a serious social problem and prompted a public outcry against them.[3]

At the same time, I want to question the negative valence of the term "scandalous" as it applies to daytime talk. I also want to question the separation of talk shows from other mass-media forms and the exclusive application of the term to talk shows alone. Just as the notion of scandal itself implies both containment and resistance, a breach of moral conduct that both challenges and reinforces social norms, daytime talk is a site of contestation, an impure space where various groups struggle to realize their own agendas and desires. The appearance of a panelist on stage is the result of intense effort and collaboration among many diverse production elements, including the guests themselves. To be sure, the tactics producers use are sometimes manipulative, their behavior with guests less than forthright and honest, and the shows they produce of questionable worth and veracity. But "othering" talk shows by emphasizing manipulation and deceit is problematic, because it tends to ignore the similar ways manipulation and deception are part and parcel of *all* media practices, not just the production of daytime talk shows, and the ways *all* media muddy distinctions between public and private, information and entertainment, the real and the unreal. It also obscures the ways in which guests have a certain amount of power and agency in this context, and can and do negotiate with producers over the terms of their performance. Guests are not cultural dopes, naively complicit in their own degradation. They have agendas of their own, and their seemingly irrational behavior makes sense when we account for their needs, desires, and material circumstances, as well as structural inequalities of access to more socially acceptable media forums.

Ordinary people on television

Ordinary people have always had limited opportunities for media exposure; historically, talk shows have been one of the few. The talk show as a broad generic category is one of the oldest and more durable electronic media forms with roots dating back to the early days of radio. While most talk radio maintained a political focus and was geared primarily toward older, affluent men, in the early 1970s the talk industry launched a new type of talk show directed at women and younger audiences, featuring light, humorous conversations about male–female relationships. Informally known as "topless radio" (and denounced as "smut" by the Federal Communications Commission), this shift marked the beginning of the genre's intensely interpersonal focus, now standard on *Oprah* et al. and on countless call-in radio sex therapy and advice programs (Munson 1993: 49).

On television, the talk show has traditionally been devoted to either light entertainment, with comedy, skits, music, and celebrity guests, or more serious discussion of news and public affairs among experts (Rose 1985). Rarely did the genre feature ordinary people; indeed, only on game shows or game/talk hybrids did ordinary people routinely play more than a peripheral role. Two such hybrid programs from the 1950s were *Queen for a Day* and *Strike it Rich*, both cited as precursors to contemporary daytime talk shows because they featured individuals willing to step forward and relate their woeful life stories on camera. On *Queen for a Day*, for example, women who provided the most harrowing tales of personal tragedy and hardship were voted "queen" by the studio audience and given prizes such as refrigerators and washing machines (Munson 1993; Priest 1995).[4]

The vast majority of daytime shows aimed at women, however, consisted mostly of chitchat between hosts and celebrity guests, along with light entertainment, cooking demonstrations, or household tips. It was not until the *Phil Donahue Show* made its debut in Dayton, Ohio, in 1967 that the concept of "homemaker entertainment" underwent a radical shift. As Rose (1985) observes, *Donahue* broke down the formal barriers of existing talk-show models, eliminating conventions such as the host's desk and opening monologue that tended to impede discussion. Guests – who were as likely to be ordinary people as celebrities, experts, or politicians – were not isolated from the studio audience but sat on stage as Donahue roamed the audience with a microphone soliciting comments and questions; viewers at home could also phone in and speak with guests on the air.[5] The formal innovation was both a cause and consequence of changes in content as well. "Donahue became a forum for exploring every issue in society, particularly the diversity of sexual lifestyles, in an open manner not previously attempted by any daytime talkshow" (Rose 1985: 338).

For almost two decades *Donahue* was the only nationally-syndicated program of its kind. By 1988, however, it had been joined by *Sally Jessy Raphael*, *Oprah*, and *Geraldo*, and as of the 1995–6 television season there were more than 20 different daytime talk shows on the air watched by millions of viewers worldwide.[6] This growth has sparked intense competition for ratings and refigured the genre in key ways. Most notably, relative newcomers like *Jenny Jones*, *Jerry Springer*, and *Ricki Lake* increasingly orchestrate conflict and confrontation in order to produce what I call the "money shot" of the text: that moment of raw emotion, from the angry denunciation to the tearful confession, the display of rage or sorrow or joy or remorse. These moments are both the hallmark of the genre and central to its trashy reputation. Talk shows are parodied on television commercials and primetime sitcoms, in comic strips and newspaper columns, in everyday parlance and discourse. Producers are called "talk-show pimps" while guests are known as "freaks of the week" or "nuts and sluts" (Kneale 1988). An essay in *Wired* magazine describes the essence of the genre as a masturbatory encounter between outraged audience and sacrificial guest (Sirius and St Jude 1994), while Dr Vicki Abt, an oft-quoted media scholar, suggests that disclosing one's personal secrets on national television is like "defecating in public" (Kaplan 1995: 12). "These days it has become standard for all sorts of people to flaunt not just their physical oddities but their stupidity, vulgarity, or sinfulness as well," writes Kurt Anderson of *Time*; "they volunteer, in exchange for attention or a few bucks, to suffer sneers and outright ridicule, so long as the medium is sufficiently mass" (1993: 94). Perhaps Jeff Jarvis of *TV Guide* sums it up best when he says, "[talk shows] are a forum for trashy people to act trashy, exhibiting their bad manners, hard hearts, and filthy family laundry before millions of viewers" (1994: 7).

Clearly what disturbs such critics is not just the public disclosure of private events, but the manner in which these disclosures are made and the kind of person making them. Thus talk shows are "scandalous" because trashy people talk trash and let it all hang out on national television. The money shot is the focus of this contempt: ordinary people's willingness to sob, scream, bicker, and fight on television. The analogy to pornography is both deliberate and fitting. The climax of most sex scenes in film and video porn, the money shot is the moment of orgasm and ejaculation offering incontrovertible "proof" of a man's – and occasionally a woman's – "real" sexual excitement and prowess. Pornography thus performs a kind of low-brow ethnography of the body, part of the documentary impulse Williams (1989) calls "the frenzy of the visible." Like pornography, daytime talk is a narrative of explicit revelation where people "get down and dirty" and "bare it all" for the pleasure, fascination, or repulsion of viewers. Like pornography, daytime talk exposes people's private parts in public. It demands external, visible proof of a guest's inner emotional state, and the money shot – the dramatic climax when the lie is exposed, the affair acknowledged, the reunion consummated – is the linchpin of the discourse.

The money shot is also the linchpin of production efforts, informing the activities of producers at every stage of the process. All the work behind the scenes – choosing topics, finding, interviewing, and rehearsing guests, coaching audience members – is done in the service of its display. Depending on the show, the money shot might be "soft-core," prompted by grief or remorse and consisting primarily of tears (as on *Diana*), or "hard-core," involving bickering, shouting, screaming, and, occasionally, physical blows (as on *Randy*). In the pages that follow I will chronicle the career of the money shot through various stages of production, illustrating how this scandalous content is accomplished in routine ways. In doing so I hope to both reinforce and challenge the framing of talk shows as media scandal by highlighting the scandalous nature of *all* mass-mediated – especially televisual – discourse.

Talk as work: routinizing the production process

Talk shows may be trashy, but trash is just as difficult to produce as more respectable forms of television, if not more so. Producers strive to elicit the money shot because they require visible evidence of a guest's emotional state. At the same time, because they tape 200 shows per year, producers must make these seemingly spontaneous and unpredictable moments predictable and routine. As Tuchman (1973) notes, organizations routinize tasks whenever possible in order to facilitate the control of work. Routinization would seem especially important – and yet especially challenging – when the work involves the intentional orchestration of volatile situations. In the world of daytime talk, "good television" requires that the money shot be genuine and spontaneous, while at the same time consistently produced. How is this delicate balancing act accomplished?

Producers draw largely on the codes and conventions of news-gathering and late-night talk. Mark Fishman (1980) and others have detailed the ways in which journalists rely on established sources and information channels in order to produce fresh news daily under the pressure of deadlines, even when the news consists of unpredictable or unexpected events like accidents, emergencies, or natural disasters. This means exposing themselves to a few key nodal points within the vast expanse of their beat territory where information is already concentrated, and then repackaging that information according to the mandates of the news organization. The world of daytime talk is also bureaucratically organized, despite the often makeshift appearance of the programs. As one producer put it, "people seem to think we pull guests right off the street like a dogcatcher picking up strays, but that's not the way it happens."

Like reporters, talk-show producers have "beat territories" they survey on a regular basis for potential story ideas – mostly magazines, newspapers, and other television programs. There is the "tabloid beat," the "hard-news-and-current-affairs beat," the "woman's-magazine beat," the "soap-opera beat," and so forth. Just as with newsgathering, there exists a potentially infinite number of available stories; in actual practice, however, talk-show topics do not come from just anywhere, but are reflexively constituted with reference to other mass-media texts, including other daytime talk shows. "There are no original topics left in this business," one *Diana* staffer confided, "it's all just variations on a theme. When I worked at *Sally*, I must have done a dozen shows on mother–daughter conflicts alone." The heavy reliance on other media as well as certain core scripts within the genre illustrates another observation made by Tuchman (1973) in her analysis of newsgathering: Variability in raw data impedes routinization. The recycling of topics (and, to some degree, guests) is less about laziness or producers' lack of imagination than the structural demands of the workplace.

In choosing topics, producers ask themselves, will the topic appeal to the target demographic (typically women ages 18–54)? If it has been done before, does it have a fresh angle? Can "real" people be found to talk about it? Most importantly, is it visual? This last question is really about the money shot, because by "visual" producers mean visibly or obviously emotional or volatile. Does the topic involve controversy, conflict, or confrontation? If not, where will the drama come from? Getting the guest to emote is the bottom line, and it cannot be left to chance. In this sense, talk shows face a dilemma diametrically opposite to that of organizations like funeral homes and hospital emergency rooms, where the goal of routinization is to minimize rather than maximize emotional displays. In both cases, however, guests and their emotions are objectified as elements of production, things to be managed and manipulated.

Another consideration is whether the topic is consistent with the image of the host and the talk show itself, for despite their seeming homogeneity, there are significant differences between shows. *Geraldo* can tackle subjects *Ricki Lake* cannot; *Jenny Jones* and *Jerry Springer* do things *Oprah* and *Leeza* do not. Each show has a unique identity, and it is the job of the executive producer to ensure that the topics, the guests, and the way both are handled support and reaffirm this identity. The executive producer at *Diana* described that show as being "classy, but with a bit of an edge. We're not one of those sleazy, tabloid talk shows, we don't ambush people and we're not confrontational – our viewers hate that. But we're not afraid to push the envelope a little either." *Diana* thus tends to avoid overt conflict, opting instead for more subtle performances. *Randy*, on the other hand, embraces it. "We always book conflict," an associate producer told me, "it's the main ingredient. Things without conflict just don't have any bearing for the show." To go back to the pornography metaphor, *Diana* is soft-core while *Randy* is hard-core, the money shot more often than not involving physical as well as emotional displays.

Once producers have been assigned a show, they rely on a number of routine sources and channels for securing guests to be on panel, the specific channel being determined largely by the topic. For serious, current-affair, or social-issue-oriented topics, more common on *Diana* than on *Randy*, the primary channel is existing groups and organizations. Producers go to the Screen Actors Guild or various publicity agencies when seeking celebrity guests, and organizations such as Alcoholics Anonymous or the local Rape Crisis Center when seeking the help and participation of experts. These experts then put producers in contact with selected "ordinary" guests, often their own clients. (Experts are thus important to the genre as much for their connections to ordinary people as for their expertise – which is why they are typically brought on stage only in the last segment of a show.) Producers can also locate potential guests through on-line databases that cross-reference stories and sources from a vast network of local and national media, or through services such as the National Talkshow Guest Registry in Los Angeles.[7] Of course, producers also rely on their own informal networks and contacts, much as journalists and other media professionals do. Sometimes these are family members and friends, sometimes former guests with whom producers have maintained a relationship, sometimes staffers at other talk shows. When in a bind, producers may rely on "stringers," individuals producers pay to find guests on short notice whom they cannot find for themselves.[8] In many cases, once producers find one guest to fit the topic, that person serves as the stepping stone or conduit to others. In this way, certain guests themselves perform much the same function as experts do for producers, or key sources for journalists.

Perhaps the largest proportion of guests, however, come from plugs, brief advertisements for upcoming topics that air at the end of every show ("Are you constantly using food as a substitute for sex? Do you refuse to date outside your race? Does your mom act younger than you do? Call 1–800-XXX-XXXX"). Plugs are used for topics that do not necessarily have an organizational base. For example, make-over shows are standard fare on *Diana*, yet, as one producer explained it, "there is no center for make-over candidates, no group or club or whatever to call. So instead of going to the guest, the guest comes to us." As an intern I logged thousands of phone calls from viewers responding to on-air plugs about forbidden relationships, compulsive lying, medical mishaps, roommate problems, interracial romance, cross-dressing, sibling rivalry, infidelity, promiscuity, dating disasters, and family feuds, among other topics.

Not surprisingly perhaps, "plug topics" have the reputation among industry insiders as the most trashy and debased, not only because of the specific content, but because, in giving ordinary people direct access and thereby bypassing official organizations and expert contacts, they require little investigative work on the part of producers. In fact, advertising for one's sources is about as far from the respected tradition of investigative journalism as one can get. It is partly for this reason, and because *Diana* defines itself in opposition to the "sleazy, tabloid" brand of daytime talk show, that the supervising producer there discouraged producers from relying too heavily on plugs to book their guests. Conversely at *Randy* – which *is* one of those sleazy tabloid talk shows (and does not pretend to be otherwise) – producers rely almost exclusively on plugs.

The blind date

Plugs are thus one of several formal mechanisms designed to streamline the difficult process of locating the kind of ordinary people producers need – those willing to talk about their personal problems, hardships, or transgressions on national television. What is more challenging to routinize, however, is the actual performance of guests once they are found. Producers thus employ various strategies to minimize uncertainty and ensure that guests will not be boring, freeze in front of the camera, or fail to show up altogether. First and foremost is an extensive pre-interview over the phone, sometimes referred to by producers as "the blind date" because they claim to know within the first minute of conversation whether the relationship is worth pursuing. If it is – that is, if the person is energetic, articulate, emotionally expressive, and forthcoming with intimate material – there are frequent follow-up conversations to iron out the exact details of the guest's story, with producers always imposing the conventional pyramid structure used by journalists to get the most important information up front. Producers may talk to other people to corroborate the story or get additional information on the guest, and they might ask for supporting documents such as letters, photographs, or videotape to use in the show. Meanwhile, the travel coordinator will have been in contact with the guest about flight and limousine arrangements.

Depending on the show's focus, producers may, like journalists, do some background research to gather facts and statistical data, especially for "social-issue" topics like rape, battery, or homelessness – again, more common on *Diana* than on *Randy*. This research usually informs the questions producers prepare for the host, and may also help producers decide on the best combination of guests for the panel. Balance of this sort is key, and is another concept familiar to journalists and other media professionals. If the issue is controversial, are both sides represented? What other elements are needed to flesh out the story? What other guests would add interest, excitement, or diversity? For example, when producers at *Diana* put together a show on teenagers with HIV, they aimed for a panel that was varied in terms of race, gender, sexual orientation, and method of contracting the virus. On *Randy*, where more energy is devoted to digging up dirt on guests than researching facts, "balance" typically means securing as many parties involved in a dispute as possible – less in the interest of fairness than of orchestrating a dramatic confrontation. As Randy himself told me: "This isn't an educational show, other than what you learn by seeing how people relate to one another. What we're discussing on any given day is the least important thing; the subject is merely a vehicle to get people to engage in certain forms of interaction."

The primary purpose of the pre-interview and other preparatory work is to solidify a structure for the show, identify the participants, narrow their stories down to manageable bits, and determine how these various bits will come together on stage in a visually compelling way. This is not so different from the assembly of late-night talk shows, described by Tuchman (1974: 131) as "the natural history of locating, preparing, and choreographing the typified personal characteristics of celebrities for public consumption." Producers of late-night talk are also concerned with, as Tuchman puts it, "designing lively interaction." They too conduct research, do pre-interviews, and strive for the proper combination of guests, especially if the celebrities interact with each other as well as the host. For that matter, so do the producers of more serious talk shows devoted to news and public affairs. And in orchestrating heated political debates among experts – which may include shouting, finger-pointing and other displays of less than "civil" discourse – they are producing their own particular version of the money shot. But the different topics discussed by ordinary people, and the kind of money shot expected of them, mean that producers of daytime talk face certain challenges the staff on shows like the public affairs debate forum *Crossfire* do not.

Given the trashy reputation of the genre, one of the biggest challenges is convincing people who may be reluctant to participate that it is in their best interest to do so or that their disclosures will serve some higher purpose. Many potential guests rightly perceive that the television industry is driven by financial rather than philanthropic concerns, and they question the motives of producers. Thus producers must be skilled salespeople with finely honed methods of persuasion. One *Diana* staffer described how he booked the cousin of the Menendez brothers after the man initially refused.[9] "I had to figure out what was going to press his buttons, what would spark some passion in this guy," the producer told me:

> So I said to him, "you know what? This whole thing with O.J. is over-shadowing the Menendez brothers, and Eric and Lyle are being forgotten. I bet people in Ohio think Eric and Lyle are sitting pretty in Beverly Hills when in reality they're sitting in prison. You should come on our show and talk about that, remind people what they're going through and how unfair it is." And you know what? He totally went for that. Because I was totally taking the side of Eric and Lyle – which I do anyway.

Because producers work in pairs, they sometimes play a version of "good cop/bad cop" with guests, where the "good" producer promises certain favors or agrees to certain conditions, and then blames the other "bad" producer when the favors fail to materialize or the conditions are not met. Depending on the situation, producers may appeal to a person's self-interest ("coming on the show may be your last chance to reconcile with your sister"; "getting this off your chest will make you will feel so much better"), altruism ("if sharing your story and educating others can help protect even *one* child, your daughter will not have died in vain") or sense of justice ("don't let your boyfriend get away with this, if you don't confront him he'll just do it again"). If a guest has initially agreed and then changed his or her mind – a common occurrence on *Randy*

– producers may stress the obligations of the informal contract, wheedle, cajole, promise special treatment, offer money (in the form of "lost wages" or *per diem* stipends), or claim their job is at stake ("If you don't show up, I'll lose my job"). Sometimes, if the story is big enough, producers will fly half-way across the country in order to beg in person. In general, the more sensitive the issue, and the greater the potential for embarrassment or exposure, the more difficult the show is to book.

Of course, the use of plugs helps bypass the potential problem of persuading guests, because most people responding to plugs are essentially volunteering their services. Nonetheless, if the topic involves conflict or the revelation of sensitive or incriminating information – and many do – then guests may reconsider their initial impulse to volunteer. Even if the person who first contacts the show does not reconsider, others connected to the story often will, and often within a day or two of the taping. Several producers mentioned last-minute cancellations, or "drop outs" as they are sometimes called, as absolutely the most frustrating aspect of the job. "I can't even put words around how frustrating that was," said a former *Ricki Lake* producer:

> It was just a nightmare. I'd book my show Friday and want to go to Cape Cod for the weekend and, you know, my show would be Monday and I'd check my voice mail Saturday night and half of them had canceled. So I'd stop what I was doing – I mean, I literally walked out of restaurants in between my appetizer and my main course and went back to work from a pay phone. It was just hateful. It was horrible.

Not surprisingly, the easiest guest to book is the wronged party, the person who wants to confront someone else about a misdeed or injustice, while the most difficult is the person being confronted. Although most talk shows now have official policies forbidding producers to lie – producers cannot tell a guest the show is about X when it is about Y, and are not supposed to lure guests on panel under false pretenses – they are nonetheless adept at withholding the full details of a given situation, choosing their words carefully to frame an issue in a particular light, and emphasizing only the benefits of participating. At *Randy*, producers will tell a prospective guest, "someone you know wants to surprise you on our show. We can't tell you who it is, or what the surprise is about – it could be good, it could be bad. But you'll get a free trip out of the deal, we'll fly you out here, put you up in a nice hotel, take you around by limousine, give you some spending money . . ."

In general, producers aim to book guests embroiled in a conflict at the last possible minute so they have little time to reconsider or press for more information. One veteran of the business, formerly with *Geraldo*, told me he used to book his best (i.e. most explosive) shows the night before taping. Producers at *Diana* are also wary of booking guests too far in advance, less because the topics are controversial than because of the simple fact that the longer people wait the more nervous they get, regardless of topic. "It's like going off the high dive as a kid," an associate producer there explained. "If you walk right up to the edge of the board and jump off, it's no problem, and afterward you're usually glad you did it. But if you stand up there staring down at the water and think about it too much, then you're probably going to back down." Another *Diana* producer said that if she books a guest more than four or five days before the show, she will chat with the person on the phone every day in order to reinforce their relationship – and the sense of obligation that comes with it.

Even when guests are perfectly willing to take the plunge – and the majority are – the very fact that they are "ordinary" people rather than experts or celebrities often impedes their easy insertion into the production sphere. Appearing on national television is not part of the daily routine for ordinary people. This is, in part, what makes them ordinary. They do not have professional media training, and their inexperience can make them high-maintenance, in need of constant attention and reassurance from producers. Nor do they have agents or publicists who handle their schedules and juggle their competing obligations. Many ordinary guests on *Diana* and the majority of guests on *Randy* are working-class individuals. They have jobs to go to, partners and children to care for, and are likely experiencing some personal problem or hardship – which is why they responded to a plug in the first place and why producers find them attractive. They may be battling cancer or AIDS; they may be homeless or abused; they may be feuding with their in-laws, cheating on their spouses, or going through an acrimonious divorce. The very things that make them willing and desirable guests also make their lives chaotic and their participation problematic. All of the communication between producers and guests prior to taping occurs by phone, yet if guests are poor or destitute they may not have a home let alone a telephone. If they are sick or addicted to drugs they may not be well enough to travel on tape day; if they have lost a child in a terrible tragedy their grief may overwhelm them; if they have multiple personality disorder, the personality who is interviewed and booked for the show may not be the same one who walks out on stage. And then there are the family members and friends whom guests bring along for support, people needing airline tickets, hotel accommodation, and special VIP seating in the audience.

People in crisis create extra work behind the scenes. At the same time they are the bread and butter of the genre, the people most likely to gain entry and the most attractive from a production stand-point. As we have seen, producers attempt to routinize their par-ticipation drawing on the conventions of newsgathering and other talk-show forms. But despite the routine procedures and all the preparatory work behind the scenes, an element of unpredictability remains. At no time are producers and guests alike more aware of this tension than on the day of taping itself.

Talk as show: airing dirty laundry

Clearly the groundwork for the money shot is laid long before a guest actually appears on stage. Producers have an easier time leading guests to an emotional brink in the moments before taping if the topic is sensitive or volatile to begin with, if the guest feels strongly about it, if producers have found others with an opposing viewpoint to challenge him or her, or if they deliberately orches-trate a surprise encounter they know will shock or provoke a vul-nerable guest on the air. Given these conditions, coaxing a dramatic performance from individuals may not seem so difficult, but this too is a challenge for producers – again, because the true stars of the show are "ordinary" people rather than experts or celebrities. Producers of late-night talk shows have long recognized that casual conversation is as performative as an entirely scripted affair, and that "being oneself is itself a constructed activity" (Tuchman 1974: 126), especially when one does it on national television. Celebrities on late-night talk shows thus rely on their acting skills to "play" themselves. Ordinary guests on daytime talk shows do exactly the same thing, but since they are not professionals, producers spend a great deal of time and energy preparing them for their roles. Indeed, this aspect of the work can be extremely stressful because, as Tuchman (1974: 122) puts it, "try as one might, one cannot accom-plish an interaction for someone else."

Although it rarely happens, producers of daytime talk live in constant fear that guests will fall apart on stage. According to one

10-year veteran of the genre, "sometimes when you sit somebody down in that chair and the lights go on and the cameras are on them and the audience is there, they freeze. I don't know if you've ever been on TV, but it's an intimidating experience. And I'm always amazed – *amazed* – that these little people from their trailer parks don't totally freak out on camera more often." "Freaking out" typically means clamming up or shutting down, or in some way failing to follow the pyramid structure of storytelling mandated by producers: not disclosing the most information first, getting the story mixed up or confused, or losing focus and going off on tangents.

To prevent this unhappy situation, all the energy expended on guests prior to taping is intensified the day of the show. It is on this day that the presentational or theatrical aspects of the genre are foregrounded, and the backstage efforts of producers come to fruition on stage. It is a day of tension and anxiety as well as excitement and drama, for staff and guests alike. Producers are on edge, making final adjustments to the script and snapping at their associates to tie up any loose ends. At some point there is a brief production meeting to go over the use of any videotape packages, stills, or live satellite hook-ups. Small crises erupt: guest no. 2 overslept and missed his flight, so he has to be moved to a later segment, and that means guests 3 and 4 cannot mention his affair until after his wife joins him on stage. Guest 5 has to stop at the pharmacy on the way from the airport to the studio because she forgot her medication, and guest 6 has changed her mind about coming altogether because she found out her sister-in-law will also be on the show. Guest 7 is in tears because the flight attendant spilled coffee on her best suit, and anything else will make her look fat on television.

When the guests begin to arrive the tension in the air increases perceptibly. At *Diana*, all guests or sets of guests have their own individual dressing rooms or trailers complete with name tag and gold star on the door. If the rooms are still in use from a previous taping (there are two, sometimes three tapings per day), they wait in the Green Room until the changeover is complete. At *Randy*, guests go directly to the Green Room or other backstage areas reserved for the same purpose, and because the topics typically deal with confrontations and surprises, producers must take great pains to keep people separated before the show. Guests whose clothes are inappropriate for television (horizontal stripes and plain white are both forbidden) or too casual (jeans, T-shirts, flannel) receive a visit from a staffer in wardrobe, and all guests at some point have their hair and make-up done. Meanwhile the stage manager wires them for sound, and the "talent coordinator" obtains written consent for their participation, along with a signed statement guaranteeing the authenticity of their story. After all this is complete, the most important remaining task is for producers to prep the guests. According to those I observed and interviewed, it is a fine line between over-rehearsing guests and providing just enough guidance so they do not freeze up. In this particular interaction, producers make a special effort to position them as both stars and experts of a sort – stars of the show and experts on their own personal experience.

The goal of backstage coaching is twofold. First, producers go over content with guests, reminding them of key points in their story and the order in which to make them. "You want guests to be fresh and spontaneous," a *Diana* producer explained:

> but on the other hand, we have very little time with these people and if they take ten minutes to answer something, it's not going to work. So I help them get to the point, I help them understand they have to start with the highlight of the answer and once they hit that they can digress all they want. You know, if the highlight of the story is that they found Jesus, I say to them, start with "I'm here today because I found Jesus." And *then* you can go back and say, "I was living on welfare in the gutter as a wino, and went through all these horrible things because I lost my job and my car and my house in a fire and da da da da da da." You know? But it's like, say what you found, and *then* how you got there. Don't build up to a point. And with some people that takes a lot of work because they want to tell you every little detail way on back to their childhood and their highschool prom and their hobbies and everything. They think they have all this time and they really don't.

Second, producers are concerned with style and performance – especially at *Randy*, more devoted to orchestrating emotional fireworks than is *Diana*. Although to a large degree the fire is built into the topic, producers use the moments just prior to taping to light the fuse. I knew the routine by heart:

> Just relax, you'll do fine. This is *your* life, you've lived it, so there's no wrong answers. Don't hold back on those emotions because this is your big chance to show millions of people you really care about this issue. If you're going to laugh, laugh big; if you're going to cry, cry big; if you get mad, show us *how* mad. This is *your* show, so take charge! If you have something to say, jump right in there, don't wait for the host to call on you, and don't let the other guests push you around. Now, when the host asks you to describe the first time you found your husband in bed with another woman, what are you going to say?

Randy guests are often carefully segregated until taping begins so the fight occurs on rather than off stage, and so producers can appear to back both sides of an issue. To the young girl and her 70-year-old fiancé in Green Room 1, a producer will say, "the important thing is to stand your ground, this show is about the two of you proving your love for each other." To the outraged mother in Green Room 2 the same producer will say, "don't be afraid to let him have it, this show is about getting your daughter away from that pedophile!"

Eventually the audience files in, while the technical crew and support staff rush back and forth, readying equipment and attending to last-minute details. *Diana* employs a comedian to warm up the audience while at *Randy* the stage manager does this job as well as his own. Both tell jokes ("your mamma is so dumb she thinks Taco Bell is a Mexican phone company") and keep up a steady stream of idle banter. Audience members are awarded prizes for singing, dancing, or telling jokes of their own. Most importantly, however, they are instructed in the finer points of audience etiquette, which forbids wearing ball caps, chewing gum, mugging for the camera, or speaking without being called on, but encourages asking questions of the panelists and giving "big reactions" (booing, gasping, clapping, etc.) to the events on stage. During the taping itself the warm-up person will often lead these reactions from the sidelines. Sometimes he has audience members rehearse the proper procedure for asking a question or making a comment ("stand up tall, lean over and speak into the mic but don't grab for it"), and he will always lead several rousing cheers in anticipation of the host's entrance. In general, the aim is to energize the audience, and to make people feel integral to the action and crucial to the success of the taping. "You can make or break this show," audience members are told. "Get involved! Show us how you feel! Ask questions! Remember, you represent all those viewers out there who can't ask questions for themselves. You represent America."

The coaching of guests and audience members, like the choice of topics, the pre-interviews, and the research, reveals the efforts of talk-show staffers to make predictable and routine what is, in the last instance, unpredictable: the behavior of ordinary people. Coaching guests increases the probability of obtaining the preferred or desired outcome on stage, and in this sense it has a number of parallels – the locker-room pep talk before the big game, or the process by which actors psyche themselves up for a dramatic performance. In my opinion, however, the most fitting comparison again takes us back to pornography. Prepping guests is not unlike preparing male porn stars for their sex scene: It gets them all "hot and bothered" so they can go out there and "show wood." With porn films, there is even a person – typically a young woman – employed on the set for this very purpose; she is called "the fluffer" (see Faludi 1995). Just as the fluffer arouses the actor to increase the probability of the money shot, producers "fluff" guests to increase the chance that they too will climax in the appropriate way. As with the male stars of pornographic films, sometimes talk-show guests can show wood, sometimes they cannot.

Most of the time – I would say 90 percent of the time – guests can. Indeed, producers have a far greater success rate than fluffers. This has to do not only with the inherent drama of the topics, but with the fact that talk-show guests, especially those responding to plugs, tend to be talk-show viewers as well. Personal crises aside, they know what is expected of them, they know what producers want, and they know how to deliver the goods. They do not need to be told to show their emotions or move their chair or stomp off the stage in a huff, because they see other guests do these things every day on television. Producers' concern about ordinary people as competent performers is thus often misplaced, for ordinary people who watch a lot of talk shows have in some sense been coached or trained long before they ever speak with a producer. (Expert guests, on the other hand, unless they have had prior talk-show experience, are more naive about the genre and may have unrealistic expectations about how an issue will be framed and their own participation managed.)

When producers put together a show they follow the same pyramid structure they urge on their guests. Thus the most "important" guest always takes the stage first, and sets the tone and framework for subsequent events (in a conflict situation, this person is typically the heroine of the story, the person who feels victimized by a past wrong or injustice). "Important" does not necessarily mean the guest has the most sensational story; it often means she is the most energetic and the best talker, and thus the one most likely to hold viewers' interest and prevent them from changing the channel. When *Diana* producers did a show about acquaintance rape, they debated back and forth about who to lead with: the woman repeatedly raped, stabbed, and left for dead, or the woman raped once by her best friend. Ultimately they decided to go with the second woman because she was a better storyteller, even though the story itself was less harrowing. Sometimes producers will switch guests at the last minute depending on what transpires in the Green Room. If guest no. 3 proves more excitable and easier to fluff, producers may bump guest no. 1 and put no. 3 in her place. According to an associate producer at *Diana*, a given show's success or failure depended in large measure on the producer's ability to make these kinds of last-minute spot decision about guests and the direction of the show. "The key is your ability to change," the producer explained:

> So you roll in that day and there's four guests there, and all of a sudden you realize the guest you thought would be in the third segment is so compelling, they're crying in the Green Room, dammit, they should be on the show first! And as a producer, that's your most important decision. Certainly planning the show beforehand is important – but you could get to the set and they [the guests] might not look or act like the person you talked to on the phone four days ago. Maybe on this day they had a bad morning, or they're PMSing, and all of a sudden they're really emotional about their kid being killed by gang members. Dammit, start with them! It's storytelling, so the most compelling story, however it's told, should be first.

In most cases the taping unfolds according to plan. Of course, when the plan itself calls for conflict or an emotional disclosure, there is still plenty of room for spontaneity. Ultimately, the tension between scriptedness and spontaneity is what many producers enjoy about the work. According to an associate producer at *Diana*:

> the fun part is to be out there on the floor the day of the show, you and the executive producer and the host, judging where the show is going, on the fly. Because – although generally you stick to your format – you've got to be able to change things. And some shows you will change a lot throughout; you'll say, "let this go long, dump that, move that." That's when it really gets exciting.

The most memorable show for a *Randy* producer had an additional element of unpredictability because of the topic: multiple personality disorder. "The show totally had the potential to be the best or the worst," the producer said:

> This girl had 15 personalities and she was confronting her mom who caused this, after she hadn't spoken to her in years. And there was a fear that, because she had multiple personalities, when she saw her mom again [on stage] she might suddenly become her two-year-old self and not talk at all. Instead of that she became her angry person and just went nuts! It was – this one scene is just like the best television moment you'll

ever see. It was so powerful and real. But she could have been, like, totally silent and withdrawn. It was just a wild card because there was so much emotion there. It was a wild card and we got lucky.

"Getting lucky" here means obtaining the money shot. But as we have seen, the money shot is really less a matter of luck and more a matter of careful design. To be sure, things inevitably happen that producers cannot foresee or control. Sometimes guests get nervous on camera and forget their training. Sometimes they get cold feet and drop out. Guests might be willing but unable to make the taping: They can fall ill, have an accident, get arrested. Someone in the audience could have an epileptic seizure during the show and unwittingly diffuse the emotion on stage. Sometimes, as one former *Ricki Lake* producer discovered, guests resolve their differences in transit and ruin the show before it even begins. "I couldn't believe it," he told me:

> This couple, they were, you know, fighting like cats and dogs 24 hours earlier and then they arrive all lovey-dovey. They're like, "oh everything is fine now, we're going to keep the baby and, you know, I'm never going to hit her again. We made up at 30,000 feet." I was like, "oh shit, come on, you're kidding me!"

By and large, however, guests and producers alike follow the script. Where guests are concerned, the venue alone – the stage, the lights, the cameras, the audience – helps to ensure compliance with producers' desires for a dramatic and compelling performance.

Talk shows and media scandal

To recap: Of all forms of television, daytime talk is considered among the most debased, characterized as trashy, sleazy, and even pornographic. Like pornography, daytime talk is a "scandalous" discourse with a bad reputation in which people display their private parts in public. More than anything else such displays have positioned talk-show guests in popular consciousness as trailer-park trash from middle America – below even talk-show viewers, who retain some vestige of dignity by remaining distanced voyeurs. The overriding assumption among critics is that guests are either naive, stupid, crazy, making it up, or deceived in some way by the production staff. Indeed, for critics who cannot fathom why anyone would go on a talk show and spill their guts unless tricked, manipulation has proved a most convenient explanation.

But the issue of manipulation and deception on talk shows is not so simple or clear cut. A certain amount of deception is inherent in talk-show production, since part of the work producers do is convince people to tell their stories on television, and then package and frame those stories as entertainment and spectacle. Every phase of the process involves the transformation and manipulation of an old reality into a new one. As one producer said to me, "asking a producer to describe manipulation is like asking a fish to describe the aquarium." As we have seen, staffers sometimes fail to give guests adequate information regarding their participation and that of other panelists – and in fact more than one guest complained to me about this. Sometimes, in order to get hostile parties together on the same stage, producers will emphasize very different aspects of the topic, as was the case for one of my informants who appeared on an episode of *Sally Jessy Raphael* about mother–daughter conflicts. Several guests have filed million-dollar lawsuits against talk shows for this very reason, claiming they were misled about the topic and then ambushed (Kaplan 1995).[10] Producers have also been known to offer bounty money to guests, if, for instance, they can start a fight with another guest in the first segment of the program. According to one informant, "punch that person out, start a fight, you get 500 extra dollars. There's no question that that goes on."

Then there is the issue of producers who knowingly book fake guests or who encourage guests to lie about their stories. One talk-show executive I interviewed admitted that, despite official policies to the contrary, some producers will "basically tell guests to say whatever they think will make a better show, whether it's true or not." I spoke with several guests who, at the urging of producers, either pretended to have problems they did not, or greatly exaggerated the details of their situation. One woman had appeared on *Ricki Lake* under the pretense of fighting with her best friend over whether or not women "needed" men. She said that not only were most of the "real" guests faking, but that the "relationship expert" on the show was actually the editor of a fitness column for a men's magazine. Likewise, when sociologist Adie Nelson appeared as an expert guest on a Canadian talk show about male escorts, she discovered after the taping that none of the panelists were in fact who they said they were. This sort of activity has led to several public exposés of talk-show fraud in recent years: ABC's *20/20*, for example, featured a number of guests from various shows – including a man who claimed to have raped more than 90 prostitutes over a three-year period – and in every case the guests claimed the host and producers knew without question the stories were fabricated.

More rarely, producers will book fake guests without knowing it, as when a comedy troupe from Toronto fooled the staff at *Jerry Springer*.[11] *Randy* staffers, too, were fooled while I was there: An aspiring actor named Tony appeared on the show with his aspiring actress girlfriend who pretended to be having an affair with Tony's ex-wife (also on panel, played by a friend of the couple). Ironically, guests of this sort often make additional talk-show appearances – starring as their "real" selves – in order to talk about why they were pretending to be somebody else. Typically these individuals are, like Tony, struggling actors or comedians. In fact, Tony later told me in an interview that he had been on four or five different talk shows in recent months in order to compile a "demo" tape for his agent. Thus deception and deceit on daytime talk shows is a complicated matter: Not only do producers sometimes mislead or lie to guests, but guests mislead producers, and producers and guests together mislead viewers.

Manipulation and media discourse

There are undoubtedly many examples of manipulation and deception behind the scenes. But I argue that focusing on the extremes of manipulation is problematic. It not only reproduces the very sensationalism that critics condemn talk shows for, it tends to mask the ways in which "manipulation" is subtle and systemic, built into the routines and practices of all media production. On talk shows, decisions are made every day about what topics to pursue, how to locate guests, what is a compelling story, and how best to tell it. Such manipulation is inescapable in a media context, and, juicy exposés of talk-show fraud aside, it is this sort of manipulation that best characterizes the daily grind behind the scenes. Daytime talk shows, like any other form of media, do not simply hold a mirror up to society, reflecting the world back to itself; indeed, if there is any way the mass media can be said to "reflect" at all, they do so, as Gitlin (1980) has noted, like mirrors in a fun house: by exaggerating, distorting, transfiguring, transforming. Guests without any media experience go on a show expecting a faithful reproduction of their stories. They are then surprised to find themselves caught in the very act of mediation. Thus when guests complain about their experience on talk shows, it is typically not about deliberate manipulation or exploitation at the hands of producers but about the ways in which the stories they tell producers on the phone become something different on stage, or about the inability of the forum to meet their goals and expectations. They complain about the process of selection and exclusion, ways of framing issues and narrating events that govern not just talk shows but the production of meaning in mass culture more generally. Indeed, deceptive practices are inherent in all human interaction, for there is no "pure" or unmediated discourse.

The ways in which talk shows mediate the experiences of ordinary people are not random or haphazard but systematic and patterned; daytime talk institutionalizes certain kinds of manipulation. In doing so, however, it has much in common with other forms of media, especially the news. Sociologists and other scholars have documented in rich detail the ways in which the news media privilege individual solutions to complex, social problems; decontextualize issues and events; maintain "objectivity" by balancing opposing viewpoints; seek to entertain audiences as well as inform them; and emphasize deviance, conflict, and violence over normal, consensual relations (Cohen and Young 1973; Tuchman 1978; Gans 1979; Gitlin 1980; Hartley 1982) – all things for which talk shows are criticized. In fact, sociologists themselves are frequently guilty of focusing on deviance, conflict, and violence over normal, consensual relations. Even a cursory glance at the monthly job bulletin for the discipline reveals that fully two-thirds of all jobs advertised are for criminologists and scholars studying crime, deviance, and social control.

One of the most common complaints among talk-show guests, especially those with an agenda for public advocacy or education, is that the genre is too much show and too little talk, that guests have too little time to tell their stories as they ought to be told. Guests typically understand they have to deliver their narrative concisely; nevertheless, they are frequently shocked at how little of what they prepared to say prior to taping actually gets said during the show. In fact, one veteran of the industry insisted this was by far the most pervasive kind of manipulation on talk shows:

Eighty percent of the manipulation that goes on, even with shows like *Ricki Lake* and *Jenny Jones*, is the manipulation to cut to the chase. In other words, we only have 42 minutes and some change to get to the point. What we want [guests] to do is cut the exposition and get to that sound bite, in much the same way politicians do, get to the sound bite so we can have a dramatic and entertaining show. That's the manipulation that goes on most of the time.

Daytime talk undoubtedly does forgo explanation and context in favor of sound bites, but this practice is not unique to the genre. As one of my expert guests insisted, he has greater opportunity to articulate and explain his point of view on a talk show like *Oprah* or *Geraldo* than he does on the CBS evening news: "I could be on a national network news program for 15 or 20 seconds, and I've been on *Oprah* for an hour!" he said. "So which one is tabloid, which one is ethical, which one is responsible? Well, from my point of view, I'd rather be on *Oprah* or *Geraldo*."[12]

Like daytime talk shows, other forms of media are self-referential or "incestuous," turning to other media texts for ideas, information, sources, and contacts. Almost all mass-media organizations seek to maximize profits, and most media professionals believe that a dramatic personal narrative will impact on people in a way that abstract generalizations and statistical data cannot. It is for this reason that virtually all media texts – especially televisual ones – deliver their own particular versions of the money shot. All "good" television is built around moments of dramatic revelation; all television, from news and documentary to soap opera and sports, aims to stimulate people visually, give people a look, let people see for themselves (hence the importance of slow motion and the close-up). Indeed, to the extent that television itself is a visual discourse devoted to making public and visible what would otherwise remain private and invisible (see Meyrowitz 1985), it can be seen as a kind of machine for producing the money shot. Desire for the money shot was the driving force behind Allen Funt's long-running *Candid Camera* series, which deliberately placed ordinary people in extraordinary situations in order to provoke them into losing their cool. This desire is also what compels television reporters to interview people immediately after they have experienced a terrible shock or tragedy – a form of ambushing if there ever was one. Randy himself made this point in our interview:

> For 10 years I used to anchor the news, and every day we would jam a microphone in the face of someone who didn't ask to be on the air – someone coming out of the courthouse, someone coming out of a divorce, out of a scandal. And you go into their homes and you ask them a question. Sometimes they're humiliated, sometimes you embarrass their families, but you do it anyway – and we say, "oh well, it's OK because it's the news."

Producing the money shot inevitably involves deceptive practices. Talk-show guests are often disgruntled or dissatisfied with the ways in which their experiences are appropriated and transformed for mass consumption: They get angry at hosts and producers for twisting their words, taking things out of context, framing an issue or event in a particular light, making their story into something it is not. These are certainly legitimate concerns, but other people appearing on TV or in the popular press complain of the very same things. Critics feel scandalized by the tendency of daytime talk to fictionalize reality, to compromise truth and authenticity for the sake of ratings. But again, pointing the finger at talk shows alone obscures the ways in which all media practices blur the boundary between fact and fiction. It also tends to ignore the structural causes for this blurring.

Talk-show staffers struggle with the issue of authenticity on a daily basis; after all, "real" stories told by "ordinary" people are the bedrock of the genre. Over and over I witnessed producers at both *Diana* and *Randy* deliberately reject people who appeared overly eager to get on TV, or whose lives seemed to fit every topic under the sun, or whose stories kept changing from one day to the next (a *Maury Povich* producer I interviewed called such individuals "talk-show sluts"). I also saw the executive producer at *Randy* cancel a show altogether only minutes before taping because it was discovered that one of the guests was lying about her identity. At the same time, the structural demands of the workplace militate against authenticity. Although producers desire real guests with real problems – people who are not slick or practiced, who express genuine emotion, are not "media savvy," and have never been on a talk show before – these are the guests who, in some ways, pose the greatest challenge to producers because the very qualities that make them "real" make them more difficult to manage in routine ways. The pressure of deadlines, the nature of the topics, and the performances required of guests actually push producers toward people who *are* media savvy, have had prior talk-show experience, and may even be actors faking their stories. Even many "real" ordinary guests have had prior media exposure, since producers often locate them in the first place by perusing already existing media texts. Thus the blurring of fact and fiction is not a conspiracy but a practicality, one that operates in other forms of reality television as well, particularly news and documentary (see Hartley 1982; Sobchack and Sobchack 1987).

The most significant feature talk shows share with other media, however, is the tendency to deny ordinary people routine access unless they engage in exceptional behavior. Talk shows are by no means alone in this regard. The mass media are generally recognized as a powerful social and cultural force, central to the orchestration of everyday life and consciousness. They select what is important to know about the world and frame how we ought to know it. Therefore coverage or exposure serves a powerful legitimating function, not only for politicians, experts, and celebrities, but for "ordinary" people as well. Unlike many experts and celebrities, however, ordinary people exist largely outside the official channels and established routines of news making and the entertainment industry; consequently they must often do and say *extra*ordinary things to gain entry. Herbert Gans (1979) noted long ago that experts and officials comprise between 70 and 80 percent of all individuals appearing in the US domestic news media, both print and electronic; ordinary people, on the other hand, obtain only about a fifth of the available time or space. And aside from a small percentage who are voters or survey respondents, these ordinary people are newsworthy precisely because they are disruptive or deviant. Thus the tendency of media critics to distance daytime talk as the "other," as if talk shows were the only discourse "othering" ordinary people, is more than a little disingenuous. Talk shows simply exaggerate or throw into high relief the manipulative practices of all media forms. Talk shows are especially maligned, however, because the particular ways in which they "other" ordinary people violate conventional middle-class standards of moral conduct and "good taste" – an issue I take up in the final section below.

Trash, class, and the money shot

I have argued that emphasizing manipulation and exploitation on daytime talk shows is problematic because it tends to mask the ways in which "manipulation" is part and parcel of all media production. But there is a second reason why this focus is problematic. Emphasizing manipulation behind the scenes, especially the ways in which unscrupulous producers deceive, and lie to, gullible guests, prevents us from seeing guests as rational human beings with desires and motives of their own, as individuals who can and do act in their own interests despite their positioning as a subordinate group in the talk-show world. It is true that guests are inserted differently than producers into this world. Although producers themselves are subject to the dictates and demands of more highly-placed industry professionals, they clearly have more power than guests to set the agenda and terms of debate, arguably the ultimate form of power in a media context. The show's topic and the way it is framed then set into motion an elaborate machinery of production that is difficult to challenge – especially for guests who are outsiders to the business. Once the day of taping arrives, the show presses forward with the inexorability of a speeding locomotive; once you get on it is hard to get off or change direction.

But the popular attitude that considers guests ignorant or duped is both limited and paternalistic. The actual appearance of a panelist on stage is the end result of a long process of negotiation, and sometimes struggle, between producers and guests. One informant described it as a kind of dance where both partners want to lead, and while producers lead most of the time, they recognize very well that without guests they do not have a show, and thus they cannot afford to upset or alienate people on a consistent or routine basis. When guests know they have a desirable story, it becomes a bargaining chip for imposing a range of conditions and demands, including airfare and hotel accommodation for friends and family, financial compensation for "lost wages," and – most significantly – increased airtime. Guests can exert pressure on producers at various points along the way, but the closer to showtime the more leverage they have. There was not a single producer I spoke with who did not acknowledge the struggle between producers and guests over the framing and telling of stories, and express frustration at what they felt was their lack of control over guests' behavior. What makes daytime talk unique and compelling – real people telling real stories – is also what introduces an element of instability into the system. I have seen guests cancel at the last minute, walk off the set in the middle of a taping, or simply clam up and refuse to talk. In general, the more volatile the topic, the greater the potential for disruption and rebellion, and staff generally have little recourse for dealing with "unsatisfactory" guests save to strike them from their Rolodex address file.

Depending on the topic, guests frequently have specific agendas for making an appearance on national television. Indeed, perhaps the most common and compelling reason cited by guests is the opportunity to proselytize, champion a cause, or make an appeal before an audience of millions. A woman may agree to appear on

a show about child-custody battles because she feels the legal system is stacked against single mothers and she wants to warn other
women; a date-rape survivor may tell a producer, "I'll come on the
show and talk about being raped, but only if I also get to talk about
how rape education policies on college campuses are in violation
of federal guidelines." Producers dislike conditions of this sort,
because on the one hand it subverts their control over the framing
of the issue, and on the other it tends to make for "bad" television,
according to the accepted norms and standards of the industry.
Producers want "real" people to provide first-hand testimony about
their personal experience as it relates to the topic at hand, the more
emoting the better. They do not want distanced analysis, or complicated discussions of politics or law.

Most guests with an agenda for advocacy or education recognize
talk shows as an imperfect forum with inherent limitations. They
understand full well that to enter this forum is to enter a world
and a reality not of their making. With 42 minutes of airtime, a
panel of four or five people plus "plants" in the audience, video
footage, and questions from audience members, any one individual
rarely has more than a few minutes in the spotlight to make a
point. "It was a circus," one *Diana* guest said in disgust, "there was
no time to really address the issue or have a serious discussion."
Thus in the clash of agendas between producers and guests, guests
often lose. But they participate anyway because they have few other
opportunities to reach a mass audience. Patricia Priest (1995) found
much the same thing when she interviewed roughly thirty guests
from the *Donahue* show, all of whom were positioned as sexually
deviant in one way or another. These guests were keenly aware of
the uneven nature of the playing field and their status as freaks,
but they willingly traded private revelations for the chance to enter
the public arena. They capitulated to the producers' (and presumably the audience's) thirst for intimate details in order to maneuver
a space, however small and fleeting, in which to educate the mainstream and contest prevailing societal depictions of their group.
As Gamson (1996: 83) puts it, "the fact that talk shows are exploit-
ative spectacles does not negate the fact that they are also opportunities" – especially for those who are silenced, marginalized, or
disenfranchised.

Of course, not everyone who appears on a talk show has such
lofty aspirations. Some just want the excitement of being on TV,
and it does not much matter what they have to say or do – they do
not take talk shows seriously and they do not expect others to take

them seriously either. Some see talk shows as a training ground for careers in the industry.[13] Some people have never to been to LA, or New York, or Chicago, and could not afford to go otherwise. Some are vengeful and have an ax to grind. Some have been wronged or victimized and want public validation for their suffering. Some turn to talk shows specifically for counseling or therapy because the health and welfare system has let them down. Some make embarrassing or shocking disclosures because the attention paid them by a producer may be the first time anyone has listened to them in a long, long, while. The price of admission notwithstanding, such guests often feel they are using talk shows as much as talk shows are using them. Indeed, their participation is a good illustration of what anthropologist Michel de Certeau (1984) calls "poaching," whereby individuals, communities, or subcultures trespass on the property of others, using it to advance their own goals and desires in ways not necessarily anticipated or sanctioned by those in control. Like de Certeau's native inhabitants who make of the rituals and laws imposed on them something quite different than their conquerors had in mind, or the reader who insinuates into another person's text the ruses of her own pleasures and appropriations, talk-show guests work within the limited space given them, making do with what they have.

It is true that guests can always say "no" and decline a producer's invitation to participate. As Randy said to me, "unlike the news, nobody gets on a talkshow by accident. You write letters, you make phone calls, you go through interviews, you get on an airplane – you have to really, really, want to be on." The fact that guests can "just say no" and do not is less a comment on how trashy they are and more a comment on the exclusivity of television and the limited access of ordinary people to media representation. Jerry Springer put it this way on a special episode devoted to talkshow guests:

> Surely the official institutions of our society have no trouble getting their voices heard. A president can hold a prime-time news conference or deliver a speech from the Oval Office. The rich and famous can find their way to a microphone or camera any time they want. Major corporations can buy all the commercial time their dollars and good sense warrant. Most people, however, don't have that kind of clout, but that doesn't mean they don't have a cause or concern or pain or view that, to their mind, deserves an audience or needs to be aired.

At the same time, talk shows do not attract just any anybody. *Who* participates in the genre is also structurally determined. Certain groups of people are more vulnerable to experiencing the kinds of problems talk shows capitalize on (which is, in part, why talk shows tackle them), and certain groups of people are more willing to talk about these problems on national television. As Ehrenreich (1995) and other critics observe, one never sees investment bankers bickering on *Geraldo*, or *Montel Williams* recommending therapy to sobbing professors. The problem with daytime talk, according to Ehrenreich, is that it goes after the most vulnerable and disenfranchised, making entertainment out of lives distorted by hardship and poverty. "With few exceptions," she writes, "guests are drawn from trailer parks and tenements, from bleak streets and narrow, crowded rooms ... This is class exploitation, pure and simple. What's next – 'homeless people so hungry they eat their own scabs?'" (1995: 92). Daytime talk *is* a discourse about class. But the fact that talk shows target waitresses and construction workers over CEOs and politicians is not simply a matter of class exploitation. Producers, scholars, and critics alike marvel at why guests do it, why they are seemingly complicit in their own degradation. But producers, scholars, and media critics typically have other, more socially acceptable forums in which to express their views. This is a matter of class privilege and deeply-entrenched distinctions between high and low culture, as is the notion of what constitutes a "socially acceptable" forum in the first place.

What most intellectuals find regrettable about talk shows is the *manner* in which ordinary people (and the issues associated with them) gain visibility on television, not the issues or the visibility themselves. To be sure, many talk shows reproduce deeply-held cultural stereotypes, since emotional and bodily displays have long been the purview of women, the working class, and people of color. In the binary organization that opposes mind to matter, culture to nature, and textuality to orality, "the body" is the domain in which these groups have been allowed and encouraged to operate (see Turner 1984; Elias 1994; Diprose 1994; Grosz 1994). Exposing their private parts in public is largely what distinguishes "ordinary" guests from other kinds of guest, especially celebrities, who are occasionally featured on daytime as well as late-night talk shows. As the talent executive at *Diana* said to me:

> if we're going to get celebrities to come in here, they're not going to come in and talk about whether they were sexually abused, raped, or whatever. You know what I'm saying? You don't go to Barbra Streisand and ask her to talk about not getting along with her mother. And you don't ask her to share the stage with a dozen other people talking about that stuff either.

In other words, the more powerful the people, the more sacred their boundaries, the less they reveal about themselves in public, and the more they control the conditions of the revealing. Celebrities and experts typically have more status, power, and prestige than ordinary people, and for this reason they are not expected to deliver the same kind of money shot. They do not – or only rarely and with great fanfare – disclose intimate or private information, admit to personal failures and transgressions, or bicker with friends and family on national television. Even when politicians or other high-status figures reveal aspects of their personal lives in public (or have aspects of their personal lives revealed by others), such revelations often function to position them as "ordinary folk" just like everybody else. Thus the fact that ordinary guests on talk shows do these things as a matter of generic expectation helps to secure and reinforce their status as ordinary people – and, more often than not, ordinary people of a particular class. The more dramatic the emotional outburst or physical display – the louder the yelling, the harder the sobbing, the more vicious the conflict or confrontation – the lower the class (and the less like celebrities) they are perceived to be. Not surprisingly, celebrity guests were rare on *Randy* compared to on *Diana*, *Randy* being the "trashier" show devoted to a hard-core version of the money shot.

On the other hand, why should emotional and bodily displays be considered trashy? As Bourdieu (1984) and others have observed, concepts of good taste, appropriate conduct, or aesthetic merit are not natural and universal; rather they are rooted in social experience and reflect certain class interests. Middle-class disgust with daytime talk is thus not unlike middle-class disgust with the tabloid press or *Hustler* magazine; all are reactions to class-conscious texts whose display of the body (and bodily functions) offends bourgeois sensibility (see Mellencamp 1992; Kipnis 1992). This sense of offense can itself reproduce and sustain class inequalities. In the realm of talk TV, contempt for airing one's dirty laundry in public reinforces the functioning of class privilege, for this reluctance is part of what constitutes one's sense of being middle- or upper-class.

This is not to suggest that talk shows are especially democratic, open, and accessible to all, or, more significantly, that talk shows are somehow authentic or accurate reflections of ordinary people and their concerns. Like every other form of representation, they offer a *mediated* reality – indeed, there is no other kind. In this sense, daytime talk is not so much a discourse about class as one about the television industry's assumptions about class, for if yelling and screaming and sobbing and bickering come so naturally to the "kind" of guest attracted to daytime talk shows, then why do producers spend so much time and energy preparing them for their roles? The fact that many guests – especially on shows like *Randy* – have to perform in these ways for the privilege of television exposure is a price they are willing to pay, not because they are stupid or naive or have false consciousness, but because they recognize they are playing a particular kind of role in a particular kind of forum. Given this, perhaps what truly scandalizes critics is the possibility that ordinary people on talk shows are *not* duped and manipulated. Perhaps what is most disturbing is that ordinary people understand the parameters, participate willingly anyway, and play their parts well.

Conclusion

To summarize, talk-show production is highly structured and constrained, characterized by norms, conventions, routines, and practices that ensure a particular kind of public space populated by particular kinds of people who do and say particular kinds of things. But if that public space is undignified or debased, it is important to ask why by looking at inequalities in society at large, as well as the entire mass-media system of which talk shows are but one part. If talk shows are to be criticized for turning the experiences of ordinary people into a circus sideshow, then the so-called respectable media must also be taken to task for rendering these people so completely invisible in the first place that daytime talk is their best or only option for public exposure. Indeed, the silence in our culture generally about the very people and issues daytime talk gives voice to plays a crucial role in shaping the genre, since the more excluded a group or topic has been, the more likely it is to appear on a daytime talk show. This is precisely what Foucault (1980) meant when he insisted that a given discourse could only be understood in relation to the interchange *among* elements, and not by reference to a level of manipulation or intentionality inherent in the discourse itself.

Never having been particularly welcome on *Nightline*, ordinary people are infiltrating the system at one of its most accommodating points. Their inclusion does not challenge the established order of the television industry, and it does not necessarily improve the representation of marginalized groups. But it does dramatize a larger conflict over the "proper" uses of television, and the ways in which ordinary people enter an arena formerly off-limits to them. As Gamson (1996) has observed, seizing the microphone is a complicated sort of power in a media culture because the voice that emerges is never only yours: If you speak, you must prepare to be used.

Notes

1 When I use the term "ordinary" to describe talk-show guests I simply mean people who are not experts and not celebrities; I am not necessarily suggesting they are average, typical, or representative of the population in general. Indeed, talk-show guests, like the subjects of most media accounts, are often chosen for their unique rather than typical qualities.

2 More specifically, I spent the entire 1994–5 television season (roughly a year) working approximately 30 hours a week as a student intern on *Diana*, and an additional two months in the spring of 1996 interning at *Randy*, both nationally televised talk shows produced in major US cities. My duties included transcribing the 1–800 telephone line for show ideas, viewer comments, and responses to on-air advertisements ("plugs") for guests; booking the studio audience over the phone; opening fan mail and filing faxes; typing thank-you notes dictated by the host to guests who had recently appeared on the show; assisting the "talent coordinator" on the set with guests by preparing the dressing rooms, getting guests in and out of hair and make-up, talking with them to calm their nerves, and generally seeing to their needs; answering the phones in the control booth during taping; and running errands and doing odd tasks to help producers, such as scanning videotapes for potentially useful footage, contacting former guests about the upcoming air dates for their shows, and occasionally pre-interviewing potential guests. During the last few weeks at *Diana* one of the producers was called out of town, and I stepped in to help her partner put together the final two shows of the season, researching the topics, finding and interviewing guests, learning how to write and edit the script, attending production meetings, and being on the set with the other producers on tape days. In my last days at *Randy* I was fortunate to have comparable access to producer–guest interactions (i.e. above and beyond that of a typical intern) when one of the associate producers allowed me to shadow him during the production of several shows. In addition, I attended more than a dozen live talk-show tapings in Los Angeles, New York, and Chicago over a two-year period, and took part in several focus-group interviews between producers and audience members at one show taped in Santa Monica, California. This aspect of the fieldwork proved invaluable not only because it allowed me to compare live performances across a range of shows (especially East Coast versus West Coast) and to note the different ways in which audiences were prepared for their roles, but also because on more than one occasion I was able to talk with the guests after the show

and before they left the studio grounds, and sometimes arrange more formal interviews with them. Finally, I interviewed a large number of people for this study, sometimes the same ones I worked with on *Diana* and *Randy*, sometimes producers and other industry professionals referred to me by my contacts at these shows. Overall I conducted about 20 formal taped interviews with producers, 10 with other talk-show staff (such as executive and supervising producers, talent executives, researchers, production assistants, etc.), 3 with talk-show hosts, and roughly 35 with talk-show guests (25 "ordinary" guests and 10 "expert" guests). While the length of each interview varied considerably, most lasted between one and three hours.

3 In early March of 1995, producers at *Jenny Jones* convinced a young man from Michigan named Jonathan Schmitz to appear on an episode devoted to "secret crushes." He went expecting a female admirer, but was confronted with Scott Amedure, a gay man from the same home town. Three days after the taping (which never aired), Schmitz shot Amedure point-blank in the chest because, as he later told police, the embarrassment of the disclosure had eaten away at him. Ignoring the homophobic nature of the crime, defense lawyers in the case blamed the producers for failing to warn Schmitz his secret admirer might be a man, and the incident sparked a nationwide media debate about the ethics and tactics of talk-show production. Thus the biggest scandal – the murder itself – was triggered by a series of smaller scandals: the show's topic, the behavior of the guests, and, most significantly, the behavior of the producers. Also, because there was little discussion outside the gay press of Schmitz's homophobia – after all, why should Amedure's admission be any more embarrassing than a woman's? – the media response to the murder was itself "scandalous" to some degree. Partly as a response to the negative press generated by the *Jenny Jones* murder, the Kaiser Foundation, a non-profit family planning organization, sponsored a two-day Talk Summit in New York later the same year which brought together daytime talk-show hosts, producers, executives, and experts to discuss the talk-show "problem." On the eve of the summit, former Secretary of Education William Bennett and Senator Joseph Lieberman staged a bi-partisan press conference to denounce daytime talk's "salacious and sensational accounts of sexual perversion, cruelty, violence, and promiscuity" (Gaines 1995). Their larger message to viewers and advertisers: "Just say no" to TV trash.

4 *Strike it Rich* was similar to *Queen for a Day* but did not last as long on the air. According to Priest (1995: 6), the producers came under considerable fire from health and welfare officials for luring the country's destitute to New York City, where they sometimes waited for weeks in the hopes of receiving money and gifts on the program. A third game/talk hybrid was called *Stand Up and Be Counted*. Less focused on tragedy and misfortune, it dealt with an "average" woman's personal dilemma, chosen from letters submitted by viewers: should Mrs Smith use her inheritance to travel the world or invest in a comfortable retirement? Should Miss Jones marry and move away or forgo the marriage and stay close to her roots? After a discussion of the dilemma between host and "contestant" on a set resembling a Victorian-style front porch, several members of the studio audience voiced their opinions, and then the entire audience voted on what the woman should do. Not bound to accept the vote, she returned the following week

to announce her decision. Viewers at home also participated by writing letters giving advice, and the best letter each week won a car, vacation, or household appliance (see Munson 1993: 54–5).

5 According to Rose (1985: 338), "Donahue was a probing interviewer who placed great emphasis on letting his studio audience (99 percent of which were women) ask the questions." In his autobiography, Donahue himself reveals that audience participation developed somewhat by accident when women began asking good questions and offering astute comments during commercial breaks. At some point both host and executive producer realized that integrating the off-stage interaction would make for a better, more interesting show (Donahue 1979).

6 King World Syndication Company estimates that as many as 50 million people watch talk shows on a daily basis. *Oprah* alone attracts between 15 and 20 million viewers in the US daily (Squire 1994; Peck 1994) and airs in more than a hundred countries, including, most recently, parts of Eastern Europe and Africa. According to Livingstone and Lunt (1994), the audience for daytime talk in Britain and the US consists largely of folks who spend at least part of their day at home: home makers, students, part-time and shift workers, the unemployed, and the retired, with gender as the most reliable demographic predictor. Goldstein (1995) cites the following statistics from the Annenberg School for Communication: 75 percent of talk-TV viewers are women, 60 percent are under the age of 54, and more than half live in households with incomes under $30,000. In a content analysis of talk-show guests, Greenberg and Smith (1995) provide an indirect profile of viewers. They report that the demographic profile of guests reflects that of viewers, which in turn is fairly consistent with the 1992 Census figures for the actual US population – the main difference being the over-representation of women and African Americans: women comprise 52 percent of the actual population but 63 percent of talk-show guests, while African Americans comprise roughly 13 percent of the actual population but 18 percent of talk-show guests.

7 The National Talkshow Guest Registry is essentially a large database of potential guests (both expert and ordinary) organized according to topic. Anyone with a "good" story or the right credentials willing to appear on a talk show can register for a nominal monthly fee of three dollars. For a larger sum, producers can purchase from the registry a list of suitable guests.

8 While Berkman (1995) reports that many guests procured by stringers are actually aspiring actors willing to assume fake identities, one of my informants, a retired producer formerly with *Geraldo* and *Ricki Lake*, contested this framing. He said it was not so much that the guests are lying or assuming false identities as the fact that they live in very different worlds than producers do, especially in terms of class and race, and producers have few other means of accessing them. "Stringers are used for certain kinds of shows," the producer said. "You know, if producers are looking for girls who dress like sluts, and the carts come up empty, they'll go to Newark, New Jersey or Detroit or someplace and they'll pay some girl 500 dollars and they'll say, 'find five girls who dress like sluts.' That happens all the time. 'Cause to be perfectly blunt, these lily white producers out of these preppy little schools, they wouldn't know the first

thing about going to the inner city and finding guests. It's the only way they can do it. You know, when you see heroin addicts and prostitutes on these shows, how else – do you think some 23-year-old Polly Pure Bread is riding around Watts, or like, you know, South Bronx? Forget it."

9 Eric and Lyle Menendez were two brothers charged with and ultimately convicted of murdering their wealthy parents for the inheritance money. When I spoke with the producer who booked the cousin on *Diana*, it was prior to the brothers' second trial and subsequent guilty verdict.

10 It is important to note, however, that the producer is not the only person responsible for deceiving the guest. When one person confronts or ambushes another, that person has typically initiated contact with the producer (by responding to a plug) and then served as a kind of accomplice or confederate by providing the producer all the necessary information to persuade the other party in the conflict to participate. So while the producer or the show itself can certainly be faulted for providing an outlet for vengeful or vindictive behavior, the confederate is also morally culpable, particularly given that he or she is often a close relative or former friend of the other guest.

11 Three members of a Canadian comedy troupe posed as guests on an episode titled "Honey, have I got a secret for you!" On the show, a man told his wife that he was having an affair with their teenage babysitter. When the babysitter was brought on stage, the wife broke down sobbing, and continued to sob with such vigor and anguish that the trio had to leave the stage after the second segment. Several days later they revealed to the *Toronto Star* that their performance was a hoax. Springer is now suing them for violating their signed release form guaranteeing truthfulness (see Slotek 1995; Belcher 1995; Zorn 1995).

12 Sound-bite manipulation occurs in academic contexts too. Talk-show guests complain that producers listen carefully to their entire stories, take everything down in detail, and then focus on only one aspect or element for the show. But sometimes I did exactly the same thing when conducting interviews and writing them up. And just as producers sometimes dropped guests from a show altogether after they arrived at the studio, I would spend two or three hours interviewing someone and perhaps not use a single word. As an ethnographer I spent countless hours in the field, took hundreds of pages of fieldnotes, and transcribed hundreds of pages of interviews – and then re-presented this material in a single book or article. All researchers, in fact, are like talk-show producers, in that they gather a wealth of information, and then sift, condense, and distill until only a nugget or drop remains at the end.

13 Indeed, a few individuals have been on so many different shows that industry insiders call them "professional talk-show guests."

References

Anderson, K. (1993). Oprah and Jo-Jo the dogfaced boy. *Time*, October 11: 94.
Belcher, W. (1995). Group springs worthy dupe on host. *Tampa Tribune*, February 11.

Berkman, M. (1995). Daytime talk shows are fraud-caster. *New York Post*, December 4.

Bourdieu, P. (1984). *Distinction: A Social Critique of the Judgment of Taste*. Cambridge, MA: Harvard University Press.

de Certeau, M. (1984). *The Practice of Everyday Life*. Berkeley, CA: University of California Press.

Cohen, S. and Young, J. (eds) (1973). *The Manufacture of News*. Beverly Hills, CA: Sage.

Diprose, R. (1994). *The Bodies of Women: Ethics, Embodiment, and Sexual Difference*. New York: Routledge.

Donahue, P. (1979). *Donahue: My Own Story*. New York: Simon & Schuster.

Ehrenreich, B. (1995). In defense of talkshows. *Time*, December 4: 92.

Elias, N. (1994). *The Civilizing Process*. Oxford, UK and Cambridge, MA: Blackwell.

Faludi, S. (1995). The money shot. *New Yorker*, October 30: 64–87.

Fishman, M. (1980). *Manufacturing the News*. Austin, TX: University of Texas Press.

Foucault, M. (1980). *The History of Sexuality: volume 1*. New York: Random Books.

Gaines, D. (1995). Jenny Jones saved my life. *Village Voice*, November 21.

Gamson, J. (1996). Do ask, do tell. *Utne Reader*, January/February: 79–83.

Gans, H. (1979). *Deciding What's News: A Study of CBS Evening News, NBC Nightly News, Newsweek, and Time*. New York: Pantheon.

Gitlin, T. (1980). *The Whole World is Watching*. Berkeley, CA: University of California Press.

Goldstein, R. (1995). The devil in Ms. Jones: Trash TV and the discourse of desire. *Village Voice*, November 21.

Greenberg, B. and Smith, S. (1995). *The Content of Television Talk Shows: Topics, Guests, and Interactions*. Report prepared for the Henry J. Kaiser Family Foundation by the Departments of Communication and Telecommunication, Michigan State University.

Grosz, E. (1994). *Volatile Bodies: Toward a Corporeal Feminism*. Bloomington, IN: Indiana University Press.

Hartley, J. (1982). *Understanding News*. London: Methuen.

Jarvis, J. (1994). Ricki Lake. *TV Guide*, July 2: 7.

Kaplan, J. (1995). Are talk shows out of control? *TV Guide*, April 1: 10–15.

Kipnis, L. (1992). (Male) desire and (female) disgust: Reading *Hustler*. In L. Grossberg, C. Nelson, and P. Treichler (eds), *Cultural Studies*. New York: Routledge.

Kneale, D. (1988). Titillating channels. *Wall Street Journal*, May 18: 1, 15.

Livingstone, S. and Lunt, P. (1994). *Talk on Television: Audience Participation and Public Debate*. London and New York: Routledge.

Mellencamp, P. (1992). *High Anxiety: Catastrophe, Scandal, Age, and Comedy*. Bloomington, IN: Indiana University Press.

Meyrowitz, J. (1985). *No Sense of Place: The Impact of Electronic Media on Social Behavior*. New York: Oxford University Press.

Munson, W. (1993). *All Talk: The Talkshow in Media Culture*. Philadelphia: Temple University Press.

Peck, J. (1994). Talk about race: Framing a popular discourse of race on *Oprah Winfrey*. *Cultural Critique*, 27 (Spring): 89–126.

Priest, P. (1995). *Public Intimacies: Talk Show Participants and Tell-All TV*. Cresskill, NJ: Hampton Press.

Rose, B. (1985). The talk show. In B. Rose (ed.), *TV Genres: A Handbook and Reference Guide*. Westport, CT: Greenwood Press.

Sirius, R.U. and St Jude. (1994). The medium is the message and the message is voyeurism. *Wired*, February: 46–50.

Slotek, J. (1995). He who laughs last: Talk show host Springer will sue over hoax. *Toronto Sun*, February 10.

Sobchack, V. and Sobchack, T. (1987). Historic overview: The development of the documentary film. In *An Introduction to Film*. Boston: Little, Brown.

Squire, C. (1994). Empowering women? *The Oprah Winfrey Show*. *Feminism and Psychology*, 4(1): 63–79.

Tuchman, G. (1973). Making news by doing work: Routinizing the unexpected. *American Journal of Sociology*, 79(1): 110–31.

Tuchman, G. (1974). Assembling a network talk-show. In Gaye Tuchman (ed.), *The TV Establishment: Programming for Power and Profit*. Englewood Cliffs, NJ: Prentice-Hall.

Tuchman, G. (1978). *Making News: A Study in the Construction of Reality*. New York: Blackwell.

Turner, B. (1984). *The Body and Society: Explorations in Social Theory*. New York: Blackwell.

Williams, L. (1989). *Hard Core: Power, Pleasure, and the "Frenzy of the Visible"*. Berkeley, CA: University of California Press.

Zorn, E. (1995). Jerry Springer gets a dose of his own talk show medicine. *Chicago Tribune*, February 11.

9 Apollo Undone:

The Sports Scandal

David Rowe

A record-breaking, gold-medal-winning sprinter is disqualified and disciplined for taking performance-enhancing drugs, makes a failed comeback, and is banned for life for the same offense. The world's best heavyweight boxer goes to jail for the rape of a "beauty queen," is released and returns to the ring, after converting to Islam. The USA's favorite basketball personality goes public with a socially-stigmatized medical condition, realizes his Olympic "dream," is then deemed to be a health risk and frozen out of domestic competition by former members of the national team, only to return as a player four years later, and then to retire "for good." An ice-skater is involved in a conspiracy to break the legs of her Olympian teammate and chief rival, seeking to pay off court fines through new careers as author, film star, and punk-rock singer, while a video claiming to cover her wedding night is circulated. A former champion American footballer turned sports commentator and film actor is tried and acquitted, after a long, televised trial, of the knife murder of the ex-wife he had previously battered and her male friend.

This is only a sample of the sports celebrity scandals which have in recent years generated and attracted the most intense media and public interest. Each has plotted a familiar, tabloid-lined path between homage and outrage, celebration and vilification, moralism and nihilism. They have taken sports news beyond the sports pages and into new realms of hyper-media, where information, analysis, censure, and pleasure intertwine in ways that defy rationalist critique. If we are to do more than remain in states of fascination and communicative ecstasy when confronted by such bizarre cultural phenomena, it is necessary to probe the sports-celebrity media scandal. Why and in which ways is sport integral to these scandals? What kinds of celebrity and sport are subject to scandal? How do celebrity sports scandals inform politico-cultural debates and discourses? These are by no means lightweight questions about ephemeral pseudo-events, because they go to the very heart of the elusive politics of the popular. Each scandal becomes an opportunity to deconstruct and interrogate those social ideologies and structures to which all forms of popular culture are tethered and from which each seeks release.

In this chapter I will analyze the concept of the celebrity and the particular variant in question, the sports star. It is necessary to outline the relationship between celebrity person and persona, and to review the terms of the "contract" between celebrities and audiences. This contract, I argue, has a specific character in the domain of sport, where heroic myths of the body are integral to the ideologies but, at the same time, are undermined by rather more prosaic and partisan forms of identification and competition. The celebrity sports scandal is a particularly dramatic exposure of the tension between those impulses which seek to place sports stars on an Olympian pedestal, those which strive to oppose and depose them, and also those which indulge in the ambivalent, if not guilty, pleasure of *schadenfreude*. The sports and general media are charged with the responsibility of covering all these angles, seeking the "serious" ramifications for sports and society suggested by a celebrity's fall from grace under the rubric of hard news. At the same time, they must honor the conventions of mock reproval, titillating detail, and ironic levity that mark the genre of soft news (Dahlgren and Sparks 1992). This dual and somehat contradictory function of the news media conditions the production, reproduction, and mutation of scandal.

The "truth" of scandal

Media scandals are constructed out of a certain moral absolutism that accompanies the condition of modernity; yet the mass-media spectacles, wild significatory spirals, paraphernelia merchandizing, on-the-street jokes, stand-up comedy routines, and induction into everyday speech that such outrages provoke are more obviously the products of the moral relativism and ironic detachment of postmodernity. A simultaneous confirmation and subversion of consensual moral order are, then, accomplished by media scandal, operating first to trace the boundaries of acceptable behavior through a process of (essentially Durkheimian) public shaming and the attachment of a "deviant" label, only to compromise the integrity of this structure of conformity and deviancy by eliciting a response of private moral ambivalence and guilty pleasure (principally of the voyeuristic gaze). In a discussion of the gossip produced by celebrity scandal, Therese Davis has noted the inherent instability of scandal's significatory spiral and ethical order, in which the scandalizing other is first alienated in binary fashion from the morally upright, only to be partially reintegrated through the collusive practice of self-recognition. The scandalized subject, she argues, comes self-reflexively to ponder the points of contact between his or her own desire/behavior and that of the scandalizing object. In this way, a gossip can be seen as a "person practised in the art of scrutinising the body for signs of 'true identity'" (Davis 1995: 200).

The bodies in question in Davis's case study materialize as the globally-published *paparazzi* images of the Duchess of York, wife of the younger brother of the heir to the British throne, in the "'Fergie' scandal of 1992 (otherwise known as the 'toe-sucking affair')," which showed her engaging in compromisingly amorous activities with a man described as her "financial adviser" while her young daughter looked on "baffled" (Davis 1995: 199, 201–2). In this scandal, the celebrity "royal" is first made newsworthy as an unapproachable (and irreproachable) other, only for the duchess to be "drawn into the world of the ordinary," so that: "while no in-depth knowledge of Fergie is claimed, what *is* known is that, naked, we are all much the same, and that all 'Truth' is a fabrication of sorts" (Davis 1995: 205).

The forms of knowledge and regimes of truth that surround celebrities – not to mention their material wealth – function to distance them from most of the population. In the absence of the dramatic downward social mobility occasioned, for example, by the collapse of a merchant bank, an insurance company, or the value of a share register, a media scandal is the most likely means by which the distance between celebrity and "common person" can be narrowed, if only in symbolic terms. The media scandal is, therefore, a way to "truth," a means by which the public façade is penetrated and privileged access gained to the domain of the private. Yet this pursuit of truth must follow the path of narrative – or, more accurately, the diverging and intersecting lines of narrativization offered up by "hard news," "soft reportage," and everyday gossip. The narrative teleology of media-celebrity scandal creates the impossibility of an appeal to a non-narrativized order of things and events. Ultimately, the scandalous insinuations, inferences, evidentiary claims, causal linkages, and "shock" revelations which comprise scandals are subject to narrative imperatives, because the only framework of meaning that can be posited against one narrativized truth claim is another narrative construction.

This alienation and reintegration of celebrities through media revelation is not confined to the beneficiaries of hereditary privilege. The twentieth century, in projecting a star system to all corners of a (hyper)commodified entertainment universe, has also enabled the proliferation of scandal. The symbolic distance which is to be breached must first, however, be reproduced in language. It is notable, for example, that monarchical connotations are frequently attached to sport, film, and musical celebrities in soubriquets such as "emperor," "king," "queen," "prince," and "pretender." It might be mentioned here that the apparently romantic relationship between Will Carling (then captain of the English rugby union team) and Lady Diana, Princess of Wales (the former wife of the heir to the British throne), constructed for the British tabloid press a sublime conjunction of royal and sporting celebrity scandals. Contemporary sport is particularly fertile ground for scandal because the bodies of these "monarchs" of the stadium – who in some sports, ironically, seek to exercise control over their own "courts" – are regularly and systematically viewed from numerous angles and speeds in ever more invasive attempts to elicit a "truth" that can be measured against their off-field conduct. I will return to this point later, but for the moment it is sufficient to note that the body of the sports celebrity, the performance of which is recorded and made routinely available for judgment, is an ideal vehicle for the carriage of media scandal.

Sport, as a key domain of popular culture, is required to perform the uncertain shuffle between ethical seriousness and naive faith on the one hand, and ethical playfulness and knowing non-commitment on the other, that characterizes commercial news. Because of the specific history of "this collective cultural creation of mid-nineteenth century Britain" (Goldlust 1987: 22), the sports celebrity scandal is one of contemporary life's most contradictory morality plays, with media, sportspeople, fans, and onlookers representing an ensemble cast adopting multiple and sometimes antagonistic roles. The movements and steps of this complex discursive dance must be tracked before addressing some exemplary instances of the sporting scandal in action.

Anatomy of a sports scandal

I have discussed elsewhere (Rowe 1994, 1995) what I take to be the anatomy – or, perhaps more accurately, the (un)natural history – of the sports scandal. Briefly, the behavior of sports stars becomes scandalizing when there is a radical disparity between their bodily dispositions on and off the field of play. The heroic mythology of sport is founded on a close matching of the extraordinary physical feats of the sportsperson *in extremis* and the imputed nobility of the performer, although there is a "deviant" variant whereby notoriety is sustained in both domains. An implied contract is drawn up between sports star and fan, the terms of which require consistency of person and persona. This contract is not so very different from that which exists between film fans and the stars who play certain typecast roles, or between pop fans and stars who have a strong on-stage image. A John Wayne or an Arnold Schwarzenegger, for example, is expected at least not to contradict off-screen his celluloid, hegemonically masculinist (Connell 1987) roles on it, while a Marilyn Monroe or a Sharon Stone is expected to play, perpetually and ubiquitously, the role of the sex goddess. Much the same might be said in the field of popular music of the masculinist image of a "metal" band such as Guns'n'Roses or of a hyper-feminine "siren" such as Madonna (*pace* assessments of her postmodern semiotic elusiveness – see, for example, Schwichtenberg 1993). In film and pop-music culture, however, there is more tolerance of ambiguity and a wider repertoire of roles to play than in sport, creating greater room for maneuver in prescriptions of appropriate front- and back-stage conduct. Male pop stars such as Prince (as he was then known), Michael Jackson, David Bowie, and Mick Jagger, for example, have all played with androgynous presentations of the self, so unsettling, if not overcoming, hegemonically masculinist and heterosexist conventionalism.

Sport, with its historically closer link to the state apparatus (through physical education and formal international representation), its rule fixation, and its affinity with patriarchal sexuality, has not yet created a wide range of subject and identity positions for sportspeople to adopt. Its founding and most enduring ideology is Olympian, constructed out of a mixture of Hellenic male body worship, neo-aristocratic British norms of edification, and French romanticism. While the body of the male athlete has long been the subject of an homoerotic gaze (Dutton 1995; Miller 1990), the culture of sport has for two centuries systematically repressed any but the most orthodox interpretations of masculinity (Messner 1992; Pronger 1990). This form of gender power found a perfect expression in the structured competition which is at the heart of international sporting practice, thereby creating the other of Olympian transcendentalism in the shape of ruthless contest, where winning is valorized and taking part devalued. Local, regional, and international sports have become more organized and rationalized at the same time as they have been figured as markers of national, social, and cultural progress or superiority (Larson and Park 1993). Out of the tension between abstract Olympianism, concrete chauvinism, and sharply prescribed private and public disciplines of the athletic body have emerged various "scandal formations." It is no coincidence that among the most prominent of these media sport convulsions are those occasioned by the most significant of all contemporary sports phenomena – the Olympic Games.

The Olympic ethic

In, according to its dust jacket, the "truly shocking account of the scandals behind the medal-giving ceremonies" provided by *The Lords of the Rings: Power, Money and Drugs in the Modern Olympics*, the authors set out the terms for the creation of a sporting scandal:

> The Olympics still hold out a special opportunity: the prospect of a better world as all our young people compete together freely and honestly every four years. That it is as important to take part as it is to win is more than a cliché, it is an ideal; this is the very bedrock of a democratic way of life. (Simson and Jennings 1992: 261)

This is the edifying philosophical foundation for the modern Olympics articulated by their chief revivalist, Baron Pierre de Coubertin. It is apparent that de Coubertin misunderstood or misrepresented the ancient games at Olympia, in particular his claim that they were essentially amateur in nature and that the ancient Greeks subordinated the value of winning to the joy of participation. This romanticized vision of the Olympics was constructed out of the unstable marriage of his "three passions [that] can be summed up as love of country, education, and love of sport" (Hill 1992: 6–9). Various historical accounts have argued that the modern Olympics were politicized from their inception, were corrupted by greed and self-interest, and exhibited a degree of brutality quite at variance with that tolerated in official, contemporary international sport. Norbert Elias (1986: 136), for example, describes the customary practice of posthumously "crowning" the victor of the pancration, a popular wrestling game-contest in the ancient Olympic Games in which contestants, often blinded by eye-gouging, could be strangled, kicked, and beaten to death. Such events obviously cloud the received images of graceful discus throwers in the ancient Olympic Games, and Elias (1986: 132) argues that the romanticization of the "game-contests of classical antiquity" creates a highly distorted tendency to treat them as "the ideal embodiments of contemporary sport." It is this nostalgic yearning at the heart of the (post)modern world's most watched media spectacle which inscribes scandal into its ethos, creating, in its very impossibility, the conditions of its own transgression. Most obviously, the explanation for this inherent destabilization of "Olympism" is its deep attachment to the concept of the corporeal ideal.

The positioning of the body of the Olympic athlete as the site of purity and transcendence of the mundane derives from the artistic representations of perfect male bodies in ancient Greece. As Dutton (1995: 36) notes:

> So thoroughly was the visible muscularity of the body itself – as distinct from its effective strength in a particular form of battle or contest – the subject of training and thus artistic depiction, that, with the exception of the runners, it is sometimes hard to distinguish in a vase painting the event in which the individual athlete was engaged: the artist was often obliged to add a discus or a pair of boxing-thongs or jumping weights to indicate the particular sport involved.

Projected onto that body across the centuries and continents is a panoply of idealizations. There is, for example, the aforementioned concept of (corporeal) democracy, with its meritocratic notions of free and honest competition in pursuit of the measurable goals of "higher, stronger, faster." This competition is conceived inside a liberal pluralist framework both within and between nation-states (Miller 1993), so that the social structural inequalities between dominant and subordinate groups (such as classes, races, ethnic groups, sexualities, and genders) or "developed" and "developing" countries (especially former colonizer and colonized) are downplayed. International sports events such as the Olympics are, furthermore, seen to function as agencies of reconciliation. The nation-state, which at the level of everyday life often seems little more than a legal abstraction, comes to life as the sporting nation united by a common interest in victory and a temporary denial of illegitimate hierarchy, inequality, and difference. At the same time as the sporting nation is displaying its physical health (not least, as Thomas Arnold, de Coubertin, and other proponents of *pedagogie sportive* believed, as a sign of combat readiness) in international sporting competition, it is encountering its erstwhile, actual, or potential enemy. If meeting the other on the sporting field is not exactly seen, in Orwellian fashion, as a gladiatorial substitute for war, Olympism regards it as an important means of acquiring the level of international understanding that would impede the nationalist processes of "enemy people" dehumanization that is usually the ideological prerequisite for warfare (MacAloon 1981). For the founders of modern sport and the Olympics, the athletic body is admired as capable of military combat while, except as a last resort, abjuring it.

Irrespective of the degree of humanization of opposing athletes, Olympian successes achieved by individual athletes and the nations they represent are not supposed to be bought or chemically manufactured. What de Coubertin called the "admirable mummy" of amateurism (quoted in Hill 1992: 8) may, in the late twentieth century, be safely interred by the sports-media complex, but monuments to it are still visible. In spite of the highly-advanced commercialization of sport, athletes are still expected to be chiefly motivated by love of sport and of nation. The financial rewards for sporting champions may be more or less sanctioned, but they are required to perform well for the "right" reasons – principally, the pursuit of corporeal excellence and as an expression of national pride. Not only are individual material interests expected to be of secondary importance, but individual performance is meant to be unenhanced. This "level-playing-field" requirement can be difficult to manage where advanced technologies, training regimens, and state/corporate-funded sports academies (such as the Australian Institute of Sport and the former GDR's sports apparatus) plainly give a competitive edge to the more affluent or "rationalizing" sporting nations. Such doubts may be handled, at least internally, by incorporating these activities and facilities within an overall, nationally-coordinated sporting effort which itself may be a source of pride. It is hard, however, to extend this approval to the practice – or, perhaps more precisely, the detection – of "cheating," especially where it involves the modification of bodily performance through the ingestion of performance-enhancing drugs.

Taking steroids and other drugs is widely judged to compromise corporeal integrity. Fixing the "correct" level of bodily manipulation to enhance sporting performance is not, however, easy. Intensive training and body-conditioning techniques, such as repetitive, minutely-prescribed gymnasium exercises and the daily consumption of a wide range of dietary supplements, constitute highly "artificial" forms of intervention. As McKay (1991: 145) notes, "The argument that drugs are 'unnatural' pales before the barrage of biological, biochemical, social, biomechanical, psychological, environmental and technological ways in which athletes' bodies are manipulated." The product of this scientistic body manufacture, with its connotations of the Gothic horror of science as popularly interpreted through the Frankenstein myth, may itself be cause for concern. Here the "extraordinary" sporting body designed for the optimal performance in sporting practice may enter the realm of the "freak," either congenitally (as in uncommon height among basketballers or the exaggerated endomorphic body shapes of some field athletes) or through intensive remodeling. The modernist horror of science's capacity for a "de-ethicized" creation of a fused body–machine is intensified by a postmodern "dread" that these are no longer categories which can be rhetorically or empirically separated, and which in any case are now overlaid with new and disturbingly "excessive" dispositions of the body. This mutation of body image becomes especially discomfiting when it articulates with concerns about appropriate gender, racial, and other ideologically contested forms of identity. Angela Nadalianis (1995: 15), for example, traces the limits of "acceptable femininity" in the self-consciously excessive realm of bodybuilding, discerning in the debates about female muscularity in bodybuilding magazines (and elsewhere) "underlying fears" of disturbing "the gender power structures" (see also Mansfield and McGinn 1993), concerns also evident in a recent controversy over lesbianism in Australian women's cricket (Burroughs et al. 1995). The limits of the sporting body, which are constantly put to the test, are endlessly productive of competing discourses of power and of scandal, especially – as in the case of the Olympic Games – when the "whole world is watching."

The Olympic scandal

The Olympics provide the greatest opportunity for scandal in sport because, as I have noted, its highly romanticized mythology lends itself most easily to the all-purpose transgression of "cheating." "Cheating" at the Olympics can take many forms, such as the manipulation of rules or the bribing of officials – but few cause as much collective angst as the use of performance-enhancing drugs. Here the prized Olympian body is most visibly compromised and the conditions for scandal most starkly revealed. The drug is taken, surreptitiously and in private, despite public pronouncements of being "clean," with all the connotations that the word entails. Proscribed drug use is "detected" (another loaded word) after official testing behind closed doors, and the results are then released to what is usually called, as in the recent case of Australian swimmer Samantha Riley, a "storm" of publicity (Cockerill 1996). The revelations are normally followed by "shock," denials, complaints about testing procedures, appeals, and so on, all of which provide enormous quantities of copy and imagery for the mass media. Because of this rationalized scandal protocol, drug testing in the Olympics, and in all major sports, is a rich source of "hot" stories. Indeed, in Simson and Jennings's (1992: 191) own breathy account of drug use by Olympian athletes in the eighties, the "scandals ground on, unceasingly," a pattern which, if it were not for the strength of the impulse to believe in "fair" Olympic competition, would surely diminish the capacity for collective outrage. There are still deep reserves of ethical anxiety available to international sport, and no sporting drugs scandal has had quite the same impact as that over Ben Johnson at the 1988 Seoul Olympics.

When Johnson tested positive for steroid abuse and was stripped of his world record and gold medal for the hundred meters, the level of media and coverage – and of scandal – was almost unsurpassed (Cashmore 1990: 107). Illicit private behavior was brought into the light in the most watched and prestigious sports event of the world's most watched and prestigious sports "meet." McKay (1991: 143–4) notes one fairly representative response in the Australian media:

> The day after the Ben Johnson scandal broke, Mike Gibson, one of Channel Ten's commentators at the 1988 Olympics, solemnly told viewers that he had just spoken to his teenage son in Australia, who asked him if it was true that Ben Johnson had been caught taking drugs. "What could I

say?" Gibson asked viewers. His son, like millions of people around the world, had put champions like Ben Johnson on a pedestal. What is it like for them, Gibson asked, to discover that their idols are fakes who cheat and take drugs? "Are we watching the greatest athletes of all time or are we watching a bunch of drugged-up freaks running around the Olympic stadium?" he wondered.

Here are the classic ingredients of the Olympian sports scandal, the sense of betrayal balancing the image of the polluted and degraded body of the athlete. Johnson's body became the subject of intense debate. His steroid use was said to be an open secret, and his body subject to its associated feminization, developing, in a graphic articulation of body panic (Kroker et al. 1989), "an enlarged left breast. He was turning into a woman!" (Simson and Jennings 1992: 195). Whatever Johnson was turning into, his public identity was also turning back, his Canadian nationality increasingly mediated in press reports by the reminder that he was "Jamaican-born." If Johnson's body was undergoing biological change as a result of the massive ingestion of Stanozolol, it was also being "re-racialized" by the Canadian media. Here the multiple transgressive possibilities of the sports scandal are highlighted – not only in the breaking of competition rules and the "spirit" of the Games, but also in the potential erosion of the boundaries between the sexes, the evocation of assumed differences between races, and a redrawing of the borders of the nation-state to exclude the once-welcomed sports migrant. This is an instance of the postmodern character of the current "age of scandal." Unlike the classic scandal of modernism, which concerned the relatively simple transgression of established ethical regimes, there is a postmodern confusion and ambivalence about precisely which of the many and shifting frontiers of self and other have to be patrolled and made secure. The Johnson affair, then, became a vehicle for the exploration of a chaotic range of social issues, spilling out from the ethics of contemporary sport to a much wider discourse of contemporary malaise.

A similar symbolic threat to social order was posed by another recent Olympic scandal, when an assailant acting on behalf of skater Tonya Harding set about fellow US Olympian Nancy Kerrigan with a police baton after she had completed a practice session on the ice. The motive, it appeared, was to counterbalance Kerrigan's advantages over Harding, which, apart from sporting performance, lay in the greater "bankability" as an endorser of corporate products arising from her more conventionally-acceptable feminine presentation of self, and the cultural – specifically, media – capital accorded by her higher class of origin (Baughman 1995). The core of this scandal lay not only in the denial of "teamship" central to Olympian competition organized along nationalist lines, but also in the eruption of privately-harbored jealousy into the public arena. The violent nature of the attack, although not conducted by Harding, enabled a mobilization of "the monstrous-feminine" (Creed 1993), with its intimations of the post-social, matricidal revenge-taking in the classical story of Medea. The celebrity sporting body is not chemically enhanced from within in the Harding–Kerrigan scandal, but subjected to the external threat of destruction at the behest of a fellow (white) American, athlete, and woman.

The Harding–Kerrigan affair did not only bring to the fore the drive in sport for personal success at the expense of collective or non-instrumental, aesthetically-pleasing triumph. It also brought into focus highly-ambivalent, binary constructions of women as inherently nurturant, passive, and non-violent or as ruthless, scheming, and beyond control. The typifications of Kerrigan and Harding have closely followed this pattern and have conditioned the trajectory of their ensuing careers, with the former assiduously maintaining an image of corporate acceptability as the latter seeks new ways of performing the assigned "bad-girl" role that she shares with, among others, pop musician Courtney Love. In following this "deviant" career – without, it seems, conspicuous material success to date – Harding's conduct illuminates another facet of the celebrity sporting scandal which is far removed from the lofty requirements of Olympism. This is the other (or under) side of sporting celebrity based on the cultivation of a postmodern form of notoriety, which threatens in the service of the scandal narrative to subvert rather than to mirror the prevailing ethical order.

The superbad, superstud scandal

Some sportsmen (the term is gendered advisedly) cultivate an outlaw, "bad-boy" image, establishing this claim on the basis of denying the hypocrisy of altruism in sport, and unselfconsciously bringing the often ugly dimensions of the private into the public sporting arena. This has been a pitch adopted, for example, by some "superbad," "superstud" black sportsmen such as basketballers Wilt Chamberlain and Dennis Rodman (whose book *Bad As I Wanna Be* (1996) actively valorizes a resistive "badness," and whose association with Madonna has turned it into a kind of locus classicus for cross-disciplinary, popular-cultural celebrity gossip). The superbad image had also been cultivated by heavyweight boxer Mike Tyson (Rowe 1994). Tyson had made few concessions to orthodox sports heroicism in his career before being tried and jailed for rape in 1992. Boxing, furthermore, is in its uncomplicated violence closer to what Olson (1996: 53) calls "sanctioned mayhem" and "public surgery" than most contact sports. Prior to this event, it would, perhaps, have been more "shocking" if Tyson had been discovered to be, in fact, privately congenial when outside the ring. Despite the seriousness of the crime, the media concentrated less on the brutality of the act than on questions of sexual protocol in the relationships between male sports superstars and women followers of sport (often described as "sports groupies"). Here, the defense-sponsored argument that "radical feminists" prejudged Tyson's guilt, in light of sexual harassment and "date-rape" accusations against, respectively, Judge Clarence Thomas and William Kennedy Smith (Kimmel 1993; McKay et al. 1994), meshed with the idea of the acquisitive sports groupie who might "set up" an unwary elite sportsman. The more enduring but less potent personal dimension of the scandal, then, was that of the radical change to Tyson's lifestyle, a rich – if unlikable and ignoble – sportsman reduced to the circumstances of a "common" prisoner.

The prime element of scandal missing from the Tyson case was that of the unveiling of the private. Tyson's ruthlessness in the ring and gracelessness out of it allowed little room for revelation – too close an alignment seemed to exist between person and persona even after the scandal broke. In the Tyson affair, the focus shifted quickly away from the perpetrator of the scandal and onto its institutional formation and exploitation. Few contributors to the debate argued that there was a "truth" about Tyson that was not generally known and required to be revealed in order to damn or exculpate him. Instead, the "truth" was institutional rather than individual – the sexual and gender structure of elite sport, the legal system, politics, and the media. This necessary feature of problematizing the "truth" of the corporeal conduct and identity of the sports celebrity was clearly present when champion basketballer Earvin "Magic" Johnson revealed in 1991 at a press conference that he was HIV-positive. Johnson's image was quite different from that of Tyson – the "most famous smile since the Mona Lisa" (Kroll 1991: 70) was used extensively in the construction of a benign, corporate-friendly image. Whereas many commentators seemed to view Tyson's crime as the convergence of private and public conduct, for Johnson there existed a much clearer disjunction. HIV–AIDS, as a condition widely associated with marginalized groups such as homosexuals and intravenous drug users, was for many admirers of Johnson a phenomenon which threatened to create a very different "truth" about sports celebrities.

"Magic" and his associates sought to manage the scandal by, first, going public about his HIV status, thus denying the media the priceless advantage of the "scoop." Next, Johnson's declarations that "I have never had a homosexual encounter. Never" and "I confess that after I arrived in L.A., in 1979, I did my best to accommodate as many women as I could" (Johnson and Johnson 1991) asserted a popularly tolerable (and inherently homophobic) picture of heterosexual promiscuity as he "truly lived the bachelor's life." Magic's dedication to the cause of safe-sex education, culminating in a short-lived membership of the US National Commission on AIDS, provided an essentially redemptive facet of the narrative, while his basketball gold medal in the 1992 Barcelona Olympics as part of "the Dream Team" presented a glorious closure to it. Threaded through the story was widespread media discussion of the "threat" posed by the denigrated bodies of the (female) sport groupies to the celebrated bodies of (male) sports celebrities. This demonization of the "infectors" allowed the "truth" of sports-celebrity victimhood to occlude other, less favorable possibilities. In this scenario, the figure of Magic's wife, Cookie Johnson (and their then *in utero*, HIV-negative child), was a necessary semiotic counterpoint to the sports groupie, redirecting the gaze from the anonymity of celebrity-sports sex to the intimacy of the nuclear family.

Finally, the Magic Johnson affair is instructive in establishing the conditions for the persistence of the sports media scandal. Most obviously, continuity can occur through the coverage of the travails and triumphs of the embodied subject. Magic Johnson's subsequent banishment from the National Basketball League, his ensuing coaching career, traveling "All Stars" venture, refusal of entry into some countries because of his HIV status, and so on can be traced as part of the mercurial trajectory of scandal. The plasticity of the material of scandal and the textual voracity of the mass media can, in journalistic parlance, give strong "legs" to particular scandal stories, to the extent that they achieve iconic status. It is this iconicity that enables the continuous invocation of a scandal that has passed its original peak media flow. For example, the

1996 revelation that the American boxer Tommy Morrison was HIV-positive facilitated the excavation of the "Magic" referent and another rehearsal of the rhetorical moves generated by the Magic Johnson story (see, for example, Vecsey 1996). This seemingly endless media scandal amplification spiral – to adapt a well-known concept developed by Wilkins (1964) – is constructed out of the frenzied intertextuality of postmodernity evidenced by the greatest sports media scandal of the nineties – the O.J. Simpson trial.

The sports celebrity murder scandal

The public image of Orenthal James Simpson was similar to that of Johnson. While he had been in retirement from the gridiron for some time and had carved out a career in film, Simpson continued to commentate on sport and, indeed, his entire standing was inseparable from it. Simpson's arraignment for the bloody murder of his ex-wife Nicole Brown Simpson and her friend Ronald Goldman was, in the first instance, shocking rather than scandalous. Suggestions of a crime of passion gradually gave way to a more scandalizing exposure of Simpson's history of spousal abuse (McKay and Smith 1995). His body, personality, and state of mind were again subjected to the kind of close interest that they had once attracted during his playing career, as his sports-related injuries, the size of his hands, his physical strength, jealousy, and violent outbursts were exhaustively examined. Once more, the scandal became a launching pad for the exploration of much wider social issues. While the Magic Johnson affair had the potential to become intensely racialized – confirming, for white racists, their anxieties about black male sexuality – it was largely contained to a scandal of sexual conduct and ultimately projected onto the nameless "buckle bunnies" who "prey" on traveling (sports) players. In the Simpson scandal, the beating and murder of women by men did not, ultimately, preoccupy public discourse. It was racial ideology that predominated, resolving itself into a dispute about whether "people of color" are the victims of "white" justice – as in the case of the Rodney King police acquittals that precipitated the 1992 Los Angeles Riots – or are able to manipulate the judicial (and, specifically, the jury) system to evade a "color-blind" jurisprudence.

The role of sport begins to look peripheral as the scandal takes on its own logics, yet its capacity to imbue individuals with the aura of the *Übermensch* is the foundation of the potent affectivity that mobilizes celebrity scandal. It was his standing in sport that enabled the Simpson affair to be generalized to the status of "an American tragedy," so that "one of the most revered idols in the American sporting pantheon" (McKay and Smith 1995: 57, 62) became the metaphorical embodiment of what is "wrong" with the contemporary US nation. Yet for many supporting "the Juice" (his football nickname) there was a simple denial of the presumption of scandal – the body that performed so majestically on the sports field and the genial persona that was marketed off it could not be construed as an instrument of death. Supporting Simpson from the bizarre moment of the televised media–police chase along the freeways of Los Angeles was, then, an extension of partisan fandom, a denial of alternative regimes of "truth" by an act of affiliation and of will. The signs declaring "GO, OJ, GO" held up on the side of the road as Simpson's white Ford Bronco sped by were the banners of devoted sports fans who supported their teams and heroes "right or wrong."

A conflation of the Olympian and partisan ideologies of sport occurs when the aura of the sports superhero has obliterated for some people even the appearance of other ways of seeing. This partisanship became evident during the 474-day trial, which transmuted into a form of sports encounter between two nations, white and black, within a nation. The subsequent verdict and its televised reaction at different, racially-"segregated" sites across America, with its jubilant "victors" and downcast "losers," resembled nothing more than the "final whistle" in a sporting contest. Racialized discourses in this instance overdetermined others, and supplied the primary (though by no means the sole) reference point from which the task of sense making in the Simpson scandal could be attempted. The "truths" of O.J., the murder of Nicole Brown Simpson and Ronald Goldman, and the state of the nation are, nonetheless, provisional and dynamic. As the Simpson case moved into the next phase of a civil trial for wrongful death, 36 Simpson-related works, ranging from comic books and memoirs of dismissed jurors to Simpson's own apologia, had already been published, with many more books to come, not least from defense and prosecution lawyers (Jerome 1995: 60). The O.J. case is now both popular scandal and industry, furnishing everyday life with a rich array of jokes and a ready reference point for moral entrepreneurs (Cohen 1972) whose agendas are radically diverse. It represents a convergence of sport, media, and scandal, destined to be invoked in numerous forms of cultural production as the *par excellence* instance of the postmodern promiscuity of sign systems and of the uncontrollable collapse of the boundaries between hard news and pliable pleasure.

Conclusion

It is not altogether easy to draw authoritative conclusions from this brief dissertation on the sports media scandal. Certainly, it is clear that sports celebrities share with those in other disciplines of fame a two-way relationship with the media, which simultaneously illuminates public conduct, imputes its connection to the private sphere (a representation of self-hood either more or less cultivated by celebrities themselves and their image consultants), and then subjects this connection to intense surveillance for signs of "contradiction." Even those celebrities who project a consistently rebellious person and persona must constantly negate alternative readings of their personality and neutralize suspicion that they may be, after all, somewhat less transparent than they seem. Sports celebrity is, however, distinctive in the integration of archival, "real" time with multi-perspectival and variable-speed scrutiny of the elite sporting body reinforced by other forms of reportage, such as the sound recording of sports contests using directional microphones. This probably unprecedented capacity for the mass assessment and interpretation of performance is coupled with a long-standing (principally Olympian) idealization of the sporting body and ethos.

The abstract exultation of the Apollonian figure of sporting excellence stands in uneasy, but nonetheless enduring, relation with the heedlesly partial affective investment of sports fandom, with its various types and levels of affiliation. The media are key conduits in the communication of the meaning of the sports scandal, patrolling and marking the ethical frontiers of sport and switching between official and popular discourses and private and public domains in a relentless quest for the "truth" of the day. The coexistence of the conditions of modernity and postmodernity is discernible in this endless redefinition of the relationship between news, citizenship, and pleasure. Media sports scandals, with their irresistible melange of high-mindedness and base inquisitiveness, are recurring and absorbing contemporary cultural phenomena of almost incredible audience "reach." The project of cultural critique is not to become nostalgic about a golden age when news discourses, subjects, and sites somehow knew their place, but to capitalize on the opportunities for critical intervention presented by the sports media scandal's effortless ability to link and problematize ideologies of dominance, technologies of the self, and rhetorics of the popular.

References

Baughman, C. (ed.) (1995). *Women on Ice: Feminist Essays on the Tonya Harding/ Nancy Kerrigan Spectacle*. New York: Routledge.

Burroughs, A., Seebohm, L. and Ashburn, L. (1995). "Add sex and stir": Homophobic coverage of women's cricket in Australia. *Journal of Sport and Social Issues*, 19(3): 266–84.

Cashmore, E. (1990). *Making Sense of Sport*. London: Routledge.

Cockerill, M. (1996). Sink or swim: The fight to save a champion's career. *Sydney Morning Herald*, February 17: 33, 36.

Cohen, S. (1972). *Folk Devils and Moral Panics: The Creation of the Mods and Rockers*. London: Paladin.

Connell, R.W. (1987). *Gender and Power*. Sydney: Allen and Unwin.

Creed, B. (1993). *The Monstrous-Feminine: Film, Feminism, Psychoanalysis*. London: Routledge.

Dahlgren, P. and Sparks, C. (eds) (1992). *Journalism and Popular Culture*. London: Sage.

Davis, T. (1995). The practice of gossip. In P. van Toorn and D. English (eds), *Speaking Positions: Aboriginality, Gender and Ethnicity in Australian Cultural Studies*. Melbourne: Victoria University of Technology.

Dutton, K.R. (1995). *The Perfectible Body: The Western Ideal of Physical Development*. Sydney: Allen and Unwin.

Elias, N. (1986). The genesis of sport as a sociological problem. In N. Elias and E. Dunning (eds), *Quest for Excitement: Sport and Leisure in the Civilising Process*. Oxford: Blackwell.

Goldlust, J. (1987). *Playing for Keeps: Sport, the Media and Society*. Melbourne: Longman Cheshire.

Hill, C.R. (1992). *Olympic Politics*. Manchester: Manchester University Press.

Jerome, R. (1995). The ordeal over, a new one begins. *Who Weekly*, October 16: 54–60.

Johnson, M. with Johnson, R.S. (1991). I deal with it. *Sports Illustrated*, November 18: 18–27.

Kimmel, M. (1993). Clarence, William, Iron Mike, Magic – and us. *Changing Men*, 25: 9–13.

Kroker, A., Kroker, M. and Cook, D. (1989). *Panic Encyclopedia: The Definitive Guide to the Postmodern Scene*. London: Macmillan.

Kroll, J. (1991). Smile, though our heats are breaking. *Newsweek*, November 18: 70.

Larson, J.F. and Park, H. (1993). *Global Television and the Politics of the Seoul Olympics*. Boulder, CT: Westview.

MacAloon, J.J. (1981). *This Great Symbol: Pierre de Coubertin and the Origins of the Modern Olympic Games*. Chicago: University of Chicago Press.

Mansfield, A. and McGinn, B. (1993). Pumping irony: The muscular and the feminine. In S. Scott and D. Morgan (eds), *Body Matters: Essays on the Sociology of the Body*. London: Falmer Press.

McKay, J. (1991). *No Pain, No Gain? Sport and Australian Culture*. Sydney: Prentice-Hall.

McKay, J., Rowe, D. and Miller, T. (1994). Sport and postmodern bodies. (Unpublished paper).

McKay, J. and Smith, P. (1995). Exonerating the hero: Frames and narratives in media coverage of the O.J. Simpson story. *Media Information Australia*, 75: 57–66.

Messner, M. (1992). *Power at Play: Sports and the Problem of Masculinity*. Boston: Beacon Press.

Miller, T. (1990). Sport, media and masculinity. In D. Rowe and G. Lawrence (eds), *Sport and Leisure: Trends in Australian Popular Culture*. Sydney: Harcourt Brace Jovanovich.

Miller, T. (1993). *The Well-Tempered Self: Citizenship, Culture and the Postmodern Subject*. Baltimore and London: Johns Hopkins University Press.

Nadalianis, A. (1995). Muscle, excess and rupture: Female bodybuilding and gender construction. *Media Information Australia*, 75: 13–23.

Olson, L. (1996). Ringside with a bloody mess. *Sydney Morning Herald*, February 17: 53.

Pronger, B. (1990). *The Arena of Masculinity: Sports, Homosexuality and the Meaning of Sex*. New York: St Martin's Press.

Rodman, D. with Keown, T. (1996). *Bad As I Wanna Be*. New York: Delacorte.

Rowe, D. (1994). Accommodating bodies: Celebrity, sexuality and "tragic Magic." *Journal of Sport and Social Issues*, 18(1): 6–26.

Rowe, D. (1995). *Popular Cultures: Rock Music, Sport and the Politics of Pleasure*. London: Sage.

Schwichtenberg, C. (ed.) (1993). *The Madonna Connection: Representational Politics, Subcultural Identities, and Cultural Theory*. Sydney: Allen and Unwin.

Simson, V. and Jennings, A. (1992). *The Lords of the Rings: Power, Money and Drugs in the Modern Olympics*. London: Simon & Schuster.

Vecsey, G. (1996). Boxing's grim future: The threat waiting at ringside. *Sydney Morning Herald*, February 17: 56.

Wilkins, L. (1964). *Social Deviance: Social Policy, Action and Research*. London: Tavistock.

10 Church, Media, and Scandal

Paul A. Soukup

From the beginning, journalists have helped bring about a convergence between religious scandals and media scandals: Aimee Semple MacPherson's disappearance, Father Coughlin's anti-Semitism, Fighting Bob Shuler's Los Angeles campaigns, and – more recently – Jim Bakker's conviction for fraud, Steven J. Cook's molestation charges against Cardinal Joseph Bernardin, and Jimmy Swaggart's tearful confession of consorting with prostitutes. Despite the common focus, the religious community and the mass-media profession have fundamentally different interests and goals when it comes to such scandals. Media scandals dealing with religion reveal a clash of social, cultural, and rhetorical forces.

In this chapter I will outline the social goals of the church and the media by sketching their background interests and ideologies as revealed by scandal; I will note how the characteristic communication patterns of each institution affect its goals; and I will examine how each institution rhetorically deals with scandal – both in exposing it and in the outcome or resolution sought. The Bakker, Swaggart, and Bernardin cases will provide illustrations along the way. Throughout I will use "religious community" as a general term to refer either to an established church and its institutional structures (for example, the Anglican Communion or the Assemblies of God in Christ) or to church members – the people sharing common religious beliefs and worshipping at a parish church or temple.

Scandal from a religious perspective

To understand how religious groups view scandal, we need to look back to the biblical basis of the term itself. To paraphrase Raymond Williams (1976), history happens in the word. Such an historical review shows that scandal emerges as a tool for establishing identity and social control within the religious community (see Thompson, this volume).

In the religious arena, "scandal" comes from the Greek noun *skandalon* and the verb *skandalizein*. While both words appear in pre-biblical Greek, they are rare; the use increases with the Greek Septuagint translation of the Hebrew Bible and becomes common in the Greek New Testament. The words originally referred to a spring-trap for prey. Because of a similarity of sound between Greek and Hebrew, the Septuagint translators used it to refer to different kinds of trap, such as those set to make people stumble – stones in a path. Some characteristic texts include Psalm 124: 7, which refers to a snare, and Leviticus 19: 14 and 1 Samuel 25: 31, which refer to a stumbling block. By extension, the term also refers to a cause of ruin, further extended to mean things that made one lose faith (Stählin 1971).

Within the Christian tradition, the religious notion of scandal finds an important expression in a saying attributed to Jesus in the Gospel of Mark and its parallel texts in the Gospels of Matthew (18: 6) and Luke (17: 1–2): "Whoever causes one of these little ones who believe in me to stumble [*skandalizein*], it would be better for him if a great millstone were hung around his neck and he were thrown into the sea (Mark 9: 42, Revised Standard Version). The text itself contains a fair amount of wordplay. As noted above, the Greek *skandalizein* refers to a trap which someone set to make the prey stumble; in Jesus's rabbinic treatment, the stone on which one stumbles gets put around the culprit's neck – an example of the Old Testament law of talion or punishment by the same tool (Derrett 1985: 218). In addition, the drowning reflects the Old Testament punishment of the Egyptians in the Red Sea, but is less severe than other forms of death prescribed in the law and so leaves open the possibilities of repentance and purification (Derrett 1985: 219). Even though the culprit receives punishment, salvation and restoration to the community – after the resurrection – remain a possibility. This is an important point to be developed later on in this chapter.

The Old Testament background sketched above helps to elaborate Jesus's meaning as well. Derrett (1985: 220) argues that Jesus's approach resembles that of Wisdom 14: 8–11, which refers us to those places in the Old Testament history of Israel that recount how various kings led the nation away from God, sinning themselves and causing others to sin. In so doing, they destroyed the community. And so, in each case punishment followed. Why a millstone? The wordplay on *skandalizein* (to trip on a stone) sets up the choice. The punishment meted out reflects the need for the community to maintain itself as faithful to God and as an integral unit.

It is clear from both New Testament and Old Testament contexts that *the key reason for avoiding scandal lies in preserving the community*. Because the actions of one affect the others, each has the obligation to avoid things that would lead others astray. In the First Letter to the Corinthians, Paul shows an acute sense of this when he claims that while there is no sin in people's eating meat from the butchers' shops – even though it might have been sacrificed to idols – the Christians should willingly avoid it if eating it would cause difficulties for others (10: 23–33). In the letter to the Romans, Paul writes, "You should make up your mind never to be the cause of your brother tripping or falling" (14: 13). The implicit reference to the stumbling stone or scandal is obvious.

At the same time there are Christian "scandals" that keep people outside of the community of believers. Jesus himself refers to the scandal that some find in himself – in his ordinariness, in his rejection by the religious leadership of Israel (Léon-Dufour 1973: 524). Paul writes that Israel stumbles (is scandalized) by the death of Jesus on the cross: "But we preach Christ crucified, a stumbling block [*scandalon*] to the Jews and folly to Gentiles" (I Corinthians 1: 23). This, though, finds its justification in the Old Testament prophecies of Isaiah (8: 14f.) where God tests the faith of Israel by being a stone of stumbling. Similarly, the New Testament notes that the stone rejected by the builders has become the cornerstone of the new faith (Matthew 21: 42, quoting Psalm 118: 22).

Two complementary things happen here: The community is built up by stones which may cause outsiders to stumble while at the same time it is preserved by avoiding stones that would trip up insiders. In the religious context, thus, scandal ultimately has to do with membership and with preserving the identity of the community. Religious institutions tend to regard scandal as behaviors that endanger the faith or commitment of church members. Predictably, they deal with scandal in two ways: urging avoidance and developing a variety of tools for reconciliation and healing.

Later Christian moral tradition, with its extensive reflection on scandal, supports the conclusion that avoiding scandal forms the basis for social control by adding an important element. Thomas Aquinas (1972: 43:3r) distinguishes between the "active scandal" discussed above (performing a scandalous act) and "passive scandal" (becoming scandalized on witnessing the act). One should arrange one's conduct to avoid both; indeed, one has obligations both to avoid giving scandal (active) and to avoid being scandalized – the passive scandal – should that weaken one's faith in the community. On the other hand, if "salutary scandal taking" binds one more closely to the community – by leading to a kind of "I don't want to be like people who act that way" resolve – it can be a good thing (Häring 1964: 487–8). In both situations scandal provides a negative guide to behavior.

Finally, the moral tradition also specifies that people have a duty to repair scandal in order to restore the community. Such reparation should be proportional to the scandal and performed publicly before the community for public scandals, or privately if the scandal is not widely known (McHugh and Callan 1929: 607–9). The mechanism for such repair takes on a certain rhetorical form, to which we shall return.

Scandal from the perspective of the news media

News media approach scandal in a very different way. While they, too, attempt to exercise their own kind of social control, scandal forms less a tool to enforce behavior within their community than a means to extend their own power to define society and situate other institutions within it. Thus, the news media tend to regard scandal as an instance of moral hypocrisy and employ public exposure, even ridicule, to develop the story. In addition, of course, many media outlets make use of scandal as a commodity – by selling scandals, they sell more newspapers and magazines, or achieve higher broadcast ratings. In doing so, they reap a double benefit, increasing both their own standing and their own profits.

How did they get to this position? The news media's approach to scandal grows out of traditional news values, a self-understanding of the press that grew up in the nineteenth and early twentieth centuries, and changes in the contemporary news business. News values guide reporters in finding stories and help editors decide which stories to run. Most journalism textbooks outline key values, such as recency, impact, importance, prominence of named people, proximity, and notoriety. However, the self-understanding of the press forms an even more powerful (though perhaps less consciously chosen) incentive for news organizations to report scandals. Four strands in the history of the news media combine to shape that self-understanding: a public service model of reporting, the background role of the press as the "fourth estate," a suspicion born of investigative reporting, and the organizational culture of the newsroom.

The public-service model of the news organization defines the news media as the group that provides what people need to know in order to act as good citizens and make informed choices (Gamson 1995: 5). That model reinforces the sense of importance of the news and positions news institutions as vital social forces. It also subtly reinforces a sense of the news organization as uniquely qualified to judge what matters for society – first, not only in politics or economics, but also in morals. Second, a relatively recent strand of the news media's self-understanding, the public-service model finds expression in the Commission on Freedom of the Press's report on the role of the press in a democratic society (1947) and in the willingness of broadcasters, for example, to support high-profile news divisions, even at a financial loss. Public-service reporting, of course, connects to the older image of the press as the fourth estate – the group that balanced or countered the power of traditional social forces (nobility, church, business) on behalf of the disenfranchised. Third, the news media understand themselves as inherently suspicious but balanced. Investigative reporting has taught editors and reporters alike to distrust official groups, sources of authority, and social institutions. Steinfels describes how such suspicion works in the case of moral teachings:

> Roughly speaking, American society is torn between two broad perspectives. One sees traditional morality as enshrining a legacy of wisdom about how we should live together and therefore challengers to that legacy as deserving of a skeptical or jaundiced examination. Another view looks on traditional morality as enshrining a host of prejudices from which we need to be liberated – indeed it considers the proudest moments of recent history to be those when people were liberated from inherited prejudices. Accordingly it looks on those who defy that traditional morality as at least deserving sympathetic attention. (1995: 16)

Each side deserves suspicion and it falls to the press to balance the two, something it usually does by quoting both, relying on an ideology of objectivity (Schechter 1994: 40). After all, who is better placed to judge than a neutral observer? Such an ideology feeds seamlessly into the fourth strand of the media's self-understanding: the organizational culture of the newsroom. "Journalistic standards call for independent, fair, and complete coverage that will maximize public understanding of important events" (McManus 1994: 35). At each stage of the news process – discovering, selecting, reporting stories – journalists base their judgments on a complex set of (often unconscious) rules learned in the newsroom. That organizational culture leads them to trust themselves and their position in society to provide a moral compass. As Lull and Hinerman argue in this volume, "mass media become reflexive agents implicitly representing those whose interests are served by the constant reassertion of dominant modes of thought, driving mainstream values and lifestyles into the assumptive worlds of audience members."

This four-fold self-understanding of the news media makes the scandal story particularly attractive, because that kind of story allows the media to legitimize their own standing as social institution, while simultaneously delegitimizing others (Tumber 1993: 346, 358–9). This works especially well in terms of religious scandals. "Practice can be counted on not to measure up to preachment, and preachment is, of course, a speciality of religion" (Steinfels 1995: 16). This is not meant to imply that developing religious scandals is an easy task, for reporting too much scandal risks a loss of trust and credibility in the press itself (Gamson 1995: 3), especially when the news media focus on highly popular or respected groups. If the public perceives the news media as too focused on the delegitimation of social institutions, they may quickly turn on the news media themselves. However, the ideology of objectivity and the norms of the newsroom do provide some measure of defense: As the *New York Times* slogan has it, news organizations neither fear nor favor any group.

Finally, a series of contemporary changes in the news business have raised the reporting of scandals to new heights. At least six factors contribute to this. First, the various media institutions today must compete more fiercely for ratings or sales (Idvsoog 1994: 38) and "scandal stories . . . help to fulfill the audience-building strategies of the press" (Tumber 1993: 352). Second, changes in ownership – particularly large corporate buyouts of media institutions and publicly-traded news companies – mean that profits (and hence audience numbers) matter more to news companies today than before (Gamson 1995: 5). In fact, McManus (1994) discusses the wider impact of this phenomenon under the rubric of "market-driven journalism." For television, such programming proves cost-effective in this environment: news shows, magazine formats, even tabloid television (for which scandal provides a key programming element) cost less for broadcasters to produce than does dramatic programming. In addition, the news companies own the final product and can continue to earn money from repeats. Third, entertainment (or "infotainment") has become the norm even in mainstream newspapers (Shaw 1994: 4; Hanson 1994: 16). In today's world:

> public service criteria (is it important? is it something citizens need to know?) are less important than entertainment criteria (is it fun? is it like a movie consumers have seen?). Disaster is good stuff, sex and crime and celebrity make terrific news, and famous sex criminals with disastrous impact are the very best. (Gamson 1995: 4)

Fourth, the fact the popular demand for scandal has increased makes the first three factors work. Scandal stories "are viewed for fun, titillation, drama, a hoot" (Gamson 1995: 7). Even if people blame the news organizations for sensationalism, the fact is that they watch the programs and buy the papers. The final two changes in the contemporary news environment that lead to more scandal stories arise out of external considerations: space and time (Shaw 1994: 4). The proliferation of newspapers and cable television, especially, means that news institutions have to provide more stories each day; scandal is easy to report and, in fact, may be "better" reported when it is not checked too carefully. Finally, short deadlines and the need to publish quickly also explain the rise of scandal stories. *Los Angeles Times* media critic David Shaw sees this as a particular problem for CNN:

> Add to this mix CNN, with its even greater demand for fodder – news every minute of every hour of every day – and it's not difficult to understand why some questionable stories inevitably find their way onto the air. But once on the air – or in print . . . – they take on a life of their own. Editors and producers at mainstream news organizations seem terrified of ignoring them. (1994: 4)

Shaw may have had a media scandal in mind, in which CNN played a leading but erroneous role. CNN aired a live interview in which Steven J. Cook accused Chicago's Roman Catholic Cardinal

Joseph Bernardin of sexually molesting him some 18 years earlier. Bernardin, who had taken the lead in the Catholic church's efforts to prevent and respond to sexual abuse by clergy, denied the charges (Chicago prelate . . . 1993: A12). The irony was not lost on CNN or on other news sources, which reported the story. Five months later, Cook withdrew his charge, noting, "I now realize that the memories which arose during and after hypnosis are unreliable," adding, "I can no longer proceed in good conscience" (Accuser drops . . . 1994: A20).

Three major factors – received news values, the self-understanding of news institutions as social guardians, and contemporary market forces – shape the media's interest in scandal. Scandals reward media institutions with standing and sales. And so, where the religious community looks on scandal as a danger, the media see it as an opportunity. But the two do more than simply compete to control the social consequences of scandals. A closer look at typical communication forms and rhetorical strategies for dealing with scandal reveals some common heritage.

Communication and scandal

Interestingly, despite their divergent goals and interests, the two groups find themselves with a shared background – the oral and folkloric background of scandals. Walter Ong's (1982) observations on orality and literacy help to situate the ways in which religious communities and the media frame scandals: Religious groups maintain a strong oral character, and media institutions a literate one. But this fundamental difference should not be thought of as totalizing or permanent. Within a complex modern society, vestiges of orality coexist with literacy and reappear in mediated communication as secondary orality, that is, as oral forms based on scripted discourse. Oral forms common to religious groups include face-to-face interaction, preaching, and simplified narratives. Oral characteristics of these forms, which surprisingly well describe how the religious community narrates scandals, involve narratives with strong characters, concrete examples, conservative outlooks, agonistic or combative style, empathy and participation, and situational thinking (Ong 1982: 37–49). Even religious groups with highly-developed literacies, complex theologies, and well-structured hierarchies maintain an oral presence in their local communities.

This presence depends on personal relationships, conversation, and preaching – all things which support oral characteristics when it comes to dealing with scandal. Television evangelists, especially those grounded in the Pentecostal tradition, demonstrate a highly-oral style, one based less on secondary than on primary orality since they preach spontaneously and not from a prepared text.

The oral culture of face-to-face communication and preaching helps the religious community maintain other attributes as well. David Payne identifies one relevant trait here: character. "Character, in this view, is a kind of least common denominator of all the socializing forces in a culture, one which seeks to instill a basis for conformity in individuals" (1991: 225). Following Riesman's typification (Riesman et al. 1950), Payne argues that oral cultures, being more tradition-directed, will highlight shame as an external motivator to enforce behavioral rules; literacy moves people more toward inner-directed behaviors, using guilt as a motivator; mass society and mass media shift people to "other-directedness," calling attention more to situation ethics, with less emphasis on enforcing behavior than on seeking social harmony (Payne 1991: 226).

As we have seen, for the religious community, scandal has two components, both of which enforce behavior: the act and the observation. Where the act is not directly witnessed – and it seldom may be – the community spreads the word through conversation or even through pulpit denunciation. Scandal, then, depends on oral forms from gossip to preaching in a fairly straightforward way. The community recounts the act in terms of unacceptable behavior and implied alternative behaviors – the scandal threatens the community while serving as a warning against similar temptations to its members. It serves at least three related functions: *warning*, for the scandal needs to generate shame and fear of transgression, lest others fall away; *justification*, for the scandal needs to reinforce the community's right to define acceptable behavior; and *entertainment*, for a good scandal story must maintain group interest and be memorable to be effective (few religious groups would admit to this label, but it seems accurate enough).

The Jim Bakker case illustrates the process. In the 1980s Jim Bakker and his wife, Tammy, founded and led a television ministry affiliated with the Assemblies of God in Christ. Originally travelling evangelists, they became regular guests on Pat Robertson's religious cable television program, *The 700 Club*. A few years later they founded their own cable television show, *The PTL Club* – short for "Praise the Lord" Club. At its peak, the program was carried on cable systems throughout the United States and claimed an audience of several million viewers. In addition the Bakkers established a theme park near their television studios in Charlotte, North Carolina.

The *Charlotte Observer* had raised allegations and questions about Bakker's financial dealings for several years before his 1987 downfall, but these did not affect his lucrative television ministry and theme park, since he had preached a gospel of worldly success and financial reward. Only when word leaked out about a sexual encounter with a former church secretary six years before did Assemblies of God officials – pushed hard by fellow televangelist Jimmy Swaggart – move to suspend him. Many church members turned against him and he eventually resigned as head of his PTL ministry. (Note that it was only when the religious community spread word of the scandal that church members were scandalized; media institutions played a role, but not a definitive one.) The accounts of those who knew about Bakker's tryst stressed the shame involved, his tearful repentance, his seeking forgiveness. However, they also included statements that shifted the blame to the 21-year-old secretary. Matters only became worse for Bakker when it emerged that the young woman was paid for her silence with a substantial settlement drawn from PTL funds. As Bakker's support within the Assemblies of God and among other televangelists collapsed, Justice Department officials scrutinized his ministry and its financial irregularities (Martz 1987).

As with all oral discourse, formulaic patterns took over – and these were primarily sexual. Scriptural links between sexual infidelity and apostasy became key frames. Such frames found support in traditional moral theology, which tends to rate sexual issues as more scandalous than other failings. Bakker's shame arose not from the money angle, but from the sex. The payoff serves to highlight the extent of the shame, as does this description of Bakker's repentance:

> Bakker told his flock that God had already forgiven him. Shortly after his tryst with Hahn, he said, he confessed his sin to psychologist Fred Gross, a member of the PTL family; and Gross told the viewers last week what happened: "He was sobbing. He was shaking so violently I had to hold him. In 10 minutes we were on the floor. His face was buried in the carpet. He was sobbing and kicking and screaming." (Martz 1987: 21–2)

For the PTL members, the description of the scandal serves as a warning to avoid adultery while at the same time justifying the ministry. And it made good television for PTL.

News organizations treated the Bakker scandal as part of a larger story about television evangelists and their financial dealings; the sexual aspect, while reported, did not dominate the coverage. This proves interesting in light of a common history. News organizations' concern for scandal arose historically from religious categories for scandal; in fact, colonial papers in America carried accounts of moralizing tales indistinguishable from those of Puritan writers like Cotton Mather and Samuel Danforth (S.E. Bird 1992: 11). The printing press allowed papers "to spread accounts of more or less typical outbreaks of murder, lust, and sin to an audience whose size was unprecedented but whose appetite for sensation was, more or less, normal" (Stephens 1988: 117). In fact, some argue that news institutions share more than just a common history with oral communities. Despite an emphasis on facts, much reporting – especially in tabloid papers or on scandals – resembles folklore. "Folklore and mass communication share common frameworks of defined situations, structure, function, and tradition" (D.A. Bird 1976: 285–6). With such a background, why would media report scandals differently?

The literate nature of news media (both print and electronic) leads them to a more dispassionate expression. Ong notes that "writing restructures consciousness" (1982: 78) and points out that it promotes a distance between the writer and the content. This leads to precision, analysis, objectivity, and closure, but also eliminates passion and the kind of involvement one finds in an oral community. In addition, Payne reminds us that literacy moves people to inner-directed behavior. Thus, we would expect news institutions to use categories of guilt rather than shame – and this is indeed how many reported on Bakker's case (see, for example, Judgment day . . . 1989: 65). In her study of tabloid newspapers, S. Elizabeth Bird confirms this, tracing how writers and editors move away from explicitly religious categories but maintain an emphasis on guilt and moralizing (1992: 14–15).

Because of the differences growing out of their literate and oral backgrounds, the functions served by scandal for media institutions differ somewhat from those found in the religious communities. Given human nature, *entertainment* remains a goal, for people do want to hear about the downfall of others; *critique* grows out of the distanciation and analysis implicit in literacy and allows media institutions to comment on society. *Exposé* forms another goal, for it serves the reporting function of the press; and *sales or ratings* a fourth, for obvious reasons. Finally, while they certainly report the scandalous act, media institutions show less interest in passive scandal (being scandalized) than do religious communities. This results from two characteristic communication patterns: First, the media have a dramatically-different sense of community since they deal with anonymous and undifferentiated groups – media institutions feel little responsibility to warn them about moral behaviors. Second, news media, pressed by deadlines and a glut of information, cannot tailor their presentations to the needs of their audiences. Their job is to spread the news (or the scandal), not prevent further scandals.

In the end, communication patterns representing the oral and literate backgrounds of the religious community and the media institutions do indeed highlight some meaningful differences between the two. Perpetrators of scandalous acts within the religious community face shame; perpetrators of media scandal face guilt and embarrassment as the media broadcast their deeds. While the former suffer a loss of standing within their largely face-to-face community, the latter may simply soldier on, find some way to explain away their deeds, or ignore the mostly anonymous witnesses to their misdeeds. Witnesses of scandal in the religious community draw warnings and behavioral lessons; media witnesses may simply find prejudices reinforced or confirmation for moral skepticism. Because of the nature of the community, religious groups respond to scandal with attempts to repair its damage and to limit its spread; media institutions respond in the opposite way – the more widely they announce scandals, the better they have fulfilled their role.

The rhetoric of scandal

The difference between religious groups and media institutions also manifests itself in the rhetorical form of scandal. For religious institutions there is a rhetorical expectation that governs talk and behavior; this in turn creates an expectation in the audience of church membership. When the expectation is violated, there again is a rhetorical form for labeling these as scandal. Finally, there is a rhetorical form of apology. The media institutions frame the second and third forms differently, providing grounds for further distinguishing the two.

The first of the three rhetorical or narrative moments that describe the scandal story is the least apparent, because most people take it for granted. For the religious community, it consists of the normal, day-to-day life of the group and might be manifest in nothing more than the harmonious life of its members – typical behaviors of faith, hope, and love, for example. Some might describe it as a life of holiness or of seeking God; at minimum, it involves avoiding sin. Different churches express these behaviors in their own ways – some use the biblical language of the Ten Commandments; others develop a more refined moral calculus. Ultimately, these narratives tell the story of what it means to belong to the group. A Catholic behaves in certain ways just as a member of the Assemblies of God follows particular teachings and behavioral practices.

Media institutions also attend to such taken-for-granted narratives of behavior, but in a more complicated fashion. Sensitive to social practices, they heed the definitions of proper behavior among the groups which constitute their audiences and monitor the environment for acts that violate community norms. The unusual – acts of destruction, disasters, crime, political turmoil, and so on – gets reported. This monitoring grows out of certain sets of values, such as those identified by Gans (1979): ethnocentrism, altruistic democracy, responsible capitalism, small-town pastoralism, individualism, and moderatism. At the same time, media institutions act out of their own self-definitions and enforce the culture of the newsroom on reporters and editors in order to foster a consistency in selecting, reporting, and presenting stories (McManus 1994). In this first moment, the religious community and the media institutions do not differ all that much, since the media institutions willingly accept behavioral guidelines for each group of their constituencies. They may not, nor must they, agree with the guidelines; it is enough that they see them as binding on the group that has proposed them. For example, a media institution or its members may feel that religious opposition to abortion is wrong; however, they will faithfully report such opposition and acknowledge that church members favoring abortion are somehow out of step with their congregations.

A second – and key – rhetorical moment comes with the naming of scandal. For religious groups, not all sin is scandalous. In fact, a religious definition of scandal limits the term and how it should be employed: "Scandal is defined as 'any conduct that has at least the appearance of evil and that offers to a neighbor an occasion of spiritual ruin'" (McHugh and Callan 1929: 584). Wrongdoing is not enough to qualify as scandal; *the wrongdoing must further lead to the spiritual harm of another*. In this light, Jim Bakker's sexual misconduct with Jessica Hahn – while wrong – was not scandalous until it became public knowledge. In fact, one could well criticize Jimmy Swaggart's publicizing the event as perhaps more scandalous than Bakker's action, since it served to do more spiritual harm to a greater number of people.[1] In keeping with limits on scandal, traditional moral teaching does identify some actions as more likely to qualify than others: attacking religion, obscenity, sexual misconduct, public disorder, injustice, bad example.

Media institutions follow a looser set of definitions for scandal, as Lull and Hinerman point out in this volume: "A media scandal occurs when private acts that disgrace or offend the idealized, dominant morality of a social community are made public and narrativized by the media, producing a range of effects from ideological and cultural retrenchment to disruption and change." Scandalous acts are those that offend some social convention. For the media institutions, key among these is hypocrisy – when a representative of a given group acts against the social norms he or she publicly upholds. This factor made it incumbent on the press to report the charges against Jimmy Swaggart and Cardinal Bernardin, whose cases I will take up in some detail in the following pages. Similarly, media institutions tend to regard secrecy or the attempt to hide actions as indicative of scandal.

The rhetoric of apology

The greatest divergence between religious groups and media institutions, however, appears in the third rhetorical moment: apology or repair. Because of their interest in maintaining community, each church has some ritual or process of repair for sin and scandal: confession, reconciliation, forgiveness, and so on. Each church usually specifies the form of the repair discourse. It typically includes naming the act, asking forgiveness, accepting punishment, and promising amendment.

Jimmy Swaggart, the powerful Assemblies of God televangelist who campaigned against wrongdoing by other evangelists, was himself caught in a sexual scandal. Despite his preaching against pornography and despite his denunciation of the adultery of others, he was photographed meeting with prostitutes, whom he allegedly asked to pose nude for him, though he denied ever having intercourse with them (Ostling 1988: 47). When the photos found their way to the Assemblies of God headquarters, the group debated the appropriate punishment: suspension, defrocking, or something in between. Swaggart preached his own confession service and made these comments illustrating the rhetoric of the repair:

> I do not call it a mistake, a mendacity. I call it a sin . . . I have no one but myself to blame. (Ostling 1988: 46)

> And to the hundreds of millions that I have stood before in over 100 countries of the world . . . I've looked into the cameras, and so many of you with a heart of loneliness that needed help reached out to the minister of the gospel. You that are nameless – most I will never be able to see you except in faith – I sinned against you. I beg you to forgive me. (Wright 1988: 100)

> My savior, my Redeemer . . . I have sinned against you, my Lord, and I would ask that your precious blood would wash and cleanse every stain until it is in the seas of God's forgiveness, never to be remembered against me anymore. (Ostling 1988: 46)

Interestingly, Swaggart omitted what most religious groups would regard as two essential elements: He never named his sin and he refused to accept the punishment imposed by the national Assemblies of God leadership – a two-year suspension. Instead, he accepted the milder three-month suspension imposed by the Louisiana Assemblies of God, a group dominated by his supporters (Wright 1988: 100). When he returned to his pulpit, the incomplete repair led one church member to disrupt the service:

> *"Brother Swaggart!"* comes the voice of a teenage boy from the balcony. *"Brother Swaggart!"* The church grows quiet. Swaggart does not turn around. "Your hypocrisy is scornful of the government of God! Liar! Hypocrite!" (Wright 1988: 103)

Just as Swaggart's confession illustrates the rhetoric of scandal repair, the disruption illustrates how well church members know the prescribed form. What Swaggart did not finish, at least some demanded.

Another repair vignette comes from the accusation of Steven Cook against Chicago's Cardinal Bernardin. Both before and after Cook had withdrawn the charges, Bernardin had attempted to meet with Cook, a meeting that took place finally on December 30, 1994, a year after the initial accusation and nine months after the dropping of charges. Bernardin's purpose was not to ask forgiveness – he steadfastly denied all charges – but to seek reconciliation.

In his statement, the Cardinal says he sought out Mr Cook last week for the express purpose of bringing "closure to the traumatic events of last winter by personally letting him know that I harbored no ill feelings toward him. . . . I also told him that while I would not want to go through such a humiliating experience again, nonetheless it had contributed to my own spiritual growth and had made me more compassionate. . . . I told him that in every family there are times when there is hurt, anger, aliena-tion," he writes, adding that the church is a spiritual family. "But we cannot run away from our family. We have only one family, so we must make every effort to be reconciled." . . .

"Never in my 43 years as a priest have I witnessed a more profound reconciliation," he writes. . . . "May this story give to anyone who is hurt or alienated the inspiration and courage to be reconciled." (Niebuhr 1995: A11)

Bernardin meant his enactment of reconciliation to serve as a les-son for the community by modeling the behavior of restoring unity after scandal. Not only does Bernardin forgive, he also sketches the benefits of spiritual growth and instructs church members on the reasons for forgiveness.

Media institutions have trouble framing this last rhetorical moment since they lack their own narratives for apology. They can and do borrow from other groups, reporting court cases, religious confes-sions, political apologies, and so on. They face the limit of merely reporting and not judging the adequacy of the apology. How could they validate Swaggart's confession? Or invalidate it, as the teen-ager in the balcony did? This leads to an awkward situation for a media scandal – it does not end. Instead, it hangs in the air until another scandal displaces it.

Conclusion

Media scandals illustrate the social, cultural, and rhetorical differ-ences between religious groups and media organizations. At the same time, they also demonstrate our inability to disentangle these powerful contemporary institutions competing for social control and influence. Where the media groups borrow definitions of scan-dal from their religious counterparts, the religious groups depend more and more on the media to communicate with their members. Swaggart's church learned the nature of his sin not from his con-fession, but from news accounts. Only a few of Bernardin's con-gregation read his reconciliation account from his pen; people across the country learned the lesson of reconciliation from news accounts of the meeting.

Because many people belong to both institutions – they are church-goers and media consumers – they have a stake in both. Such membership may make it easier for them to move between the two or it may make it more difficult to fully accept the definitions and social control of either. Church members may resist and resent media reporting of church scandals; non-church members may find it hard to make sense of seemingly restrictive church teachings. Their positioning vis-à-vis each institution will largely predict how people react to media scandals.

Finally, the differences between the two institutions revealed by their reaction to scandals (reporting, repairing, manifesting, minimizing, and so on) highlight the need for each to better understand the other. And, sadly, that does not happen often, as Steinfels testifies: "Religion and the media is a topic surrounded by hypersensitivity, if not downright paranoia" (1995: 14). Perhaps scandal, revealing something to each, could ironically become common ground and a site of reconciliation.

Note

1 Some did question Swaggart's motives, both in regard to Bakker and in regard to another evangelist he had earlier charged with adultery (see Martz 1987; Wright 1988).

References

Accuser drops abuse charge against Cardinal in Chicago. (1994). *New York Times*, March 1: A20.
Aquinas, Thomas. (1972). *Summa Theologiae*, vol. 35: 2a2ae. 34–46. London: Blackfriars.
Bird, D.A. (1976). A theory for folklore in mass media: Traditional patterns in the mass media. *Southern Folklore Quarterly*, 40(3, 4): 285–305.
Bird, S.E. (1992). *For Enquiring Minds: A Cultural Study of Supermarket Tabloids*. Knoxville, TN: University of Tennessee Press.
Chicago prelate is accused of sex abuse and denies it. (1993). *New York Times*, November 13: A12.
Commission on Freedom of the Press. (1947). *A Free and Responsible Press*. Chicago: University of Chicago Press.
Derrett, J.D.M. (1985). Two "harsh" sayings of Christ explained. *Downside Review*, 103: 218–29.

Gamson, J. (1995). Incredible news: Tabloids meet news. *Current*, 370: 3–7.

Gans, H.J. (1979). *Deciding What's News: A Study of CBS Evening News, NBC Nightly News, Newsweek, and* Time. New York: Pantheon.

Hanson, C. (1994). How to handle dirty stories (and still feel clean). *Columbia Journalism Review*, 32(6): 14–16.

Häring, B. (1964). *The Law of Christ: Moral Theology for Priests and Laity*. Vol. 2: *Special Moral Theology*. Tr. E.G. Kaiser. Westminster, MD: Newman Press. (Original work 1960).

Idvsoog, K. (1994). TV sitting on stories to improve ratings. *Nieman Reports*, 48(1): 38.

Judgment day. (1989). *Time*, October 16: 65.

Léon-Dufour, X. (ed.) (1973). *Dictionary of Biblical Theology*. 2nd edn, tr. P.J. Cahill. New York: Seabury Press. (Original work 1968).

Martz, L. (1987). God and money: Sex scandal, greed and lust for power split the TV preaching world. *Newsweek*, April 6: 16–22.

McHugh, J.A. and Callan, C.J. (1929). *Moral Theology: A Complete Course*, vol. I. New York: Joseph F. Wagner.

McManus, J. (1994). *Market-driven Journalism: Let the Citizen Beware?* Thousand Oaks, CA: Sage.

Niebuhr, G. (1995). For cardinal and accuser, a profound reconciliation. *New York Times*, January 7: A11.

Ong, W.J. (1982). *Orality and Literacy: The Technologizing of the Word*. London: Methuen.

Ostling, R.N. (1988). Now it's Jimmy's turn: The sins of Swaggart send another shock through the world of TV evangelism. *Time*, March 7: 46–8.

Payne, D. (1991). Characterology, media, and rhetoric. In B.E. Gronbeck, T.J. Farrell, and P.A. Soukup (eds), *Media, Consciousness, and Culture: Explorations of Walter Ong's Thought*, 223–36. Newbury Park, CA: Sage.

Riesman, D., Denny, R. and Glazer, N. (1950). *The Lonely Crowd: A Study of the Changing American Character*. New Haven: Yale University Press.

Schechter, D. (1994). TV news with a conscience. *Nieman Reports*, 48(1): 39–42.

Shaw, D. (1994). Surrender of the gatekeepers. *Nieman Reports*, 48(1): 3–5.

Stählin, G. (1971). σκανδαλον. In G. Friedrich (ed.), *Theological Dictionary of the New Testament*, vol. 7: 339–58. Grand Rapids, MI: Wm B. Eerdmans. (Original work 1964).

Steinfels, P. (1995). Religion and the media: Three 70th anniversary forums keynote address. *Commonweal*, February 24, 122(4): 14–19.

Stephens, M. (1988). *A History of News: From the Drum to the Satellite*. New York: Viking.

Tumber, H. (1993). "Selling scandal": Business and the media. *Media, Culture, and Society*, 15: 345–61.

Williams, R. (1976). *Keywords: A Vocabulary of Culture and Society*. New York: Oxford University Press.

Wright, L. (1988). False messiah. *Rolling Stone*, July 14–28: 96–110, 151–2.

11 Pushin' it to the Limit:

Scandals and Pop Music

Javier Santiago-Lucerna

This chapter focuses on the way scandals articulate both the production and consumption of popular music in society. Scandals are examined as part of the *desiring production* of pop music. Although they have formed an essential part of pop music since its beginnings, two particularly striking examples will be emphasized here: the Sex Pistols and the punk revolt created during the late 1970s, and Madonna's visit to Puerto Rico during her Girlie Show tour. I hope to show how scandals work as a crucial part of the seductive modus operandi of popular music. The first part of this analysis, thus, dwells on how scandals fuse with pop music as part of an overall commodity configuration within the cultural media. Second, specific illustrations of this discourse are considered.

Let us recall three particular moments from media history to demonstrate the power and prominence scandals have had on the early success of pop music in the United States. It was television, not the music industry, that provided a certain platform for the possibility of pop-music scandal. By watching the *Ed Sullivan Show*, many fans were able to establish visual "contact" with pop-music stars. The show was a trampoline for new bands as they were able to reach a huge audience in one shot, thus greatly enhancing their chances for stardom. Even the Beatles benefitted tremendously. While the Fab Four were already popular before traveling to the States, their performance on the *Ed Sullivan Show* gave them a unique opportunity to exhibit the complete package; now they were not just a pop band, but a phenomenon surrounded by hysteria. In order to move to this next level, the remarkable sight and sound of screaming girls as background to the music was needed. In the realm of popular culture, what happened that night on the *Ed Sullivan Show* was a scandal.

The Beatles' television performance created quite a stir, mainly because the mainstream, adult world could not understand what the hysteria was all about. Was it simply a matter of innocent, pre-pubescent, and adolescent adoration directed toward four harmless guys from "over there?" Or was it something more, something quite threatening? At the heart of the adult incomprehension was a very particular fact: only the kids understood what the frenzy meant. It was the frenzy that separated children from their parents, and the parents could not control what was happening.

Later came the same opportunity for that other band from England, the Rolling Stones. This time, however, the scandalous nature of the appearance on the same show had less to do with what they did, more with what they did not do. While the Rolling Stones were invited by Sullivan's staff to sing their hedonistic anthem to pubescent lust, "Let's Spend the Night Together," the band was forced to alter the key lyric to "Let's Spend Some Time Together." This, the band was told, would be necessary so as not to offend the national television audience. Mick Jagger's face on the tube that night told the whole story: it revealed both disappointment and burlesque as he mocked the conservative cultural decision. In the end, Sullivan helped demarcate pop culture from authorized culture. The Rolling Stones' authentic music had been labeled inappropriate for consumption by the general public. Parents were pacified; teens were outraged.

The third example also draws from the archive of the *Ed Sullivan Show*. The singer of the Doors, Jim Morrison, was asked by Sullivan to alter the lyrics to the classic "Light My Fire." While the band agreed to change beforehand, when they took the live TV stage the Doors performed the song with full integrity. Sullivan was incensed, swearing that the Doors' career was simply over. The Doors broke the rules and created a scandal in the process. Of course, this incident only contributed to the rebellious image and ethereal mysticism that surrounded Jim Morrison and the Doors during their heyday and beyond; it continues even today.

These three significant events point to different kinds of scandal. Each scandal set in motion a foundational feature of rock music

history. The Beatles rocked the cultural sphere by their very presence. The Stones had been censored, but took an irreverent, even
disrespectful, attitude toward mainstream cultural practice. The
Doors openly disobeyed cultural authority. Each of these scandalous events helped shape the way we experience popular music today.

The screaming and the commotion broke any pretense of inter-
generational harmony for those who were not tuned into what was
happening. For the participants, however, the frenzy was itself an
emotional medium for conveying the ecstasy of pop music and
culture from one person to another. If scandals such as these are
experienced by the body, then they are aesthetic. They relate more
to what we feel than to what we think. In this sense, the scandals
were accumulating historically to articulate the experiences of young
people under an increasingly unified cultural code. These musical
experiences made their participants – both musicians and fans –
feel different: defying of adult authority. They were true sensory
experiences. They articulated, reinforced, and extended a growing,
restless consciousness among youth. But let us not forget, the Beatles,
the Stones, and the Doors were (and are) part of an economic
enterprise too. Scandals still operate not only as emotional and
cultural magnets for youth, but as profitable ploys for the music
industry as well.

Popular music, the rock apparatus, and commodity aesthetics

I began this chapter by discussing examples derived not solely
from music but from television, in order to illustrate the pervasive
presence and significance of popular music. Music is important not
only in terms of sound. In fact, much popular music is very simple
musically. As Hill argues: "What we should notice first about early
rock and roll music is that it was less a breakthrough at the level
of musical form or language than a series of transformations in the
way in which popular music was produced and disseminated"
(Hill 1991: 679). Contemporary popular music too derives its meaning not from the realm of words set to melodies/sounds, but from
an ever-expanding consolidation of various technologies, symbolic
forms, and cultural impulses.

Certainly in order to grasp the way popular music articulates the
tension of its audience we must listen carefully to the lyrics, the

beat, the melody, the arrangement. But the release of tension is also linked profoundly to the visual realm. There lies the importance of style, movement, social space, class, race, attitude, and ideology. These cultural features are all clustered around an even more encompassing imaginary that gives life to popular music's cultural practices. Larry Grossberg calls this ensemble of sites the "rock apparatus." He defines this apparatus as a device that:

> brings together musical texts and practices, economic relations, images (of performers and fans), social relations, aesthetic conventions, styles of language, movement, appearance and dance, media practices, ideological commitments, and sometimes media representations of the apparatus itself. It is not merely a set of codes or resources that a particular audience brings to the text. (Grossberg 1984: 101)

In recognizing its intricate relation with mass media and technology, contemporary popular music must be understood as part of a much broader transformation of social space, work, and everyday life. It is related to what several social critics call "consumer society," the relatively unobstructed circulation of commodities through social space, and the "symbolization and use of material goods as 'communicators,' not just utilities" (Featherstone 1991: 84). This means that, first of all, there is a need to recognize that the popularity of music derives not from its direct relation to the people who create it and listen to it, but rather from the way it reaches masses of people through vast territorial extensions. This is made possible by its commodification and the advent of consumer culture, which allows commodities to circulate freely through different and spatially-separated groups of people. But in order to incite consumption, commodities need a symbolic dimension with which consumers can relate. This symbiosis is crucial in order to understand the relationship between pop music and the media scandal.

In his book on U2, Flanagan discusses the group's image change during the 1990s, and argues that:

> The emotional directness, the simplicity, that rock and roll got from blues and country is always at the heart of the music's appeal. It only took a few years for people to get used to the sound of basic rock and roll before its directness began to seem clichéd. So new angles had to be found to surprise the ear and keep music fresh without corrupting rock's directness ... From Hendrix to country rock to reggae to the Sex Pistols to *Achtung Baby*, rock and roll has come up with sonic innovations that allow us to hear a simple song as if we have never heard it before ... The ideas

> that make them innovative records are finally important only because
> they allow us to hear the songs with fresh ears. (Flanagan 1995: 153)

What Flanagan calls "angles," "sonic innovations," and "ideas" are all part of the process of symbolization that brings meaning to what in a strict musical canon does not appear to have much significance at all. If pop music is considered first and foremost a commodity (rather than a musical object), "symbolization" is the operation by which that particular object is rendered likable to the potential consumer.

Haug calls this particularity of commodities in contemporary society "commodity aesthetics," meaning that a sensual understanding "developed in service of the realization of exchange value, whereby commodities are designed to stimulate in the onlooker the desire to possess and the impulse to buy" (Haug 1986: 8). In other words, the process of symbolization imprints on the commodity a certain alchemy (or "aura" as Walter Benjamin would call it: Benjamin 1968) that attracts consumers toward it. This aura need not reside in the object *per se*, but in the way the commodity is wrapped and marketed.

So, in order to conceal what in musical terms would be pop's structural simplicity, the industries that produce it must create images and discourses that make such a simple symbolic form desirable. Pop music's commodity aesthetics thus resides not in the musical realm, but in the way the genre is portrayed in public space. The rock apparatus exists to produce the right (read "profitable") aura for the musical object. As Flanagan (1995) points out, part of the aura of rock music surely is built within the timbre, but the production of commodity aesthetics encompasses many other domains of representation. Grossberg (1984), for example, has suggested that the symbolization of pop overflows into sensuality and visuality. The symbolization also includes clothing, television, print media, and cinema as media of exposition, spectacle, and performance. The main objective of the apparatus is to render popular music likable to its target audience, to make it desirable.

Now, the immediate question that comes to mind when discussing the way popular music makes itself desirable is: How is such a weighty task accomplished? Medovoi suggests that since its inception, rock has used "shock" as a strategy to embellish its commodity status and stimulate consumption (Medovoi 1991/2: 159). He relates this approach to the style of the avant-garde, where the intention was to offend the bourgeoisie, noting that rock's real critique is against the very social conditions which create it:

Rock and roll then utilizes shock tactics as had the historical avant-garde, but its narratives aim at a different target: intentional rudeness that flaunts a refusal of blandness and conformity through such devices as obscenity, crude irony, electronic feedback and distortion, sexualized performance, high volume, even screaming. But it directs all this not at the sanctity of art, but at the sanctity of life – at what it considers to be the banality of a pop existence. (Medovoi 1991/2: 160)

The contempt, thus, is directed at social institutions, including mass media and the culture industries, but at the same time it contributes to the wealth of the mass media and related entertainment industries. Worth noting are the shock tactics. Obscenity, crude irony, the sexualized performance, and screaming are all commonly perceived within normative society as disruptions – scandalous behaviors that fracture the stability and harmony of everyday life. Pop music fastens its symbolic power to such disruptions by adding technical elements – feedback, distortion, high volume – to the mix. We are led to the inescapable and important conclusion that the commodity aesthetics of popular music is rooted in its potential to disrupt the flow of everyday life – its ability to scandalize civil society.

Consider this proposition in light of pop music's crucial early moments. The uproar Elvis Presley created with his pelvic twists and thrusts, for instance, actually became a mechanism intended to represent the sexual curiosity and restlessness of American teenagers in the 1950s. It was scandalous. Since its inception, rock music has depended on creating an audience for itself separate from fans of the sweet melodies left over from the Tin Pan Alley era. The audience for rock was constructed as different from other real and possible audiences. If rock was to be a site where, among other things, sexuality was to be embodied (at least discursively), it was not just any kind of sexuality. It was adolescent sexuality. It was also important for rock to construct the adult world as something different, something that did not and could not relate well to adolescents. In this sense, pop-music scandals work in two ways: by rendering pop music and its culture incomprehensible to adults, and as a desiring production meant to stimulate participation and cultural possession by youth.

Many examples come from cinema, where the tension created by rock's sensual content is filtered through the lens of public opinion. A good early example is the film *Blackboard Jungle* from the 1950s, where an intimate association between rebelliousness and youth is contemplated. The movie was among the first to use rock music as its soundtrack, constructing through it a significant liaison between the emerging musical genre and the scandalous behavior of youth depicted in the movie. The film was meant to show the crisis of mid-century American youth, their demeanor, their wicked values. By framing adolescents as the "other," it contributed greatly to the scandalous aura that rock and roll, and American youth culture generally, was erecting for itself.

Rock's controversial nature can also be productively evaluated by reviewing the polemic over its censorship in the 1950s. Most of the censors' arguments derived from those aspects where rock's shock tactics were most apparent: the beat, its "jungle strains," and its association with youth riots (Hill 1991: 682–7). The public was alarmed by the way the music effectively summoned teenagers' bodies and their sexual energy. It was a major disruption to the socialization process of a society where sexuality was concealed, even repressed. Because of the way it was structured musically and performed, rock also integrated the presence of black culture into white teen awareness, a development that some white adults surely regarded as damaging to their children. Furthermore, there were traces of juvenile delinquency that rock and roll evoked through its structure of feeling, including especially the visual aspects – the tough look, the hoods, the outsiders. All these elements worked effectively as commodity aesthetics of the genre because through them "teenagers could exercise the body and . . . indulge its sexuality" (Hill 1991: 680).

The Sex Pistols and the punk revolt as pop scandal prototypes

To take punk as an illustration of how scandals work as a commodity aesthetic for popular music is risky. This is because punk was supposed to function outside the corporate culture industries. Still, punk is instructive because it shows very explicitly the role scandals play in how popular music is configured as a desiring object. Its case reveals how artists actually need industry to construct certain forms of attention. Thus, the genius of Malcolm McLaren is not that he "discovered" the Sex Pistols (indeed, he created the band in many respects), but that he was able to create a stunning myth that contributed greatly to what became known as the "punk revolt." In a vivid account of the radical cultural developments of the 1970s in England, John Savage (1992) tells how McLaren mastered the business of creating scandals. McLaren started not in the music business, but in the fashion scene. He owned a clothing store on King's Road in London. By giving the store various names (the best known was "Sex"), McLaren was able to sell clothes through shock appeal. Scandals were created by the way the sexy garments were displayed in the store windows. Police even confiscated some of the most radical outfits in the name of public decency. The ensuing controversy contributed much to the notoriety the shop was getting, enticing consumers from all over the world to spend money there.

Fully conscious of the way fashion articulates into popular music, McLaren decided in 1975 to expand his operations within popular culture. That was the moment he decided to support a band Steve Jones and Paul Cook were putting together. McLaren's interest in the project focused on the image of the band, not so much the music. His fascination with John Lydon – the way he dressed, his language, his attitude – signaled how he would package the Sex Pistols: much the same way he had designed and displayed clothing – as a scandal. John Lydon became Johnny Rotten.

The Sex Pistols would shake British society and the world. The road to superstardom, however, began only after a now-famous incident on the television program *Today*, hosted by Bill Grundy. At the time, the Sex Pistols were *potentially* one of the hottest items on the British music scene; they had just closed a deal with EMI, one of the most prestigious record companies in Europe. The record company's executives managed to book the Sex Pistols on *Today*, as they were searching widely for new avenues of exposure. The executives never realized what a mess the Sex Pistols were about to make on national television. Rotten and his mates made numerous obscene utterances and gestures. Bill Grundy became livid. All of England was abuzz about these "irreverent punks." Given our discussion here, the result is perhaps predictable. The Sex Pistols had created a scandal of such magnitude it seemed to secure their success: "from that day on it was different . . . before then, it was just music; the next day it was the media" (Savage 1992: 260).

As the Sex Pistols' uproar reached maximum volume young fans identified more and more with what was at stake. The punk band and its growing number of followers were considered outlaws against proper English values and behavior. But from a marketing standpoint, the *Today* incident and all that followed signaled exactly how things should be handled from the point of view of the band. From that time forward the Sex Pistols intentionally accumulated scandal after scandal, and with the history they were writing their popularity grew by leaps and bounds. Even when they resurfaced in 1996, the Sex Pistols could best be understood as a scandal waiting to happen.

But this strategy in the realm of popular music does not always work to the advantage of the musicians and the economic forces behind them. The scandal-on-purpose approach, for instance, was used in the Sex Pistols' tour of the United States in 1977. McLaren advised the band to play not only in places where attendance was assured, and where fans would be knowledgable, but in obscure places along the southern belt where the sole purpose would be to annoy the audience. As a result, the Sex Pistols became embroiled in controversies they could not control. Struggles in the ideology, management, and performance of the band then began to infect the success. Johnny Rotten quit; the Sex Pistols' magic faded away.

Malcolm McLaren understood the way popular music works in the commercial emporium. He had manipulated the media in such a way that it constructed the Sex Pistols primarily as an object of sociocultural disgust. The strategy guaranteed short-term success, but it eventually led to failure. But the larger point is that the whole Sex Pistols experience helped many youth redefine and reconfirm what it means to be young. If at its beginning rock music conveyed an energy and spirit of things to come (as Grossberg suggests: 1992), then punk became a forum where the young could exteriorize their frustration with social conditions. The scandals created by the Sex Pistols and other punk bands represented a kind of authenticity that bolstered their acceptance among young people, and encouraged the music industry to pay attention too.

Upon historical reflection, however, the importance of punk must also be understood in terms of how scandals reach their limits as commodity aesthetics. The same media the Sex Pistols had manipulated so effectively at the beginning later started to undermine their economic and cultural potential. For example, industrial plate-makers refused at first to create the proper materials for cutting one of their singles, "God Save the Queen," which was being prepared just in time for the celebration of the Jubilee of Queen Elizabeth. Radio refused to play the song during Jubilee week (Savage 1992: 349, 365). While the song worked to reinforce the band's scandalous image, it also gave government authorities and mass media a reason to derail the Sex Pistols' influence. From that moment on, the Sex Pistols suffered censorship at the hands of British authorities so harsh they had to stop playing live shows. Even EMI buckled under the pressure. The Sex Pistols' contract with the music giant was canceled. In the end, not only government but the culture industries had retreated from the band that abused them.

I will return later to this discussion of the limits of scandals within the desiring production of popular music. For the moment, it must be said that at the same time the Sex Pistols showed their power, they also met its confines. As Hill (1991) notes regarding rock's censorship during the 1950s, rarely did civic authorities censor specific cases (bands, records, concerts); they executed their crusade much more generally against the whole idea of rock and roll. But in the case of the Sex Pistols, censorship was brought to bear on the performers themselves. The Sex Pistols exceeded the limits of tolerance and brought a new variety of censorship into consideration and action. Such a change in society's attitude toward the supposed dangers of popular music will now be explored in my second key example.

Express yourself: Madonna's Puerto Rican flag incident

Throughout her career Madonna has used scandals and the media in a way exemplary of the influence exerted by the Sex Pistols and the punk revolt. Even the not-so-innocent, girlish look she showed the world when arriving on the pop music scene was produced in part by punk's subversiveness. The world of pop had been transformed by the Sex Pistols' antics, and any performer or group hoping to reach stardom needed to stir some kind of controversy to get sufficient attention.

Madonna picked up the cue beautifully. After her first album she began to get away from all traces of innocence, lest they be wrongly interpreted as submission. Even her video portrayal of a virgin was ambivalent: she appeared in the "Like a Virgin" clip in lingerie and an aerobics outfit. Madonna then went from virgin to material girl to seducer to slut to unwed mother. She has endured so long as a pop-culture heroine through constant changes not only in music, but in image.

The Girlie Show tour of 1993 was ripe for scandal in Puerto Rico. Madonna's controversial album *Erotica* had just been released. It was joined in the cultural sphere by the movie *Body of Evidence,* where Madonna played a lethal seductress, and by a book of semi-pornographic photographs of the pop star, *Sex*. Through all this Madonna had become an evil vamp, a ruthless man trapper constantly searching for new varieties of forbidden fruit. Earlier, *Justify My Love* had become the biggest seller in the history of the singles format after it was banned from MTV Music Television for being too sexually explicit. The MTV ban forced the public to either buy or rent the video in order to see what was so controversial. The ban itself then became big news, adding to the Madonna mystique. While she may have appeared to have been a big loser when the MTV ban was first announced, she ended up profiting greatly from the situation as audio and video versions of the sexy song sold in retail outlets skyrocketed. The big payoff from *Justify My Love* incited her to push the limits of her image even more. With so much marketing foreplay, it became obvious that the the Girlie Show tour was going to be wild.

The official announcement for the concert date in San Juan was made on August 12, 1993, by promoter Larry Stein. Soon many Puerto Rican civic organizations raised their voices against the concert.[1] They argued that Madonna was a horrible role model for Puerto Rican youth. They questioned her musical ability. Some groups called for a concert boycott and a ban on the promoter. Later, island government officials said that although they could not stop the concert, they agreed it was not good for young people.

The concert controversy, of course, created just the effect Madonna and her promoter wanted. The show sold out so quickly the promoter scrambled around to book even more mega events in Puerto Rico.[2] Meanwhile, Madonna's fans defended her vociferously against charges of immorality, arguing for tolerance and respect.

On the night of the concert, several civic and religious groups picketed and prayed outside the stadium, desperately trying to dissuade the audience from attending. Some sang religious hymns, attempting to drown out the blasphemous ritual going on inside. News reporters from all over Puerto Rico swarmed the grounds. Because of the sharp conflict between pro- and anti-Madonna forces, they expected a confrontation, maybe even a physical fight. Television stations covered the show from helicopters whirling overhead.

Something important did happen that night, but it had nothing to do directly with the kind of hostility I have described above. About two-thirds of the way into the show, with Madonna singing the hit *Holiday*, and with her dancers dressed in military outfits under a giant American flag, Madonna took a Puerto Rican flag from someone in the audience. In front of everyone, she slowly pulled the flag between her legs.

There is a lot at work here in the context of Puerto Rican politics and culture. Since the invasion of the American troops at the end of the nineteenth century, Puerto Rico has been a colonial territory of the United States. Political debates on the island throughout the years have oscillated between the desirability of colonial status (which, of course, has been modified from the original situation), annexation or statehood (with full representation in the American congress), and independence from the United States. Of the three options, statehood has the biggest following among Puerto Ricans, although the proponents of independence also have a strong voice. The complex struggle between forces of change – between advocates of statehood and those of independence – contributes to a powerful and perplexing ambivalence in the political and cultural identity of island inhabitants. This is a long-standing and emotional issue for all Puerto Ricans, so any action by a "mainlander" certainly will be interpreted at least partly in terms of this sensitivity.

The live concert audience barely noticed what Madonna did with the flag. People continued to dance and scream. But the media, especially television, became acutely aware of what had happened. When the concert was over reporters asked fans about the "flag incident." Representative David Noriega, a member of the Puerto Rican Independence Party, called for a public reprimand of the singer. He asked that criminal charges be brought against Madonna for offending Puerto Ricans. Other politicians agreed, including even the pro-statehood governor. The incident also regenerated a huge debate about identity politics among Puerto Rican intellectuals (Román 1995; Pabón 1995). Interestingly, the heated discussions concentrated on how the event shifted the focus of contemporary Puerto Rican identity struggles away from the political sphere to the cultural sphere. The fact that so many diverse politicians, intellectuals, and civic representatives were offended by Madonna's gesture – all for their own reasons, but still somehow united – illustrates plainly how serious the struggle for island identity is, and what a complex thing the media scandal can be.

The scandal traveled far beyond Puerto Rican shores. It was reported in the *New York Times*. David Letterman commented on it the following week. Dennis Miller joked about it on *Saturday Night Live*, wondering "whatever happened to the flagpole?" The Brazilian parliament passed a law prohibiting Madonna or anyone else from using the Brazilian national flag in offensive ways. Media from around the globe began to track Madonna's footsteps ever more closely.

Regardless of Madonna's intentions, the "flag incident" clearly shows the disruptive potential of popular music. The consequences, however, are not easy to predict. Scandals do not always work in favor of the scandalizer. If what Madonna wanted to create onstage in San Juan was a rude act designed to enhance the appeal and value of her commodity aesthetic, then within the Puerto Rican political and cultural context this was a mistake. More likely she simply intended to add another suggestive dimension to the sexual atmosphere of the concert, quite fitting to the sensuality of Puerto Rico. Maybe she intended to insult those who were protesting the concert outside, who knows? Whatever the motivation, Madonna touched a raw nerve in Puerto Rico – the political and cultural ambivalence, and uneasy relation to mainland USA, that the territory has been going through for an entire century. The "flag incident," thus, reveals both the symbolic triumphs and limits of the media scandal as a culturally-situated phenomenon of popular music seen as a commodity aesthetic.

Pushin' it to the limit: the boundaries of scandal in pop

> We're fat, forty, and we're back. Nobody likes us, but we don't care.
> *Johnny Rotten during a concert on the Sex Pistols reunion tour in London, June, 1996*

One way that the popular music industry tries to sell its product is by creating commotion. The commotion is not just about musical aesthetics; it also affects the consumer at the discursive level. Pop-music scandals can even dramatically influence the way young people construct their values and their everyday lives.

Media scandals have been an important part of the popular music scene since the 1950s. Beginning back then, scandals have been incorporated into the way music is made and presented to the public. Scandals help young people *feel* popular music. The combination of pop music's sensual content and the shock appeal of scandal incites audiences to participate in the imaginary of pop, thus forging them as consumers of certain kinds of culture.

There are important, substantial differences, however, among the types of pop-music scandal and the means by which they influence listener/consumers. We must be careful not to collapse all kinds of pop-music or media scandals into a single category. For example, consider our two main examples, the Sex Pistols and Madonna, as scandal producers. While the Sex Pistols violated the rock-music establishment, they scandalized its musical code as well as its style and manner of professional conduct. Madonna, on the other hand, has mainly affected only the style and manner. These differences shape discourses that give life to pop music while they promote diverse ideological impacts.

Finally, to look closely at the changing nature of the media scandal, especially its shifting boundaries, sheds light not just on the workings of popular music as an art form and industry, or on the media, but on the nature of consumer society. The history of censorship surrounding pop music reveals how the dominant moral code has changed through time. As I discussed earlier, such ideological and cultural dynamics related to music get worked out strenuously in relations between youth and their elders. The pop-music scandal brings questions of cultural identity right to the surface, as was the case with Madonna's appearance in Puerto Rico.

Ideological and cultural hegemony thus is made problematic through the discourses of the media scandal. Despite such challenges to the status quo, however, the media scandal in popular music also reminds us of what Walter Benjamin intended throughout his oeuvre. Buck-Morss (1992) insightfully suggests that Benjamin's work is an exercise aimed at discovering how capitalism has shaped the cultural experiences of people through "shock." Popular-music scandals, in a very similar manner, seduce consumers into possessing goods by submerging them in the undeniable sensuality of the art form and the shock of marketing appeals. The rational capacity of the human being, Benjamin warns us, becomes obliterated in the process. Perhaps that profitable, shocking journey is precisely what Elvis, the Beatles, the Stones, the Doors, the Sex Pistols, Madonna, and all other pop-music scandalizers have in common.

Notes

The author wishes to thank James Lull, Stephen Hinerman, Nydza Correa de Jesús, M.T. Martínez, and Maria Judith Rosa for their suggestions.

1 The first letter opposing the concert was published September 17, 1993, in the local newspaper, *El Nuevo Día*. From that point forward a tremendous reaction took place as many different persons and organizations expressed their opposition to the concert.
2 He booked Michael Jackson for a show in San Juan, but the event was called off because Jackson had been accused of child molestation charges (see Hinerman, this volume), and the tour was abandoned.

References

Benjamin, W. (1968). The work of art in the age of mechanical reproduction. In H. Arendt (ed.), *Illuminations*. New York: Shocken Books.

Buck-Morss, S. (1992). Aesthetics and anaesthetics: Walter Benjamin's essay reconsidered. *October*, 62: 3–41.

Featherstone, M. (1991). *Consumer Culture and Postmodernism*. London: Sage.

Flanagan, B. (1995). *U2 at the End of the World*. New York: Delta.

Grossberg, L. (1984). I'd rather feel bad than not feel anything at all: Rock and roll, pleasure and power. *Enclitic*, 3: 94–111.

Grossberg, L. (1992). *We Gotta Get Out of this Place*. New York: Routledge.

Haug, W.F. (1986). *Critique of Commodity Aesthetics*. Minneapolis: University of Minnesota Press.

Hill, T. (1991). The enemy within: Censorship in rock music in the 1950s. *South Atlantic Quarterly*, 90(4): 675–707.

Medovoi, L. (1991/2). Mapping the rebel image: Postmodernism and the masculinist politics of rock in the U.S.A. *Cultural Critique*, 20: 153–88.

Pabón, C. (1995). De albizu a Madonna: Para armar y desarmar la nacionalidad. *Bordes*, 1: 22–37.

Román, M. (1995). El *Girlie Show*: Madonna, las polémicas nacionales y los pánicos morales. *Bordes*, 1: 14–19.

Savage, J. (1992). *England's Dreaming*. New York: St Martin's Press.

Index

Allwood, Mandy, 70–1
Andersen, R., 113
Anderson, B., 72
Ang, I., 135
Antoun, R.T., 107
Aquinas, T., 225
Aristotle, 137
Ashdown, Paddy, 63
audiences, 145–6, 159; for scandal, 13–19; scandal relevance to, 71–82
Austin, J.L., 44
authenticity, 146–9, 154–5

Bakker, Jim, 99, 106, 109, 115, 222, 230–2, 234–5, 238
Barings Bank, 66, 68, 75–7
Barthes, R., 79
Bascom, W., 105
Baughman, C., 214
Bauman, Z., 74, 81
Beatles, 240–2
Beck, U., 2, 68, 69
Benjamin, W., 244, 253
Bennett, L., 135
Bennett, W., 135
Bernardin, Joseph, 222, 228–9, 236–8

Bird, D.A., 232
Bird, S.E., 100, 101, 104, 117, 161, 232
Birth of a Nation, 85, 92, 95–7
Blair, Tony, 72
Bobbitt, Lorena, 24, 25, 27, 109, 114, 115, 166
body, and scandal, 22–3
Boethius, U., 6
Bourdieu, P., 195
Bowser, E., 161
Boyne, R., 138
Brummett, B., 141
Buck-Morss, S., 253
Burke, K., 135
Burroughs, A., 211
Butler, J., 96
Buttafuoco, Joey, 23–4, 110–11, 114

Callan, C.J., 225, 234
Campbell, R., 118
Carey, J., 105
Carter, S., 135
Cashmore, E., 212
celebrity, 17, 20, 21, 22, 90, 91–2, 122–42, 204–7, 217–19
character, 122–42

Charles, Prince, 47, 53, 66, 78, 108, 114
Clinton, Bill, 18, 42, 47, 72, 118, 122–42
Clinton, Hillary, 1, 98, 126–31, 134
Cohen, S., 4, 187, 218
commodity aesthetics, 242–6, 252
community, 25–8
Connell, I., 108, 149, 207
Creed, B., 214
cultural studies, 105
Czilli, E.J., 99, 102, 106

Dahlgren, P., 204
Dardenne, R.W., 101
Davies, C., 116
Davis, T., 205
de Certeau, M., 100, 193
Derrett, J.D.M., 223, 224
deviance, 5–6
Diana, Princess of Wales, 47, 53, 66, 78, 83, 108, 114, 206
Diprose, R., 194
discourse, media, 186–96; opprobrious, 45, 54; televisual, 170
Donovan, P., 76
Doors, The, 241–2
Durkheim, E., 57
Dutton, K.R., 208, 209
Dyer, R., 146, 147

Ed Sullivan Show, 240–2
Elias, N., 194, 209
Ellis, B., 115
ethics, 130–41
ethos, 136–8, 141

Faludi, S., 182
Featherstone, M., 243
Fisher, Amy, 23–4, 103, 104, 110–11, 114
Fishman, M., 170
Fiske, J., 16, 85, 100, 117, 118
Flanagan, B., 243–4
Flowers, Gennifer, 42, 125–35
Foucault, M., 196

Gamson, J., 192, 197, 226, 227, 228
Gans, H., 113, 187, 190, 234

Garfinkel, H., 124
Giddens, A., 26, 66, 80
Gilmore, D.D., 107
Gitlin, T., 186, 187
globalization, 65–84
Gluckman, M., 105–6, 107
Glynn, K., 100
Goffman, E., 8
Goldlust, J., 206
Goodwin, A., 143
Goodwin, J.P., 116
gossip, 7, 45, 106–7, 119, 205
Grant, Hugh, 21–2, 91, 101, 109, 115, 116, 148
Gray, H., 94
Greenberg, B., 199
Gripsrud, J., 113
Gronbeck, B., 137
Grossberg, L., 94, 243, 244, 248
Grosz, E., 194
Guerrero, E., 88, 96
guilt, 25–8
Gurevitch, M., 72

Habermas, J., 71
Hall, E., 129
Hallin, D., 118–19
Hamilton, P., 161
Hanson, C., 228
Harding, Tonya, 24, 116, 148, 213–14
Haring, B., 225
Hartley, J., 187, 189
Haskins, J.B., 100
hegemony, 2–6
Helms, Jessie, 94–5, 98
Hill, C.R., 209, 210
Hill, T., 242, 246, 249
Hirsch, P., 28
Hogshire, J., 105
homosexuality, 94–5, 98, 198
Hoskins, C., 71

Idvsoog, K., 227
image system, 21–2, 145
Internet, 29
Iran–Contra affair, 46, 56, 66

Jenny Jones, 166, 198
Jerry Springer, 2, 186, 193, 200

Johnson, Ben, 212–13
Johnson, Magic, 22, 66, 215–17
Jones, Paula, 122–4
journalism, 53–4, 77, 90–2, 143–63,
    170–1, 225–33; investigative,
    28–9; and morality, 131–5

Kern, M., 138
Kerrigan, Nancy, 24, 116, 148,
    213–14
King, A., 68
King, Rodney, 9, 85, 86, 89, 91, 97,
    98, 217
Kipnis, L., 195
Kneale, D., 169
Kroker, A., 213

LaClau, E., 5
Langer, J., 99–100, 114, 115
Larson, J.F., 208
Leon-Dufour, X., 224
Lewin, R., 136
libel, 7
Livingstone, S., 199
Lull, J., 16, 21, 25, 70, 161
Lunt, P., 199

MacAloon, J.J., 210
McGinn, B., 211
McHugh, J.A., 225, 234
McKay, J., 211, 212, 215, 217, 218
McLaren, Malcolm, 246–9
McManus, J., 227, 228, 234
McRobbie, A., 5, 6, 28
Madonna, 21–2, 207, 240, 249–52,
    253
Mansfield, A., 211
Mapplethorpe, Robert, 98
Maradona, 32, 154–5
Martín-Barbero, J., 107–8
media organizations, 49, 234–5
Medovoi, L., 244–5
Mellencamp, P., 99, 106, 195
Mellor, David, 44, 62–3
melodrama, 107–9, 115–16, 117–18
Menem, Carlos, 31
Mercer, K., 161
Messner, M., 208
Meyrowitz, J., 8, 188
Miller, T., 208, 209

Mirus, R., 71
modernity, 7, 20–1, 26; global,
    66–7
"money shot," 168–70, 171, 184,
    188–90, 195
morality, 11–12, 16, 22, 39–42,
    65–82, 86, 89–92, 123–4, 128–31,
    205–7; in postmodernism, 2–6
moral panic, 4–6, 18, 27, 28
Morley, D., 70, 74, 78, 83
Munson, W., 167, 168, 199
Murphy, P., 76

Nadalianis, A., 211
narrative, media, 3, 13, 15–17, 23–5,
    53–5, 77–80, 101–5; oral, 107–9;
    tabloid, 143–67
National Enquirer, 108–19
Newcomb, H., 28
Nixon, Richard, 18, 42, 52
Noonan, P., 135
North, Oliver, 47, 99, 106, 109, 113,
    124

Odwalla, natural juice scandal,
    10–13
Olympic ethic, 208–11
Olympic scandal, 212–14
Ong, W.J., 229, 232
orality, 104–5, 107–8, 117–18,
    229–33
Oring, E., 116

Pabón, C., 251
Park, H., 208
Parkinson, Cecil, 62
Parnell, Charles, 34–6, 40
Payne, D., 230
Pearson, G., 4
Peck, J., 199
Phil Donahue Show, 168, 192, 199
pornography, 169–70, 181–2, 184
Postman, N., 135
postmodernism, 2–7, 135, 213–14
Presley, Elvis, 245
Price, V., 99, 102, 106
Priest, P., 168, 192, 198
production, TV talk show, 170–200
Profumo, John, 35–6, 42, 52, 58,
    124

Pronger, B., 208
Puerto Rico, 249–54
punk rock, 246–9

Queen for a Day, 168, 198
Quindlen, A., 126–7

race, 85–98, 217–18
racism, 19, 27
reception, of scandal, 100–1
Reimer, B., 32
religion, 37–9, 68–9
reputation, 46–8
rhetoric, of scandal, 233–7
Riesman, D., 230
Riggs, M., 94
Robins, K., 140
rock apparatus, 242–4
Rolling Stones, 241–2
Román, M., 251
Rose, B., 168, 199
Rose, T., 94
Rowe, D., 207, 215
royalty, 8–9, 47, 53, 66, 78–80, 83,
    205, 206
rumor, 4, 45

Savage, J., 246–7, 248
scandal, biblical references to,
    223–5; and blackness, 82–98; and
    black popular culture, 93–5, 97;
    and culture, 104–5; definition of,
    3, 4, 7, 9–19, 25, 37–48, 166–7,
    223–5; discourse, 29, 85–98; and
    distancing, 115–16; ecology of, 17;
    hierarchy of, 17–19; institutional,
    19–25, 55, 58; intertextuality of,
    17–19; and locality, 71–82;
    management of, 15–16; and
    middle-order moral events, 67–71;
    and music, 93–4, 143–63, 240–54;
    origins of, 37–9; personalization
    of, 12, 75–80, 82, 111–16; and
    pleasure, 114–15; political, 18,
    40–1, 47–8, 50–1, 57, 59–60, 61–2,
    122–42, 249–53; and polysemy,
    17–19; psychodrama, 20–5; and
    the public sphere, 71; and
    religion, 222–39; and sex, 21; and
    speculating, 109–11; and sports,

203–21; star, 20–5; susceptibility
    to, 17–19; technology, role in,
    14–17, 29, 45–6, 51–5; and trust,
    58–60; and truth, 155–61, 204–7,
    215–16, 218–19
Schechter, D., 227
Schutz, A., 73
Schwichtenberg, C., 207
Sex Pistols, 240, 246–9
shame, 25–8, 205
Shaw, D., 228
Silverstone, R., 71
Simpson, O.J., 14, 19, 24–5, 27, 28,
    31, 66, 68, 89, 96–7, 99, 116, 175,
    217–18
Simson, V., 208, 212, 213
Sirius, R.U., 169
skandalon, 37–8, 224
slander, 7, 39
Smith, S., 199, 217, 218
Sobchack, T., 189
Sobchack, V., 189
Sparks, C., 204
Squire, C., 199
Stahlin, G., 223
Steinfels, P., 226, 227, 238
Stephens, M., 117, 232
St Jude, 169
storytelling, 101–21
Swaggart, Jimmy, 223, 235–7, 238
symbolic capital, 47–8
symbolic power, 8–9, 47–8, 63

tabloid, 7, 54, 68, 90–2, 99–121,
    143–63, 232
talk shows, 4, 97, 118, 164–202;
    guests, preparation, 178–84;
    guests, selection, 172–8; and
    social class, 190–6
Tarbuck, Jimmy, 108–9
Taylor, C., 96
Tebbel, J., 7
Texaco, racial scandal, 9–20, 29
Thatcher, Margaret, 62
Thompson, J.B., 8, 67, 73, 79
Thornton, S., 5, 6, 28
Thorpe, Jeremy, 52, 63–4
Tomlinson, J., 83
Tongues Untied, 94–5, 98
Tyson, Mike, 215

Tuchman, G., 170, 171, 174, 178, 187
Tumber, H., 227
Turner, B., 194

United States, military scandal,
    9–20
U-2, 243–4

visibility, 8, 14, 20, 36, 40–1, 43,
    49–51, 67, 79–80

Walser, R., 94

Watergate, 18, 28, 42, 46, 52, 56, 57,
    64, 66
Watney, S., 4
Whitewater, 1, 71–2, 117, 123
Wilkins, L., 217
Williams, L., 169
Williams, R., 223

Young, J., 7, 187
youth culture, 5–6, 240–54

Zuckerman, M., 100